RETAIL LOCATION AND RETAIL PLANNING IN BRITAIN

Retail Location and Retail Planning in Britain

CLIFFORD M. GUY
University of Wales
Institute of Science and Technology
(UWIST)

Gower

Published by
GOWER PUBLISHING COMPANY LIMITED
Westmead, Farnborough, Hampshire, England

 British Library Cataloguing in Publication Data

Guy, Clifford
    Retail location and retail planning in Britain.
    1. Retail trade - Great Britain - Planning
    I. Title
    381'.0941   HF5429.6.G7

ISBN 0 566 00270 1

Printed in Great Britain by David Green (Printers) Limited
Kettering, Northamptonshire

Contents

List of Tables

List of Figures

Acknowledgements

The work involved in the preparation of this book commenced during a three-year period as Social Science Research Council Senior Research Fellow in the Department of Geography, at Reading University. I would like to thank the SSRC for their financial support, and Professor Peter Hall and Dr Sophia Bowlby for their stimulating and thorough supervision of my research programme and their continuing interest subsequently.

I have been fortunate in being able to continue this work within a congenial environment for teaching and research at UWIST. Particular thanks are due to Ian Bracken, Patrick O'Farrell and Richard Spooner for reading and providing valuable comment on draft chapters. I take full responsibility however for any errors, omissions or misrepresent-ations. Grateful thanks are also due to Myrtle Robins for her immaculate typing and to Gareth Jones for the preparation of some of the Figures.

Finally my greatest debt is to my wife Kathleen for her constant interest and encouragement.

1 Retail change and retail planning in Britain

1.1 RETAIL PLANNING IN BRITAIN

1.1.1 Definitions

The term 'retail planning' has become commonly used in recent years but may still need some explanation. In its widest sense it concerns the planning of all future activity in the retail sector, but it frequently involves two more specific elements. The first is the spatial distribution of retail activity, taken as a whole rather than for individual firms. The second is the involvement of the public sector, both in assisting retail firms in their planning, and in controlling the   X results of such planning in the interests of society as a whole. 'Retail planning' thus involves both public and private sectors, ideally in some form of joint attempt to provide a geographical system of retail activity which is of maximum benefit to the public.
  This book is written in the belief that the provision of shopping is too important to be controlled entirely by the decisions of the private sector - property developers and retail firms in particular. This is because shopping is a fundamental activity whereby the people of this country obtain the goods they need; it is justifiable for the state to be concerned whether the satisfaction that shoppers derive from the retail system is at its highest possible level, within constraints necessary for the economically efficient running of the system as a whole.
  However, government intervention in Britain - particularly at the local level by land use planning authorities - does not yet appear to have led to the ideal situation indicated above. This is clear from the extent of the current controversies in retail planning, of which more below. If intervention has not been fully effective, then it is important to investigate why, and at the same time to attempt to improve the process. This book is intended to assist these objectives, firstly in its explanation of the major trends that have contributed to the formation of present patterns of retail location in Britain; and secondly, in its discussion of the rationale for planning intervention in the retail sector, firstly in general, and then in the context of particular issues of current concern.

1.1.2 Changes in the retail environment

As a prologue, it is worth examining briefly some major changes in the retail sector which have occurred since 1945 in Britain, in order to be able to structure the more detailed discussion in subsequent chapters. These changes may be classified under three categories: retail distribution, consumer behaviour and the external environment. The following discussion may be read in conjunction with Figure 1.1, which depicts some interrelationships between these changes.
  Retail distribution has undergone important changes since 1945. The total number of shops in Britain has declined considerably, despite the growth in population, and substantial rises in real incomes. The number of firms involved has also shown a decline, since most of the closures

Figure 1.1   Retail change in Britain, 1950-1980

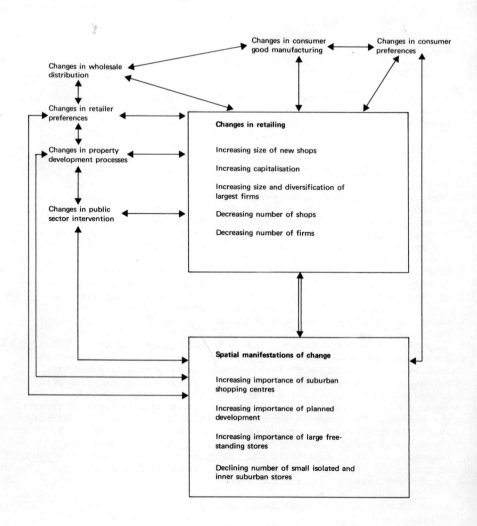

Changes in consumer
good manufacturing

Changes in consumer
preferences

Changes in wholesale
distribution

Changes in retailer
preferences

Changes in property
development processes

Changes in public
sector intervention

Changes in retailing

Increasing size of new shops

Increasing capitalisation

Increasing size and diversification of
largest firms

Decreasing number of shops

Decreasing number of firms

Spatial manifestations of change

Increasing importance of suburban
shopping centres

Increasing importance of planned
development

Increasing importance of large free-
standing stores

Declining number of small isolated and
inner suburban stores

have been in small firms, often owning just one shop. Accordingly, the
multiple firm has grown rapidly in importance, assuming a larger and
larger share of the market. This has been due partly to the expansion
of long established firms, involving in some cases their loss of identity
as retailers within giant multi-national corporations; and partly to
the establishment of many new firms, often as innovators selling new
types of goods or using new methods. The average size and real turnover
of the British shop has also increased considerably. Firms have become
far more conscious of a need to reduce costs of operation: this has
been achieved by using more economical methods of selling goods, and
also by operating from larger premises in which certain economies of
scale are possible.

Consumer behaviour has also changed in several very broad ways. There
has been considerable growth in real disposable income, such that luxury
goods in the 1940s had become essentials by the 1970s (television sets,
for example). At the same time, expenditure on food and some other
household necessities has scarcely risen in real terms. These trends
have affected the retail sector, such that food and household goods
shops have undergone severe decline while the number of durable goods
and clothing shops has increased steadily over most of the post war
period. A second type of change has been in the increasing use of the
private car for shopping purposes. This has allowed shoppers a far
wider choice of shops than in pre war years: the increasingly varied
demands of shoppers can now be met by travelling to relatively remote
specialist shops or large shopping centres, and the shopper need no
longer rely on local centres. This trend has led to important changes
in the locational policies of retailers, many of whom now regard good
car access as essential. A third broad change appears to have occurred,
though it is less easily detectable. This is an increasing consumer
consciousness of price of goods, and a decreasing attention paid to the
standards of service provided in a shop. This trend is clearly due in
part from changes in retailing methods, and particularly the introduction
of self service and of discount stores.

Finally, the external environment has changed. This includes the
institutions which govern the activities of retailers and consumers.
Here the three most important changes have probably been the introduction
of comprehensive town planning control over development and change of
use of land and buildings; the rise in importance of the property
developer as provider of new shopping space; and increasing intervention
by central government, including the imposition of new charges and
responsibilities on the shopkeeper, such as the collection of value
added tax.

1.1.3 Changes in retail location

The changes outlined above have contributed to a number of general
changes in patterns of retail location: these are summarised in Table
1.1, which represents a concensus view of the Shopping Capacity Sub
Committee convened by the National Economic Development Office in 1970.
Although presented as a series of broad forecasts for the 1970s, it is
clearly based upon events in the 1960s, and as such forms a useful
summary for our purpose.

It is unnecessary to discuss each item in this table, as they will be
dealt with in later chapters. However two important general points
emerge. The first is a trend towards a net outward movement of shopping
facilities within urban areas: this consists broadly of decline in
inner suburbs and the establishment of new shops in outer suburbs. This

Table 1.1   Shopping centres: anticipated changes in trade 1970-1980

1 Areas unlikely to change their share of trade much
   (a) Central shopping areas
   (b) Shops in villages and small towns

2 Areas likely to increase their share of trade
   (a) Suburban shopping centres

3 Areas likely to lose trade
   (a) Street corner shops
   (b) Shops in intermediate areas adjacent to town centres
   (c) 'Parades' of the type built in the 1930s

4 Areas whose performance will depend on the attitude of public
   authorities
   (a) 'Off centre' stores
   (b) Free standing superstores
   (c) Out of town regional shopping centres

Source: Distributive Trades E.D.C., 1971, p.51.

---

has been associated with a net outward movement of residential
population, such that falling population in inner suburbs has led to
reduced demand, and growth in outer suburbs has justified the
construction of new centres. Other important factors have been slum
clearance and other redevelopment in inner areas; the effects of rising
car ownership; and the emphasis on economies of scale in store
management, which has led to the establishment of large new stores on
cheap outer suburban sites.
   A second important feature is summarised in the table as 'the attitude
of public authorities'. It is mentioned particularly with respect to
control over the development of 'off centre' stores, free standing
superstores, and out of town regional shopping centres. But the
discussion upon which the table is based (Distributive Trades E.D.C.,
1971, Chapter 6) indicates that public authorities, and especially local
authority planning departments, are involved in almost every aspect of
change in retail location. This is the case for town centre shopping,
where planning policies for expansion of shopping areas or for traffic
improvements or pedestrianisation are of vital importance; and also for
inner urban shops, which have been affected by redevelopment and other
planning policies.
   Planning policies appear thus to have retarded, accelerated or even
caused change in patterns of retail location in Britain since 1945,
probably to an extent greater than in other developed countries. Despite
this, there has been little academic attention given to the purposes and
effects of this degree of intervention.

1.2 THE PURPOSES OF THIS BOOK

1.2.1 The field of enquiry

It follows from the discussion above that planning intervention, especially at local level, and its effect upon patterns of retail location in Britain is a valid field of enquiry. Much descriptive work has taken place on the results of certain types of intervention, for example in town centres or in connection with hypermarkets and super-stores. Such work is often characterised either by a lack of justification for the ideological stance taken with respect to planning intervention itself, or by a lack of understanding of the operations of the private sector: retail firms and property developers.
   This book is intended to supply a broad context for detailed studies of retail planning and retail location in Britain. It attempts basically to describe and explain the major factors that have helped cause the present geographical pattern of retail location in Britain. This explanation then leads to conclusions about possible future events and their implications. These are discussed in relation to the involvement of public sector planning, past, present and future. The field of enquiry thus is firstly, the retail sector in Britain; secondly, shops and their locations; thirdly, the wider social effects implied by such patterns of locations; and fourthly, relationships between locations, effects and public planning policies.

1.2.2 The method of enquiry

This field of enquiry is clearly very broad, and definitive answers cannot always be sought or given. While it is hoped that any tentative or generalised conclusions are valid and of use to policy makers, in some areas of investigation no conclusions may be possible. In these instances it will be necessary instead to raise further questions, which can be answered only through further and more specific research. Thus more questions are likely to be posed than answered.
   Having set a very broad field of enquiry, it follows that almost all of the empirical findings discussed must be drawn from existing sources. This inevitably raises problems of comparability between different studies, using various methods, and set in various localities and at various times. These problems are discussed in the text. However, the act of synthesis allows one to build up a convincing overall picture of attitudes, behaviour and interrelationships within which some anomalous results may lead to further insights.
   The discussion of empirical work is of little value unless it is set within some broad theoretical framework, which can allow questions to be posed, hypotheses tested and predictions made. In retailing, one feature that is common to all the 'actors' involved is the need to make decisions: the location of a shop; the choice of goods to sell; the place to go shopping; whether to permit a new shopping centre to be built. It seems appropriate therefore to base a study of changes in the retail sector upon theoretical frameworks involving decisions themselves and ways in which they are taken. This serves to structure any analysis of observed decisions by suggesting a sequence of stages within the process of decision making, and also ways in which the decision is influenced by characteristics of the decision maker and the environment within which the decision or sequence of decisions is made.
   This concentration on decision making as the focus of attention

determines the way in which this book is organised. Chapter 2
introduces the material reviewed in later chapters, by presenting a
description of aspects of theory on decision making, and by summarising
the approaches to the study of the retail sector that have arisen from
a number of academic disciplines. Chapters 3 to 6 examine empirical
evidence of decisions, the ways in which they are made, and their effects,
on the part of property developers, retailers, consumers, and land use
planners, respectively. The chapters on developers and retailers
concentrate on decisions involving the location of shops, although these
are shown to be subsets of wider decision structures in respect of
property development and methods of retailing. The chapters on consumers
and planners discuss theories of consumer behaviour and planning
intervention, respectively, which are well developed and can provide
useful insights into the more narrow focus of attention in this
investigation.

Chapters 7, 8 and 9 discuss three important issues in which changing
circumstances have led to increasing difficulties for some of the actors
involved. These are also areas in which past planning intervention
appears to have had particularly important effects. In these discussions
- on town centre redevelopments, the hypermarket controversy, and local
shopping problems respectively, the description of events is set within
the framework of the decision making behaviour of the various actors
involved. This leads to examinations of the ways in which these actors
are in agreement or contention, and finally to some recommendations for
policy. Chapter 10 summarises the preceding material and presents some
tentative conclusions, about the possible course of events in British
retailing in the near future, and the stances that local authority
planners and other decision makers might usefully take with respect to
these events.

2 Research into decision making and retailing

2.1 INTRODUCTION

The purpose of this chapter is to establish a context for the following
four chapters, which review the evidence concerning decision making by
the 'actors' involved in retailing. Sections 2.2 and 2.3 attempt a brief
summary of relevant aspects of decision making theory. These sections
demonstrate that there is generally a wide disparity between the
behaviour of the 'ideal' decision maker, and that of actual decision
makers, whether in commercial or domestic circumstances. This disparity
is of interest, partly because it suggests that when faced with the need
to make decisions, people will adopt strategies for simplifying the task
of making them. These strategies are likely to involve distortions of
the processes of perceiving and selecting those factors which should
influence their decision. If we can begin to detect systematic variation
of such distortions among decision makers, then we may be able better to
understand and predict their decisions, and the resulting patterns of
behaviour.
   Sections 2.4 and 2.5 summarise theoretical approaches and empirical
research concerning the retail sector. The social science disciplines
of economics, psychology, sociology and geography have each provided
some insight into the activities of retail producers and consumers.
Attempts have been made to put these insights to practical use,
particularly in the study of 'marketing', which is concerned among other
things with the management of retail firms. However, relatively little
of the marketing literature is concerned with decisions or behaviour that
have some direct spatial connotation. The spatial perspectives have been
provided largely from the discipline of human geography, and thus the
geographical literature is given a somewhat longer review. However, this
and the other reviews in this chapter are of necessity cursory, and serve
mainly to draw attention to the types of assumption used in different
treatments of decision making or behaviour in retailing. Comparison of
these treatments suggests that much can be gained from combinations of
approaches from different disciplines, and indeed some of the most recent
work has been inspired by such combinations.

2.2 NORMATIVE DECISION THEORY

2.2.1 Decisions and decision theory

Before considering theoretical approaches to decision making, it is worth
attempting to define decisions, and to suggest that all decisions have a
common broad structure upon which theoretical constructs may be based.
   A decision may be defined as:
      'a conscious choice between at least two possible courses
      of action' (Castles, Murray and Potter, 1971, p.11)
   It follows that the decision maker (i) must feel some need to take a
decision; (ii) must be able to define at least two possible courses of
action; (iii) must have some estimate of the likely outcomes of these
courses of action; (iv) must have some set of rules or criteria for
choosing between the courses of action. This implies that (v) he has

some overall purpose or objectives in mind. We may thus summarise
elements of the process of decision making in the following formal terms:
    '1. A search process to discover goals.
     2. The formulation of objectives after search.
     3. The selection of alternatives (strategies) to
         accomplish objectives.
     4. The evaluation of outcomes.'   (Scott, 1967, p.219).
    The distinction between goals and objectives is important. The search
for goals is, according to Scott, initiated because of dissatisfaction
with outcomes within an existing set of goals. Objectives on the other
hand relate to the decision in question, and imply the existence of
values which are held by the decision maker.
    In selecting from alternatives, the decision maker will be aware that
attached to each alternative is one or more <u>outcomes</u>. Each outcome may
be expressed in terms of monetary or other <u>gain or loss</u> (<u>payoff</u>).
For each payoff there is a <u>probability</u> of its occurrence, which the
decision maker may attempt to estimate. Finally, the alternative will
have a <u>value</u> attached to it: this value reflects some combination of
the payoff and probability of the alternative. The decision maker
chooses that alternative with the highest value.
    Having established a common structure for decisions, we may now examine
the two broad theoretical approaches to the study of decision making.
Firstly, <u>normative</u> decision theory:
    '... is concerned with the way a rational decision maker
     should analyze a problem and reach an optimum solution
     given a particular situation and specified information'.
        (Castles, Murray and Potter, 1971, p.11)
    The emphasis here is on 'should'. The basic purpose of normative
decision theory is to provide decision makers with the conceptual
equipment to enable them to make 'better' decisions (however defined).
<u>Descriptive</u> theory of decision making, on the other hand,
    '... is concerned with how decisions are made in practice
     and also with what decision-making structures operate'. (<u>ibid</u>,p.11)
    This area of theory seeks essentially to explain how decisions
typically are made, not how they should be made. It also seeks to
investigate ways in which decisions are influenced by the organisational
environment within which they are initiated, taken and evaluated.
    The contrast between these two approaches extends to their academic
backgrounds. Normative theory relies heavily on economic and statistical
theory, and its major precepts are formed by deduction. The main
propositions of descriptive theory are drawn largely from the social
sciences of psychology and sociology, and owe much to the findings of
empirical research.

2.2.2 Normative decision theory

The following account discusses some essential elements of normative
decision theory, in the context of a hypothetical case study - that of
a shopkeeper choosing a location for a new shop. (1)
    A comparison of definitions of the decision making process and of
normative theory (2.2.1) leads to certain inferences. First, the search
process to discover goals. The 'rational' decision maker will wish to
maximise over a period of time the utility which can be derived from
those activities about which decisions are to be made. 'Utility' is
where possible expressed in monetary terms, although it may include
non financial elements of 'satisfaction'. For example, a shopkeeper may
intend to maximise profits from his retail business, or possibly maximise

a more complex utility function which includes (for example) the
satisfaction derived from selling certain types of good to knowledgeable
customers. Generally these types of goal are likely to be constant in
the short or medium term. However, decisions may involve the setting
or revision of more immediate goals: for example, a decision to move
to larger shop premises within a given period of time may follow from
a general goal of increasing sales (Figure 2.1). For a 'rational'
shopkeeper this goal serves the purpose implied by his overall goal of
maximising profitability: however he will be prepared to modify or
abandon it in the light of new information.

The other elements of the decision making process (the formulation of
objectives, selection of alternatives, and evaluation of outcomes) may
be regarded as parts of a cyclic process whereby the nature and scope of
the decision or decisions concerned are clarified in the light of
assessment of outcomes and collection of further information. Initially
the decision maker may select a small number of alternatives for analysis.
He may be aware of a small number of possible outcomes and be very
uncertain of the probabilities of each one occurring. By using
techniques such as the formulation of decision trees (Moore and Thomas
1976, Chapter 4), he can in effect break the overall decision down into
a series of sequential decisions. For each decision the range of
outcomes and the probability attached to each outcome should be clearly
specified. From examination of the initial decision tree it will usually
become clear that certain alternatives are likely to produce undesirable
outcomes and need not be investigated in detail. For other alternatives,
sensitivity analyses incorporating a range of estimates of probabilities
attached to outcomes can be employed. Where the choice between
alternatives appears to be sensitive to the probabilities assumed, then
it may be worth delaying the decision until further information becomes
available. The costs of acquiring the information, and delaying the
decision(s) concerned, can also be estimated. These costs then are
incorporated into the decision tree so that it can be decided whether to
seek further information or not.

To illustrate, the 'rational' shopkeeper mentioned above would perhaps
obtain a short list of vacant shop premises from which to choose his
new location. He would attempt to estimate the costs and revenues that
would be derived from operating his shop at each location: the surpluses
of revenue over cost, expressed perhaps as rates of return over a
specified number of years, form a set of outcomes. The shopkeeper would
be wise however to consider the results of alternative assumptions of
future growth in consumer expenditure, or of future increases in labour
costs or rent. This would suggest several possible outcomes at each
location, each of which would have a level of probability attached to it.
The shopkeeper would then calculate the value derived from each
alternative. This is normally found by adding the products of the
monetary value or payoff from each outcome, and its probability, to
form the expected monetary value (EMV) of the alternative. (2) This
process is depicted in Figure 2.2, a simple example of choice between
two new shops or remaining in the present shop.

At this point the shopkeeper may decide to seek further information,
either because he wishes to consider further alternatives (for example,
other possible locations); or because he wishes to assign higher
probabilities to certain outcomes (for example, obtain better estimates
of receipts at certain locations). Before so doing he would estimate
the cost of seeking the information required, and also the opportunity
costs of delay (for example, losing an opportunity to acquire a very
promising location). In the example shown in Figure 2.2, there is

Figure 2.1　Goals and decision problems for the 'rational' shopkeeper

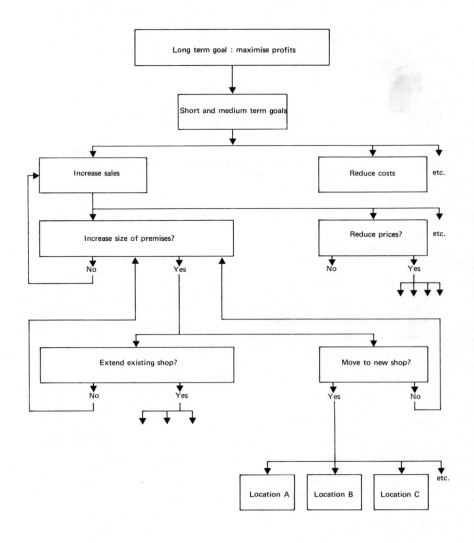

Figure 2.2   Comparison of outcomes at different locations by the
              'rational' shopkeeper

Location	Outcome	Probability	EMV
A	20	0.25	(20 x 0.25) +
	12	0.5	(12 x 0.5) +
	8	0.25	(8 x 0.25)
			= 13.0
B	16	0.25	(16 x 0.25) +
	12	0.5	(12 x 0.5) +
	10	0.25	(10 x 0.25)
			= 12.5
No move	12	0.5	(12 x 0.5) +
	10	0.5	(10 x 0.5)
			= 11.0

Notes:

1. Location A is a high-rent shop in a town centre.
2. Location B is a low-rent shop in a suburban area.
3. Outcomes are expressed as expected percentage p.a. rates of return.
4. Estimates of outcomes and probabilities are derived as follows:
    the shopkeeper's current rate of return is 12%. In his present shop
    this may continue, or decline to 10% because of increasing storage
    problems for new product lines. If he moves to larger premises, he
    can expect his current rate of return to be maintained, but with
    less certainty: at A, he may benefit from the greater accessibility
    of the town centre, or suffer from the increased costs, while at B,
    the margins of uncertainty are somewhat less.

clearly a need to refine estimates of outcomes and probabilities, since
there is little difference between EMV's.

Eventually however our shopkeeper would complete his analysis, and then
attempt to purchase that shop which offered him the highest EMV. This
account is of course highly simplified: in particular it takes no
account of the bargaining which often occurs in property deals. Here,
using further methods of decision analysis, our shopkeeper would be able
to estimate the maximum amount that he should offer for each of the
properties under review, under various assumptions about the strategies
likely to be adopted by rival shopkeepers and the vendors of the
properties.

The essence of modern decision analysis (for which the above treatment
is no more than a highly simplified introduction) lies in its treatment
of risk (to which prior probabilities can be given) and uncertainty
(which comprises factors which cannot be given probabilities of
occurrence). The traditional economic theory of the firm held that for
any decision a set of goals and objectives would immediately be apparent,
and that the outcomes of alternatives could be accurately assessed by the
decision maker without the incursion of any extra costs of information
seeking. Normative decision theory allows that outcomes are uncertain,
and that information seeking does in fact impose extra costs upon the
firm. The vital advance has been the direct incorporation of these
problem areas into the analysis.

2.2.3 Alternative goals and criteria

The rational decision maker will act such that his expected utility from
the result of the decision is maximised. This may involve the
calculation of the expected monetary value (EMV) which arises from each
alternative,or more complex methods of risk analysis (Moore and Thomas,
1976, Chapter 11). A problem that many decision makers have to face is
that certain courses of action appear to carry unacceptable levels of
risk, even though they should be <u>expected</u> to give maximum benefit.
It follows that the criterion of expected monetary value (EMV) is not
always appropriate for judging between alternative outcomes. Instead,
it may be necessary to avoid the possibility of highly unsatisfactory
outcomes rather than to find that likely to be the most satisfactory.
Although this type of behaviour is not fully rational (according to
economic precepts), it can be accommodated within the framework of
normative decision theory.

The term 'unsatisfactory' can be defined here in two ways. First, it
can denote financial or other loss. Most individuals will take steps
to avoid even a remote probability of heavy financial loss: hence the
popularity of insurance policies, although the EMV of taking out a policy
is likely to be less than that of not taking one (Moore and Thomas, 1976,
p.31). More generally, the decision maker can choose that alternative
which offers the highest (i.e. least bad) minimum outcome (ibid, p.42).
In the example shown in Figure 2.2, the shopkeeper might reject location
A because it carries the risk of a low rate of return. A move to B
is then preferable to no move, since its EMV is higher. (3)

The second definition of 'unsatisfactory' relates to the level of
opportunity costs incurred through experiencing certain outcomes. This
cost is defined as the difference between the highest and lowest outcomes
which, it is estimated, may occur under one alternative. The decision
maker may wish to choose the alternative which presents the least
opportunity costs: in decision analysis this course is termed
minimisation of regret (Moore and Thomas, 1976, p.43). To illustrate,
our shopkeeper (Figure 2.2) might choose to remain in his current
location, where he would have lost relatively little if his pessimistic
estimate turned out to be correct.

These examples indicate ways in which normative decision theory may be
adapted to suit the requirements of those whose methods may be less than
fully rational according to the conventional economic criteria. However,
consideration of these matters ultimately forces one's attention upon
the goals and objectives of the decision maker. It is reasonable to
suppose that he who decides so as to reduce either risk of failure or
possible 'regret' to a minimum, is also likely to be a 'satisficer',
content to accept the first satisfactory solution to his problem (2.3.3).
It may be doubtful then whether he is likely to specify clear goals, or
to reconsider these in the light of former decisions. These conclusions
take one further away from the world of the normative decision maker.

It is clear however that decision analysis is a valuable aid in
situations where goals and objectives can be defined unambiguously, where
most of the values involved are monetary, and where clear criteria can be
used for choosing between alternatives. It consists of a set of
techniques to be used consciously by the decision maker. It may also be
used to examine actual decisions or sequences of decisions which have
been made, not necessarily using explicitly the techniques involved.

2.3 DESCRIPTIVE DECISION THEORY

2.3.1 Introduction

'Descriptive' or 'behavioural' decision theory does not consist of a
clear set of axioms and postulates leading to conclusions which can be
put into operation, as with normative theory. Instead we find a wealth
of empirical material describing and interpreting evidence of decisions
made by actual individuals and organisations. From these descriptions,
and aided by other areas of theory, notably in social psychology, some
general concepts have emerged. The purpose of much of this work has
been not to provide instruction on decision making, but to advance the
state of knowledge in the social sciences concerned.
   In an introductory chapter of this type it is clearly impossible to
give a full review of empirical findings and the development of theory
in this subject. Instead it may be useful to discuss briefly three
issues, each of which will be of considerable importance in the chapters
to follow. These are:
   i)   How do decision makers collect and use information ?
   ii) How and to what extent do decision makers search for alternative
        solutions ?
   iii) How are decisions affected by the nature of organisations within
        which they are made ?

2.3.2 The use of information

If a problem requiring decisions is at all complex, then its complete
analysis is likely to require a quantity of information that is
impossible to obtain or evaluate. Information itself often needs to be
purchased, and its evaluation takes time which may be needed for other
tasks. This means that decision makers have to adopt 'strategies' for
using a limited quantity of information to the best possible effect.
Observations suggest that the quantity and nature of the information
obtained are not necessarily suitable for the purpose of producing
unbiased estimates of outcomes and probabilities. Firstly, the quantity
of information which decision makers can handle may be small, and
inadequate for a rational decision to be made. Secondly, the selection
and use made of information are both likely to be subject to bias. In
other words, the decision maker may ignore certain items of information
of relevance to the problem, and put an incorrect interpretation upon
other items. Simon (1957a) has introduced the concept of 'bounded
rationality': the decision maker's selection and perception of
information is limited by his interests and experience, and by the
amount of time available to him. Within these limits he attempts a
rational decision making procedure.
   For example, our shopkeeper needs information about shops which are
available for purchase or rent. The extent of information of this kind
in a large town is likely to be considerable: therefore it is worth his
while to select a sample of the available information, peruse it and then
seek further more detailed information on any shops which appear to show
promise as new locations for his business. Strategies for taking a
sample of the information available would include the use of estate
agents; but the use simply of one agent, who was a personal friend of
the shopkeeper, would seem to be both inadequate and biased. Further
bias might occur in the choice of properties for further enquiry, for
example in the rejection of all properties in a particular shopping
centre because of erroneous opinions about the level of incomes of those

who shop there.

It is likely here that large organisations possess considerable advantages over the individual. In an organisation the tasks of collecting information and making decisions can be given to separate persons or groups, and the resources available for information collection and digestion may be considerable. Organisations are likely however to possess disadvantages in certain respects (2.3.4).

2.3.3 The nature and extent of search

The term 'search' here refers to the analysis of alternatives rather than the formulation of goals or objectives (2.2.1). The search is thus either for acceptable alternatives from which a final choice must be made, or for the final choice itself.

The discussion of search activity in the recent literature has been greatly influenced by the work of Simon (1957a, 1957b). He introduced the concept of 'satisficing': the individual would search until a satisfactory alternative was found. The further effort involved in finding an 'ideal' solution would not be worth while. This concept stems from two lines of approach. Firstly, psychological theory suggests that individuals' motives stem from drives, which can be fulfilled after appropriate action: whether fulfilment occurs or not depends upon an aspiration level which varies between individuals and which will also vary over time for each individual, according to experience (Simon, 1959). Secondly, the bounds upon information usage discussed in 2.3.2, of which the individual is partly aware, limit the value of striving for a utility maximising solution.

These concepts of search behaviour are important in providing a 'descriptive' or 'behavioural' theory of decision making which can, like the normative theory, be tested against empirical evidence. It is certainly not hard to find examples of behaviour which corresponds to this theory. To return to our shopkeeper, he might thus decide to buy (or rent) the first property which appears satisfactory to him, in terms of price, size, location, and other features. He may feel in any case that the advantages of one location over another are relatively slight, and that any location which does not have clear disadvantages will prove adequate.

2.3.4 Decisions within organisations

In the simple economic model of the business firm, and also (by implication) in case studies of normative decision analysis, it is assumed that the firm acts as an individual - it collectively considers the requisite information, and reaches a decision which reflects the best interests of the firm as a whole (Lipsey, 1975, p.210). The research into behavioural aspects of decision theory has added two important modifications to this view of the organisation. Firstly, the principles regarding bounded rationality, search behaviour and satisficing have successfully been applied to organisations as well as to individuals (Simon, 1957b; Cyert and March, 1963). It is accepted that organisations:

'1. ... make extensive use of programmed decisions, which involve reasonably well-structured patterns of search ...
2. ... often use rather simple rules of thumb to make decisions as well as the complex analytical frameworks that are so often attributed to organisational decision making ...
3. ... make decisions that are bound and biased by the local rationality of the decision unit ...

4. ... engage in directed search for relevant alternatives ...
5. ... learn from and adapt to their environment.'
(Harrison, 1975, pp.8-9).

The second modification stems from a recognition that individuals working within the firm (or organisation) are likely to differ in their approach to problems and decisions: hence, the nature of decisions made by organisations is likely to depend partly on how many, and which, people have been involved in defining and considering the problem, collecting information, and making decisions. While every individual may exhibit to some extent the tendencies towards selective perception of information and limited capability for search, as discussed above (2.3.3), each will vary in these respects. Thus, for example, certain information may be filtered out at an early stage and thus be unavailable to other persons who value it more highly.

Another factor which may affect the quality of ultimate decisions lies in the possible conflicts between individuals in the organisation, which can lead to distortion or withholding of information. In general individuals will have personal goals, which may be optimising (for example, promotion) or satisficing (a quiet life). These goals may or may not allow behaviour consistent with the goals of the organisation itself.

For example, if we switch our attention from the individual retailer to the large 'multiple' retail firm (4.3), the simple descriptions of decision making used in the illustrations above are no longer adequate. The large firm may receive information about possible new locations from a variety of sources: these locations will be considered by one branch of headquarters management which is responsible for locational assessment, and then another which is responsible for negotiation over property, and eventually to senior management and the board of the company. The firm will probably develop routine procedures to ensure that suitable opportunities are evaluated as quickly and accurately as possible; but these procedures may be corrupted by personality clashes or eccentricities within management.

2.3.5 The value of descriptive decision theory

It should be clear from the discussion above that descriptive decision theory is less precise and more subtle than the normative theory. In studies of the type attempted in this book, it is however essential in providing a basis upon which to explain certain features of locational behaviour on the part of actors in retailing. For example, the evidence about locational decision making among independent retailers (4.4) is fragmentary, but evidence of their behaviour in general suggests a predominance of risk avoidance and satisficing criteria for decisions. This indicates that their <u>locational</u> decision making is likely to be guided by these principles, such that in many cases decisions are made not to move shop at all rather than to find a new location, even if the latter appears economically justified.

2.4 ASPATIAL ASPECTS OF RETAILING: A LITERATURE REVIEW

This and the following section have two principal aims. First, it offers a brief discussion of some of the most important literature on the retail sector: it is not intended to give detailed reviews here. The second aim of these two sections is to discuss the extent and nature of the literature on decisions and behaviour of those actors involved in the retail sector. Detailed discussion of certain findings in this area will be carried out in later chapters: at this point the intention is to discover the amount of emphasis that has been placed upon <u>explicit</u> consideration of decision making and behaviour, as opposed to <u>implicit</u> assumptions about behaviour which are often made in theory construction, or in explanations of aggregate findings.

This section deals with material on the structure of the retail sector as a whole, and with aspects of behaviour which have no particular spatial manifestations: section 2.5 deals specifically with spatial aspects. In both sections the source material is ordered by academic disciplines. This treatment emphasises the approaches and assumptions typical of each discipline. It also reveals some inconsistencies and gaps in knowledge which have resulted from the fragmentation of approach between the various disciplines involved.

2.4.1 The economic approach

When one considers the importance of retail distribution in the economy of most nations, it seems surprising that more attention has not been devoted to this topic by economists. The sale of retail goods is divided amongst very large numbers of firms, such that one might expect models of perfect competition to be appropriate. However, shops are generally recognised by economists as holding to some extent a monopoly position, partly because no two shops are likely to sell exactly the same combination of goods, and partly because the location of a shop may confer a competitive advantage over other shops (2.5.1). These theoretical problems may have been responsible for the relegation of the retail firm to something of a fringe topic in classical economics.

A representative selection of the work of economists on the retail sector in general, and the retail firm, is provided in the reader 'Economics of Retailing' (Tucker and Yamey, 1973). Most of the papers in this anthology tend to be normative. Typical problems tackled are the optimal size (optimal in terms of productivity) of the retail firm (Douglas, 1962; Winsten and Hall, 1971), or the optimal mix of retail goods to be stocked in a supermarket (Holton, 1957). A second area of concern is the impact upon profitability of changes in retail management policies (Baumol, 1967), or in instruments of public policy (Gould and Preston, 1965). In all of these areas there is scope for the economist to provide greater understanding. There appears to be less interest demonstrated however in description of the retail sector as a whole, or of the behaviour of retail firms. In general, economists seem reluctant to seek convincing empirical evidence for their theories, as has been pointed out by many authors, including Simon (1959).

Economists have offered an important contribution in the theory of 'consumer' or 'household' behaviour. This deals with the processes by which the rational consumer should decide how much to spend upon various types of goods and services, proceeding by means of the concepts of total utility, marginal utility, and the household's demand curve (e.g. Lipsey, 1975, Chapter 15). Specialist treatments have included discussions of the timing of purchases, household decisions on savings, methods of holding wealth when faced by uncertainty, and the evaluation of the efficiency of an economic system in terms of effects upon consumers (e.g. Brown and Deaton, 1972; Green, 1976). Clearly the consumer is expected to have full knowledge of marginal utilities and costs of goods, and the capability of applying this knowledge correctly in a given situation. While this appears unlikely as an explanation of individual behaviour, economists would argue that over a large population, aggregate behaviour will tend to approach that of the rational consumer multiplied many times over.

Recently several writers have attempted to modify the model of the fully rational consumer, by examining issues such as consumers' perception and valuation of time (e.g. Lowe, 1973); limitations on the ability of consumers to compare goods (Nelson, 1970); and consumers' reactions to pricing policies (Gabor, 1974). Thus, the strict economic approach in this area is becoming more applicable to the individual case, by taking aboard some of the concepts derived from behavioural science (2.4.2-3).

2.4.2 The psychological approach

The behavioural science of psychology has provided three important areas of insight. The first is the 'descriptive theory' of decision making, which has been summarised above (2.3). This has hardly been applied yet to the study of decision making in retail firms, but is becoming increasingly used in the study of spatial aspects of consumer behaviour (2.5.3). The second and third concern the analysis of individual consumer behaviour; the contrast here is basically between qualitative and quantitative modes of explanation.

The qualitative modes derive from the main stream of psychological theory. Although a number of strands of psychological thought are involved, it is probably fair to state that most of the theoretical and empirical development has been connected with the concepts of need (or drive), stimulus (or cue), response, and reinforcement. These concepts are discussed in more detail below (5.2): it is sufficient here to refer to the existence of many texts on consumer behaviour, mostly for an intended readership of advertising, marketing or retail students and managers (e.g. Britt, 1970; Kassarjian and Robertson, 1973; Foxall, 1977). The nature of these texts suggests a close relationship between the psychological approach and the applied sciences of marketing and market research.

The basic principle in market research is that in order successfully to sell consumer goods to the public, one should understand the aspirations, motivations and perceptual processes of individuals. This is partly so that appropriate markets can be found for particular goods, but also so that consumers can be persuaded into buying more of Brand X than of any other brand. Some have claimed that a principal aim of market research is to improve methods of manipulating consumer demand to suit the requirements of consumer goods manufacturers (Packard, 1957). An example of this approach at its most cynical is the well known 'Handbook of Consumer Motivations' by Dichter (1964). The profession itself would however claim that market research is essential in allowing the manufacturers to adjust their products according to consumer needs and preferences.

It should be recognised that the work of applied psychologists in market research has been of considerable importance in helping to explain aspects of consumer behaviour, particularly those which the economic approach (2.4.1) cannot easily deal with. Surprisingly though there appears to have been little attempt to integrate this work with the contributions of Simon and others to descriptive decision theory. One would expect market researchers to be concerned to know the extent to which consumers may conduct searches, and accept satisfactory rather than optimal solutions.

Quantitative models of behaviour have also been developed by psychologists (or 'psychometrists'). Two formulations have particular relevance to consumer behaviour, as they both attempt to model processes of decision making. The first is in the area of 'choice theory' (Luce, 1959; Luce and Suppes, 1965). This is developed from the premise that the probability of an individual choosing one stimulus from several presented to him is directly related to the utility derived from that stimulus, compared with the utilities derived from the other stimuli in the choice set. (4)   It is further assumed that the utility of any stimulus depends upon attributes of that stimulus, and upon characteristics of the individual. This theory has clear applications in the study of brand choice, and choice of shopping centre (2.5.3).

A second type of formulation has been of the stochastic model of buying behaviour (Ehrenburg, 1969; 1972; Massy et al, 1970). This work has concentrated on methods of predicting aggregate behaviour over periods of time. The emphasis is on <u>regularities</u> in aspects of, for example, repeat purchasing of brands, rather than the identification of differences between individuals, as in the more qualitatively inspired work described above.

To summarise, the psychological approach has provided considerable insight into aspects of consumer choice of retail goods, and to a lesser extent, of spatial consumer behaviour (2.5.2 and 5.2). The habitual application of concepts or findings to practical marketing problems tends however to inhibit the development of an integrated theory of individual consumer behaviour.

2.4.3 The sociological approach

The approaches outlined in the above two subsections have been concerned to hypothesise and explain behaviour of the individual involved in selling or buying goods. Sociological studies are likely to take a broader view, examining ways in which behaviour is related to the individual's social environment of family, peer groups and neighbours. There appear to be two different areas of interest here.

Firstly, academic sociologists have shown some interest in the retail sector. The 'small' or independent shopkeeper does not fit easily into the conventional system of social classes, and hence his behaviour and values deserve special attention. However, this topic seems to be of fringe interest, and has progressed in Britain mainly through the attention of one group of sociologists (Bechhofer et al, 1971; 1974a; 1974b), whose findings are discussed below (4.4).

The other area in which sociological concepts and findings have been applied is in market research. Firstly, it is recognised that aspects of consumer behaviour are often statistically related to measurable demographic and socio economic characteristics of the consumer. This theme will be evident in the discussion of evidence on spatial aspects of consumer behaviour in Britain (below, 5.4). Secondly, market researchers have drawn upon broad areas of theory in social psychology, such as role theory (Goffman, 1959) and direction theory (Riesman et al, 1961). Here it is suggested that the consumer's 'self image' is affected not just by his own needs and drives, but also by the nature of the roles he has to adopt in society, and by the influences of family, colleagues and peer groups.

These concepts are again applied by authors such as Schewe (1973) to help improve sales of branded goods. This approach should thus be regarded as an adjunct to the psychological approach (2.4.2). It is probably fair to conclude that mainstream sociology has so far provided little enlightenment upon retailing and consumer behaviour.

2.4.4 The retail management approach

The approaches described above all stem from academic disciplines, each
with its own methods of theory construction and empirical research.
In addition there exists material written for those engaged in retailing,
and which usually has little explicit theoretical content.

One theme here is advice to those wishing to become retailers (e.g.
Jensen, 1963; Fiber, 1972). This type of book will contain straightforward instruction on raising capital, choosing and controlling stock,
keeping accounts, management of staff, etc.

A second area of literature on retailing is of interest more to the
large retail firm. A number of books and journals report new or improved
methods of management, and also describe changes taking place within
certain firms, or within the retail sector itself (e.g. Thorpe, 1974a).
In recent years two important studies have been commissioned by
government agencies in Britain: the report on 'The Future Pattern of
Shopping' (Distributive Trades E.D.C., 1971), and the research carried
out for the Bolton Committee on Small Firms, among which is to be found a
useful study of the retail sector (A.D. Smith, 1971).

These and similar studies are of considerable interest, but contain
little material on decision making processes within the retail sector.
It will become clear from a study of the following chapters that the
absence of empirical evidence on such processes is one of the main
deficiencies in our knowledge of retailing.

2.4.5 Conclusions

The discussion in this section has been somewhat artificial in its
deliberate omission of material on spatial aspects of retailing and
consumer behaviour. However, a number of problems have emerged. In
relation to the purposes of this book, two problems stand out. The first
is the fragmentation of empirical work on the retail sector, resulting
from the peripheral involvement of several academic disciplines. The
behaviour of actors in retailing has tended to be studied either to
demonstrate the value of concepts whose main applications are elsewhere,
or to help improve the profitability of manufacturing and retail firms.
Thus there has been little apparent need for writers to step outside the
bounds imposed by their own academic paradigms, or practical objectives.

The second problem to be found in reviewing the existing literature
on retailing is the general lack of explicit investigation into decision
making. The economic and psychological paradigms involve contrasting
assumptions about consumer decision processes. In both disciplines the
modification of theory arises from further deduction, or from inference
of decision making processes gained from studies of the behaviour of
firms, households and individuals. The important work of Simon and his
associates appears to have gone untested so far in research into the
retail sector.

2.5 SPATIAL ASPECTS OF RETAILING: A LITERATURE REVIEW

This section follows a course similar to 2.4, in examining existing
material on spatial aspects of retailing. The attention thus is on
variations in behaviour where some specific choice of location is
involved. All the disciplines mentioned in 2.4 have some interest in
this topic. A further discipline - geography - is given extended
treatment below, because of its special interest in explaining spatial

variations in economic activity. It will be found that geographers have
been concerned mainly to describe and explain physical patterns of retail
outlets and shopping centres, but that in recent years more attention
has been focussed on the behaviour of the actors involved in retailing,
with most of this attention being devoted to consumers.

2.5.1 The economic approach

It has already been stated (2.4.1) that retailers are held by orthodox
economists to hold partially monopolistic advantages, because their
location will (other things being equal) ensure the custom of those who
live or work close to the shop. The force of this argument was weakened
by the theoretical findings of Hotelling (1929) that firms selling
identical goods would cluster together so as to ensure that their
competitors did not capture an excessive share of the market. Later
authors have developed the analysis of location for several firms
selling similar products (Lösch, 1954; Devletoglou, 1965), but there
has been no concensus as to whether a dispersed or clustered pattern is
more likely to develop (for detailed reviews, see D.M. Smith, 1971,
pp.130-147; Cooper, 1975, pp.29-30).

This theoretical work is in general characterised by naive assumptions
about locational decisions of retailers and consumers. These assumptions,
some of which are implied rather than stated, appear to include the
following: retailers are fully aware of the advantages to be gained
from finding an optimal location: they can move short distances to an
improved location, following certain actions of competitors, with
minimal costs; alternatively, retailers not located in optimal sites
will inevitably fail; consumers obey simple rules governing their
choice of location, usually that they visit the nearest shop offering
the good required.

There appears to have been little enthusiasm among economists for
testing theories of retail location, or for integrating them with
analyses of other aspects of retail management. Among the few articles
that attempt the latter are Baumol and Ide (1956), in the American
context, and Lewis (1945) in the British. The latter article, despite
its age, is still useful as an analysis of retail distribution in
Britain: among other things it holds that small shops are far too
numerous for efficient operation, and predicts a rapid decline in their
numbers. The post war experience has confirmed this hypothesis (9.3).

2.5.2 The social psychological approach

Both the psychological and sociological approaches (2.4.2-3) have little
to offer specifically on spatial aspects of decision making. These
approaches remain important however in providing much of the insight
necessary for one to understand spatial aspects of consumer behaviour.
For example, some market researchers have examined the 'images' that
various types of retail store may induce in the consumer (e.g. Berry,
1969; Grubb and Grathwohl, 1967; Lessig, 1973). This topic obviously
has spatial implications, as consumers' trip destinations may be those
stores which possess the most attractive images.

2.5.3 The geographical approach

Geography is the one discipline that is explicitly concerned with spatial
aspects of behaviour, and with retail location as a subject for study in
its own right. Therefore it is of crucial importance here, in adapting

theory from other disciplines, and in formulating its own theories and methods of analysis. As there already exist two works which provide full reviews of the application of geographical thought to the study of retailing (Scott, 1970; Davies, 1976a), the following review will summarise the main themes of geographical research.

Geographers have shown enormous interest in patterns of retail location since around the mid 1950s. This interest was stimulated principally by the discovery of the work of Christaller (1966) by American researchers. Christaller's central place theory had been developed in the 1930s to explain regularities in the size distribution and locational pattern of settlements in southern Germany. The theory was adapted to the case of 'tertiary activity location' (retail and business activity) within urban areas, by Berry and Garrison (1958). This in turn stimulated much empirical measurement of characteristics of shopping centres and consumer trip patterns, examples of which are reviewed in Scott (1970, Chapters 9-10) and Berry (1967). Detailed commentaries upon central place theory, including the work of Lösch (1954), are given by Beavon (1977) and Carter (1975, Chapters 5-7).

As with the economic theory described above (2.4.1; 2.5.1), central place theory is deduced from simplistic assumptions about the behaviour of retailers and consumers. The empirical research into characteristics of settlements and shopping centres has generally given only weak support, if any, to the predictions of the theory (Beavon, 1977, Chapter 4). This has led geographers to question the assumptions of uniformly 'rational' behaviour by retailers and consumers. It was shown firstly that the policies of property developers and major retail firms could have important effects upon the location and size of new shopping centres, and upon the prosperity of older centres in an urban area (Cohen and Lewis, 1967; Thorpe and Rhodes, 1966). Secondly, surveys of consumer behaviour in space showed that a considerable minority, if not majority, of shopping trips were of greater length than the minimum required to purchase the goods or services in question (e.g. Golledge Rushton and Clark, 1966; Clark, 1968). This finding led to the identification of two further areas for research. First, consumers' perceptions of the opportunities available in shopping centres, and of their distances from home, might be both biased and partial. Second, there might be attributes of shops or shopping centres which consumers would regard as more important than distance from the home. It became inevitable that psychological and sociological concepts would be necessary in the development of theory and empirical methodology. Thus, the geographical research has in recent years begun to attempt the analyses of spatial aspects of consumer behaviour, which the psychological and sociological approaches have been unwilling to investigate (2.5.2).

Most of the recent geographical research thus stems from a relatively new stance in geography, which recognises that consumer behaviour is affected both by the spatial disposition of shopping centres available, and by personal and social characteristics of the consumer. There are however two basic approaches to this type of research. The first is that the underlying factors affecting choice of shop or shopping centre can be inferred or 'revealed' from analysis of actual behaviour, usually at aggregate level (e.g. Rushton, 1969). This assumption has in itself met with considerable criticism, summed up by Pirie (1976); and in addition, Rushton's work should be criticised because variations between individuals are assumed to be unimportant. However, formulations which allow for variation in perception of opportunities, and/or in variation according to personal and socio economic characteristics of the shopper, may become very complex (Pipkin, 1977; 1979).

21

The second approach has been to carry out interview surveys designed to elicit the factors which individuals consider important in influencing their choice of shop and centre. These may be questioned directly (Bruce and Delworth, 1976; Bowlby, 1979; Downs, 1970), or may be derived indirectly from analysis of comparisons between shop or centre types (Hudson, 1976; Spencer, 1978). This approach lies open to charges of bias, either because of restrictions over choice of answer in the direct approach, or because of the necessity for interpretation by the researcher in the indirect approach.

Two other topics of recent research are linked with these basic approaches. The first is the study of dynamic sequences of choice of shop or shopping centre, related to various models of learning processes. This work has been pioneered by Burnett (1973; 1977; 1978; see 5.3.4). The second topic, related more to the second broad approach, is of consumers' perceptions of shopping opportunities. The initial work of Horton and Reynolds (1971) on 'action space' and 'activity space' has been extended by several researchers (e.g. Bowlby, 1972; Smith, 1976; Potter, 1977, 1979), and is discussed further in 5.3.5.

At the same time, geographical research into the supply side (developers, retailers and planners) appears to have made little progress since the late 1960s. This seems surprising, because in recent years much of the study of industrial location has been characterised by research into the decision making processes of industrial firms (e.g. Townroe, 1972; Cooper, 1975). Cooper's study of industrial firms in the Midlands and North-West of England which had recently moved their location made explicit use of descriptive decision theory (2.3) in its investigation of information seeking, search processes and learning from experience. Similar studies of decision making and locational behaviour on the part of retail firms would be valuable.

This brief review of the geographical approach has concentrated on the development of theory and the recent trend towards more explicit studies of decision making and behaviour. It has omitted discussion of other material of considerable interest, but which is intended mainly to provide more precise description of patterns of location, rather than theoretical explanation. The important work of 'marketing geographers' will be discussed in the next section.

2.5.4 The retail management approach

At this point, as in Section 2.4, the attention shifts from essentially academic studies of the retail sector, to work which has a more normative purpose. The focus in this subsection is on material which describes methods of selecting appropriate retail locations. Since a summary of this material is to be given below (3.2), it is necessary here simply to relate it to the topics already discussed in this chapter.

Much of the development of methods of assessing and choosing locations for retail development, especially in the United States, has been the responsibility of 'marketing geographers' (Davies, 1976a). These methods usually make indirect use of central place theory, in their reliance on the definition of 'market areas' or 'trade areas' for stores and shopping centres. A recognition of the diversity of behaviour amongst consumers has led to increasing reliance on surveys of consumer behaviour and attitudes as a prelude to the defining of market areas: thus, 'primary', 'secondary' and 'fringe' areas often have to be determined for existing shopping centres (Thorpe and Rhodes, 1966). The extent of market areas may be estimated from a combination of methods: surveys of consumer behaviour, or recognition of a central place hierarchy and the resulting deduction of the size and population of market areas, or the use of 'Reilly's Law' to determine the boundary between market areas of two centres (Reilly, 1929; Thompson, 1966; Davies, 1976a, pp.32-34). American marketing geographers have written many articles describing their methods (e.g. Applebaum, 1961; Kornblau, 1968).

Much has been written also on the evaluation of sites for specific types of store (e.g. Ransome, 1961; Kane, 1966; Epstein, 1971). The fullest treatment, and one which has influenced many authors, has been that of Nelson (1958), which is discussed below (4.2.1). In this and other such works the emphasis tends to be upon drawing criteria and guidelines from analogy with successful firms, developments, etc., or simply from experience. Explicit references to theory of retail location or consumer behaviour is uncommon.

In contrast, there is little published material on store location research in Britain. Only one book appears to deal specifically with this topic (Cox, 1968: discussed below, 4.2.1).

The important development of spatial interaction models for use in retail forecasting, although pioneered by Huff (1966) for use by retail firms, has been applied most thoroughly in public sector retail planning. Thus it will be mentioned in the following subsection.

It is worth noting finally the almost complete lack of concern of centre and store location experts with any elements of the psychological or sociological approaches to retailer or consumer behaviour. Thus we may find one set of consultants advising a firm on store 'image', and another on store location, without any joint discussion of the concepts and methods used by the two sides. (5)

2.5.5 The town planning approach

A full discussion both of the rationale for town planning intervention in the retail sector, and of methods of analysis used by planners, will be held in Chapter 6. A few general points may be noted here.

Town planning as an academic discipline has to rely for its interpretation of urban society on the established social science disciplines discussed above. Its main focus of attention has been the development of methods whereby certain societal goals and problems can be defined and the impact of planning policies on these goals and problems can be determined. In this respect the retail sector can be seen both to provide its own needs or problems (some of which are discussed in Chapters 7-9) for the attention of planners, and also to have impact on other foci of planning concern, such as traffic problems.

In general town planners have been slow to develop an explicit concern for the retail sector itself. However, some attention has been paid to the 'forecasting' of changes in retail provision among shopping centres. The use of methods derived from central place theory, similar to those of marketing geographers, is common in Britain (Davies, 1976a).

Another important set of methods has been that associated with spatial interaction theory (Davies, 1976a, Chapters 2, 8). Its application to retail forecasting has derived both from its early use by marketing geographers (2.5.4) and from the development of 'gravity' models for use in transport planning. Following the well known paper by Lakshmanan and Hansen (1965), the first to use a spatial interaction model of the retail sector in the assessment of alternative proposals for development, much effort has gone into theoretical refinement (Wilson, 1970; Senior, 1979) and into solving problems of measurement and calibration (e.g. Openshaw, 1976; Batty, 1976). Rather less effort appears to have been

made to ensure that results of direct application in the planning
process are produced (6.2.4); or to acknowledge their simplistic
assumptions of consumer behaviour (Huff, 1966) and of retailers'
adjustments to changes in consumer demand patterns. Some researchers
have however used spatial interaction models deliberately to explore
facets of consumer behaviour that do not correspond to the models'
assumptions (e.g. Bucklin, 1967; Schiller, 1972).

The town planning approach then is one where future events in retailing
are usually forecast in a rather simplistic manner, and policies
designed accordingly. In some instances planners are prepared to have
special surveys of consumer shopping behaviour carried out, usually in
order to calibrate interaction models for forecasting purposes. Surveys
are also used in attempts to estimate the impact upon shopping patterns
of new major retail developments (Chapter 8). The design of such surveys
may be sophisticated, but the information collected is often no more than
physical details of shopping behaviour and some demographic and socio
economic data. There is thus little indication that planners are fully
aware of the findings of market researchers on variations in aspiration
and perception among consumers (2.4). There is even less evidence that
most planners understand the decision processes of developers and
retailers, although they may have some first hand experience through
attempting to negotiate with them. This lack of understanding is not
surprising, since there has been little serious attempt to apply
established theory of decision making to the activities of developers
and retailers.

2.5.6 Conclusions

The conclusions regarding the published material on spatial aspects of
retailing are similar to those in the previous section (2.4.5). The
development both of theory and empirical research has, with a few
exceptions, been inhibited by academic demarcation lines, and a
comprehensive understanding of spatial choice patterns either of
retailers or consumers does not yet exist. One way towards this goal
appears to be in the construction and testing of models of choice
processes, using normative and/or descriptive decision theory. While
some of the work reviewed above makes reference to decision theory
concepts, much remains to be done in this area.

A disparity exists also between the 'academic' and 'practical' work on
topics such as assessment of store location. The published work written
by or for the practitioners (which may here be defined to include town
planners) makes use of very simple models of spatial structure and
consumer behaviour. Reliance is placed upon rules of thumb and analogies
with past events. The degree of success of such methods may be
satisfactory to those concerned, but only in situations where
expectations and behaviour are likely to remain stable over time.

2.6 SUMMARY AND CONCLUSIONS

This chapter has attempted an overview of the theories which are of
actual or potential use to those who attempt to describe and explain
patterns of retail location and consumer behaviour over space. In
Chapter 1 the view was put forward that such patterns can be interpreted
as the results of decisions by those actors involved in retailing.
This view necessitates an examination first of decision theory (2.2,
2.3). Here it is found that although there seems to be general

agreement over what constitutes a decision and what basic thought processes are involved, there is an important distinction to be made between normative and descriptive theory. The former is intended to guide decision makers into making their decisions as 'rational' as possible, given imperfect information. The latter draws upon theory and techniques of observation from behavioural science rather than economics, in suggesting strategies that decision makers commonly use in order to simplify the task of decision making. These strategies are not perfect, and lead to distortions of 'rationality'.

In 2.4 and 2.5, the contributions of several social science disciplines to the study of the retail sector have been examined. The distinction is drawn between work which has been carried out mainly to advance the state of knowledge in the discipline concerned, and work which attempts to improve performance of those involved in the retail sector itself. It is found that the academic approaches have largely remained separate, and that each has led to a set of methods used by practitioners. It is also found that, although the practical aspects would seem to be largely a matter of advising decisions, there is little regard paid to either normative or descriptive decision theory. Both branches are however making some impact on the recent geographical research into aspects of consumer behaviour in space.

These conclusions suggest elements of a new approach to the study of the retail sector, which is to be developed in the next four chapters of this book. Because of the lack of application of decision theory in the existing literature, it is necessary to explore the possibilities of such application. This entails the examination of some rather fragmented evidence of behaviour by the actors involved, and the inference from this evidence of typical sequences of decisions. This in turn may suggest a need for the further development of theory in relation to the different actors.

However, it is hoped also that even at this stage an increased understanding of the retail sector may emerge from the analysis. This understanding is put to the test in the final chapters, in which a number of current problems in British retail planning are examined.

NOTES

(1) For detailed presentations of normative decision theory, the reader is referred to standard texts such as Raiffa, 1968; Lindley, 1971; Moore and Thomas, 1976; Kaufman and Thomas, 1977.
(2) Decision criteria other than EMV can be used: these involve departures from 'pure rationality' and are discussed in 2.2.3.
(3) In contrast, an 'optimistic' decision maker would choose A since it may offer the best outcome of any location.
(4) This may be compared with economic theory, which would predict a deterministic choice such that the stimulus with the highest utility is always chosen (Stopher and Meyburg, 1975, pp.4-12).
(5) These two areas of concern may in fact be strongly linked: see 4.2.2.

3 Attitudes to retail location: the developer

3.1 THE PROPERTY DEVELOPER IN BRITAIN

This chapter examines the behaviour of property developers in Britain
in their role as provider of new shopping facilities. In this section
some principles of property development are discussed, together with
a brief description of the 'shopping precinct' that has been one typical
result of developers' activity. The following section reviews some
evidence concerning the decisions of developers about location and
siting of developments with a substantial retail component. Section 3.3
examines the typical processes of negotiation with retail firms and
public sector agencies (usually local authorities) that developers have
carried out. The final section attempts to relate these findings to the
more general issues discussed in Chapter 2, and also provides some
tentative conclusions about future changes in processes of shopping
centre development.

The approach used in this chapter thus follows the framework discussed
in Chapters 1 and 2, with an emphasis upon the processes of decision
making adopted typically by 'actors' in the development process. The
chapter should ideally be read in conjunction with other accounts which
emphasise the economic and political aspects of property development,
and in particular the effects of changes in the sources of capital, and
its availability to developers, in inducing changes in methods of
development (e.g. Ambrose and Colenutt, 1975; Massey and Catalano,
1978).

This chapter also serves as introduction to the detailed discussion,
in Chapter 7, of the postwar history of retail development in British
town centres.

3.1.1 The rationale for property development

The property development company (or 'developer', (1) to use common
terminology) is essentially an intermediary in the process by which
land users find locations for their activities in capitalist economies.
The developer provides space, in the form of houses, shop units, office
accommodation, etc, on land which has either previously been devoted to
some other use, or which has been devoted to the same use, but in a
manner which most users would consider to be of inferior quality. The
rationale of the developer may thus be seen as the making of profits as
a direct result of increasing the value of a parcel of land, (2)
because of its development. Table 3.1 describes the development process
in general terms.

Profits are made from development in two ways. Firstly, the developer
may seek an annual income from the developed site, in the form of rents
paid by users, which exceeds the annual repayments of the capital needed
to finance the purchase of land, and the construction of the development
itself. The difference between income and costs, averaged over several
years, may be termed 'developer's yield' (Cadman and Austin-Crowe, 1978,
pp. 32-33). Secondly, the developer may seek an increase in the value
of the land itself, such that he can make a capital profit by selling
the site after its development. There is a connection between these

Table 3.1   The development process

Stage in process	Actors involved
1. Perception and estimation of demand for new commercial buildings	(E) (P)
2. Identification and securing of sites on which buildings might be constructed to meet that demand	O (P)
3. Design of accommodation to meet the demand on the sites identified	P (A) (T)
4. Arrangement of short and long term finance to fund site acquisition and construction	I
5. Management of design and construction	C
6. Letting and management of the completed buildings	T

E   economic consultant
P   local authority planner
O   landowner
A   consultant architect
I   investor
T   tenant(s)
C   construction company

Notes

1. ( ) denotes involvement in certain instances only.

2. The developer who may either be a property company or any one of P, L, I, T or C, is involved in all stages.

3. Source: Based upon the Pilcher Report (Department of the Environment, 1975), pp. 49-50.

---

two types of financial objective, since the value of a developed site is linked to the level of income that can be expected from its users over a period of time. Even if a developer retains ownership of the site, he can benefit from the increase in value, to the extent of being able to secure loans for further development elsewhere.

3.1.2 Property development in post-war Britain

As a prelude to the examination of retail development schemes, it is worth briefly summarising the postwar history of property development in Britain. This account draws mainly upon the material in Marriott (1967) and Massey and Catalano (1978, Chapter 6).

Property development firms existed before the war, but it was common then for users desiring new accommodation to buy freehold sites and carry out development themselves. The postwar opportunities for redevelopment, caused by war damage, were gradually taken up in the early 1950s. aided by the relaxation of earlier legislation restricting the level of construction activity. Local authorities were enabled to buy war damaged sites through compulsory purchase, thus initiating the

powers of site acquisition to be used more extensively in the 1960s.
At the same time a number of individuals – often estate agents – foresaw
rising demands for modern office and shop property in central areas and
began to accumulate suitable sites for development. With the successful
completion of such schemes, a number of property development companies
expanded their activities rapidly, since they now possessed credibility
in the eyes of bank managers and other sources of finance. Existing
developments were used as security for the loan of further capital.

The early 1960s was probably the heyday of the property development
company, with a few developers making capital profits of several millions
of pounds on single schemes. Provincial shop and office developments,
more modest in scale, were also becoming commonplace.

The results of the success of the larger companies were an increasing
pace and scale of development, as more financial institutions sought to
benefit from investment in property. During the middle and late 1960s,
insurance companies and pension funds invested significantly more in
property than hitherto, and increasingly sought to benefit from
increases in rents and land values rather than simply accept loan
repayments. Landowners and construction companies also sought
development gains.

The effects of these trends were somewhat detrimental to property
development firms, who found that intense competition now existed for
developable freehold sites. This forced up prices, thus reducing
development gains; and the demands of financial institutions meant that
smaller proportions of gains devolved to developers. They were, until
1973, shielded from the full extent of these effects because of the
continual increase in land and property values. This was fuelled by
expectations that current rapid increases in rents would be maintained
well into the future. Developers also increasingly sought the security
of 'partnerships' with local authorities, in which the problems of land
acquisition were ameliorated (7.3.3), although financial institutions,
construction companies and landowners were also becoming involved in
partnership schemes.

In 1973-74, a combination of events occurred which significantly
worsened the position of the developer. These events included the
imposition of government control over commercial rents, changes in the
taxation system for property companies, rapid increases in interest
rates, and general investment uncertainty allied to an international
economic recession. It became clear that expectations of continually
rising rents were false, and thus the value of property companies at
the Stock Exchange fell dramatically. New development, in almost all
instances, became financially infeasible. Several firms collapsed and
others were taken over by insurance companies, multinational enterprises
or foreign governments.

In the late 1970s there is evidence that rents are beginning to rise
in real terms, and that the new Conservative government's attitude to
property development will be more benevolent than Labour's. This has
led to expectations of the renaissance of property development. The
events of the 1965-1973 period seem unlikely to be repeated however,
unless interest rates can be reduced and stabilised; and clearer
indications of increasing demand by users for new floorspace will be
necessary to justify the risks involved in large schemes.

3.1.3 Attitudes to property developers

A notable feature of the literature on property development in Britain
is its critical or even polemical stance (e.g. Ambrose and Colenutt,

1975). The strongest criticism has been reserved for certain developers who have made profits of several millions of pounds from single developments, usually of offices in central London (Marriott, 1967, Chapters 11 and 12). But two more general arguments should also be mentioned.

The first is that the inflow of funds into property development, particularly in the early 1970s, represented a diversion of financial capital from the more socially justifiable function of supporting industrial investment in plant and machinery.

The second argument is that increases in land value which arise from the community's agreement to property development, should be returned to the community as a whole. This sentiment is expressed as an objective of the Community Land Act (Department of the Environment, 1974, para 16).

These criticisms appear to have led developers to adopt defensive postures in their dealings with public sector agencies and the public. Developers try to foster public images of themselves as ordinary businessmen trying to make 'normal' profits, despite government hindrance; or even as public-spirited benefactors who single handed have dragged Britain's cities into the twentieth century. In reality the developer habitually takes substantial risks, since neither the costs of development nor the future level of income from a developed site can be estimated with any degree of certainty. Therefore he aims for a profit much higher than that which the conventional investor would accept. There are two further effects of this situation, which make the task of reviewing the developer's decision processes (3.2 and 3.3) rather difficult. Firstly, developers tend to be secretive in their operations, and are often reluctant to provide information either on their financial dealings or their methods of locational assessment. This they would regard as action to preserve their competitive position. Secondly as mentioned above, developers tend to lay stress on their value to society. Their own publications cannot therefore be regarded as wholly reliable records of their objectives and methods.

3.1.4 Retail development: the shopping precinct

One important type of user who is willing to rent space provided by the developer is the retailer. In Britain a particular physical form has become associated with developments carried out wholly or partly for retail use. This is the pedestrian precinct, in which shops are built facing a pedestrian way. Large schemes may be built around a number of pedestrian ways, occasionally on two or more levels. A report by the Economist Intelligence Unit (1973) estimates that in the twenty years (approximately) to 1973, no less than 300 of these precincts had opened in British town centres, with a further 160 in suburban locations.

The typical precinct is built in one operation, and consists of one or more large stores and several small shop units. Table 3.2 provides a summary of the planning process necessary for a successful shopping centre development. The large store is usually let to a multiple retail firm (the 'major space user') at an early stage in the process of development, and the small units are let at later stages. It is normal for the developer to retain possession of the land, as freeholder or leaseholder, after completion of the development. He may then provide management and publicity services for the precinct (or 'centre') as a whole. In these respects the British precincts are similar to 'planned centres' in the United States. The contrast lies mainly in their typical location, as American examples are almost all in suburban or out-of-town locations

Table 3.2   An idealised development process for shopping centres

Stage of process	Questions to be answered	Actors involved
1. Initiation	Can land be acquired ?	(O)
	Will planning permission be obtained ?	(P)
2. Potential and suitability	Is there a need for a new centre ?	E
	What potential is there for profit ?	E
	Will a shopping centre serve the needs of the developer, tenants, local authority, and community at large ?	P (T)
3. Size of gross retail area	How large an area ?	E
	How many levels ?	
	Will it be viable ?	E
	How much will its construction cost ?	Q
	What are the requirements for access and parking ?	P
4. Type and character	Should centre be covered ?	(P) (T)
	Should centre be air conditioned ?	(T)
	What shape should it have ?	P
	What physical appearance ?	P
	Should there be a design 'theme' ?	
5. Preliminary breakdown of space users	Number and size of major space users ?	E
	Type of major space users ?	E (T)
	Any special features ? (e.g. retail market)	(P) (T)
	Number, size and type of smaller units ?	
	Length and type of lease (e.g. fixed or turnover rents)	
6. Selection of key tenants	Which 'key' tenants ?	L T
7. Schematic layout	What form of layout ?	A D
8. Selection of tenant mix	Which types of tenant and in which units ?	D Q L
9. Development to completion		

O   landowner(s)
P   local authority planner
E   economic consultant
T   tenant(s)
Q   quantity surveyor
L   letting agent
A   consultant architect
D   consultant designer

Notes

1. The 'developer' may internalise any of these functions except T.

2. Source: Based upon Northen and Haskoll, 1977, pp. 84-87.

(Davies,1976a, Chapter 6). The reasons for this contrast are discussed
in Chapters 6 and 7 below.

3.1.5 The public sector authority as developer

Many precincts have been developed partly or wholly by the public sector
in the form of local authorities, or development corporations in new
towns. This influence ranges from 'partnership' schemes with developers
(7.3.3) to schemes in which the authority takes full responsibility and
full risk for the development, although relying on financial support
from the private sector. These types of scheme are explained in detail
by Stocks and Gleave (1971).
   The public sector authority is obviously motivated by broad goals
different from those of the developer: it should strive to meet the
needs of the community rather than aim for substantial long term profits.
But so far as the details of retail development are concerned, there is
often little difference between public and private sector operations,
in respect of precinct design, typical rent levels, types of retail
firm involved, etc. There are probably two main reasons for this
similarity. Firstly, the public sector authority will feel obliged to
make a profit from each of its commercial schemes: this may be required
by central government and is likely to be supported in principle by
local political interests. This normally entails the charging of
'realistic' or 'market' levels of rent to the retail and other occupiers
of a scheme. Secondly, public authorities often use private sector
consultants to advise on design, tenant selection, rent levels, etc.,
and these consultancy firms are also employed by private developers.
Hence a similarity in visual appearance between public and private
sector precincts, especially in town centres.
   For these reasons, the distinction between public and private sector
developers will not generally be made in the remainder of this chapter.

3.2 THE DEVELOPER'S PERCEPTION OF LOCATION

This section discusses methods used typically by developers in reaching
decisions on the location and scale of developments with a major retail
component.

3.2.1 The developer's locational decision

It is said that when any private developer is asked which are the three
most important requirements for a successful shopping centre development,
he will reply 'Location, location and location'. Most experts in this
field are quick to give examples of 'badly located' centres, especially
after they have been open for some time and still contain a high
proportion of vacant shop units. It appears more difficult though to
identify 'good' locations in advance of development.
   To examine this point it is necessary to consider the general nature
of the opportunities which are made available to developers. It is

probably rare for developers of retail schemes to take a positive role
in accumulating sites for development, by purchasing land from several
landowners, in the manner of some office developers. It is more common
for developers to be offered an option to purchase a site, usually on a
long lease. That site may be surplus to the requirements of a landowner:
an example is the Whitgift Centre in Croydon, developed on land formerly
owned by a private school (Marriott, 1967, p. 220). Alternatively, the
site may have been purchased from several landowners by a local authority,
in the interests of 'comprehensive redevelopment' (7.2.2). In this case
the authority may wish to constrain the developer's freedom of choice
still further in stipulating the amount of space to be developed for
various land uses, or other conditions.

Thus the developer has to estimate the costs of development and future
rent income from a site of which he has little prior knowledge,
frequently under conditions of pressure. Usually information about the
site is being provided to several developers so that they can each
'tender' their offers of a purchase price for the lease, and details of
a scheme. These decisions are influenced by the knowledge that a time
limit has been imposed by the landowner or local authority, and that
other firms are involved in similar decision processes. Despite
uncertainty about costs and returns from an unfamiliar site, little time
is available for collecting information about the site or the town in
which it is located. In order to reduce the degree of error and
uncertainty in his estimation of outcomes of development, the developer
can pursue two strategies. The first is to establish a general set of
'rules' for estimating outcomes: these rules are connected with various
locational attributes of a site. The second strategy is to hire a firm
of consultants to estimate these outcomes, using perhaps similar sets of
rules.

The following two subsections discuss the 'rules' that appear typically
to be used by developers or consultants in assessment of sites,
particularly in respect of potential retail use. Finally in this section
an attempt is made to consider the extent to which these rules are in
fact used by developers, and from this consideration some further
conclusions are drawn.

3.2.2 Locational assessment

In considering any possible site for retail development, the developer
must have regard, firstly, to the potential that the shopping centre
and town, of which the site forms part, has for growth in retail
provision; and secondly, to the location of the site itself with
respect to the rest of the shopping centre and town. This is simplifying matters, but seems a valid distinction, particularly for town centre
development, where the site is likely to be small in comparison with the
existing shopping centre. This subsection is concerned with assessment
of a shopping centre or town as a whole.

This assessment is similar to that which can be made by retail firms
in considering new locations for stores. Such methods are discussed
by authors such as Nelson (1958) and Cox (1968) (4.2). One method used
specifically to advise developers is that devised by a firm of estate
agents, and described by Langton (1973). Here, a town centre is given
up to 500 'points' in the calculation of an 'index of retail attraction',
whose components are listed in Table 3.3.

Table 3.3   Components of 'index of retail attraction'

1. Existing retail representation:

Department stores	30 points
Bazaar stores	20 "
Specialist stores	15 "
Convenience shops	5 "
Supermarkets	10 "
Durable goods shops	10 "
Non-retail trades	10 "
	100 points

2. Accessibility:

Access by private transport, and car parking	80 points
Access by public transport	70 "
Access by pedestrians	30 "
	180 points

3. Amenities:

Diversity of retailing	35 points
Ancillary facilities	50 "
Span of opening hours, concentration of shopping, weather protection	60 "
Price levels	30 "
Design and 'atmosphere'	35 "
Adjacent office accommodation	10 "
	220 points

Source: Langton (1973), p. 29.

In Langton's account the precise basis for awarding points is not made clear; presumably, a centre is given maximum or near maximum points for levels of 'representation', 'accessibility', and 'amenities' which are judged to be excellent. Clearly an index of this kind cannot easily be calibrated from existing data, or used precisely with any confidence. The awarding of points on each criterion, as well as the choice of maximum values as listed in Table 3.3 must follow the results of past locational assessments, as well as reflecting a number of value judgments. In view of the emphasis that Cox (1968) and the American 'marketing geographers' (2.5.3) have put upon the application of central place theory in locational assessment, it is interesting to note its virtual absence in this index. Earlier writers such as Diamond and Gibb (1962) stressed the importance of existing levels of population within the catchment area of a town centre, and of probable growth rates in population and expenditure. It may be argued that the 'representation' components reflect the existing demand for retail facilities, which is strongly linked with population levels. But the other components, which carry four fifths of the total weight, are only tenuously linked with population levels. The main assumption underlying this index appears to

be that the shopper will discriminate in favour of a centre that can
offer a high quality environment for shopping and for other forms of
business and pleasure. This seems reasonable where the centre concerned
is one of several of similar importance in a relatively small geographical area, such as the suburbs of London or of a major regional capital.
But it should still be recognised that many towns are relatively
isolated, and in these cases population levels and rates of growth must
be important factors to take into account in assessing the potential for
development.

The situation with respect to a self contained suburban or out of town
shopping development differs from the above in certain respects. Such
centres are designed to be accessible to motorists from surrounding
suburban areas: for example, a requirement for a 'modern,self contained
district centre' is a catchment population of at least 70,000 within
10–15 minutes drive(URPI, 1977a, p. 35). Existing features of the
immediately surrounding area are of little importance in such a
development decision.

3.2.3 Site assessment

When the general location of a potential redevelopment site appears
suitable, the developer still needs to be sure that the site itself
possesses no major disadvantages. One of the main features to consider
here is the geographical relationship between the site and the rest of
the shopping centre within which it lies. Alternatively, it may be
intended to build an entirely new centre, but similar criteria apply to
some extent. In both cases, the major criteria are of accessibility.

For the town centre pedestrian precinct, the three main site requirements appear to be first, proximity to major shopping facilities;
second, proximity to adequate car parking facilities; and third, a
good position with respect to major pedestrian routes, for example a
route between existing department stores, or between a car park and the
central part of the shopping centre.

So far as suburban centres are concerned, car parking facilities and
accessibility by road appear to be the major requirements for a site.
For smaller centres, pedestrian access from nearby residential areas is
important.

3.2.4 Locational and site assessment in practice

The previous two subsections have discussed methods of assessment as
recommended by writers in this field. These methods all involve, to
varying extents, the concepts of population catchment, attraction of
existing facilities, and site accessibility. Practitioners would
experience problems in attempting to carry out assessments, using any
of the published methods. This is because the methods are not generally
described clearly enough to be of direct use. The experienced developer
or consultant is thus likely to work out his own methods of assessment,
relying to some extent on rules of thumb and comparative judgments.

There appears to be no empirically based review of methods actually
used in locational assessment in advance of retail development. It is
impossible therefore to suggest which methods are most commonly used and
by whom. It can be suggested that in some cases methods of locational
and site assessment have been poor, or non existent. Even this has to
be shown largely by inference.

It seems, firstly, that there is so much variability between methods

34

used by different 'experts' that the success or failure of a scheme may depend upon whose advice one adopts. Cole (1966) has demonstrated enormous variation in assessments of recommended floorspace increases in a number of shopping centres, when the methods used by different consultants or local authorities are compared. The apparent viability of a scheme would thus seem to depend upon the choice of advisor as much as the merits of the location itself.

Secondly, it appears that in some cases, developers have not made any attempt at all to estimate the locational characteristics (as defined above) of a town centre in judging whether to prepare a scheme; or, they may receive unfavourable advice, ignore it and go ahead with the scheme (Marriott, 1967, Chapter 15).

Similarly, Likierman and Wilcock (1970), in an examination of three suburban precincts, criticise the methods of demand forecasting and financial appraisal used by developers and local authorities alike. They suggest that in these examples 'the actual shopping area was determined quite arbitrarily' (p. 140).

Where site assessment is concerned, the nature of the typical town centre site offered to developers is likely to present problems. Such a site will usually be very large, in relation to the area of a single shop, and is unlikely to have been used for intensive retail purposes prior to redevelopment. It will probably be on the edge of, or outside, the traditional shopping centre, and may suffer problems of pedestrian access. If this is so, then site assessment may be crucial to the correct estimation of outcomes, as shown by the success or failure of the centre after redevelopment. This view is held by a number of writers. For instance, Langton (1973) gives an example of two developments in Burton on Trent. The first to be built was unsuccessful, in that many of its shop units remained vacant. This scheme is sited 'some distance away from the established shopping area', and has 'little parking to offer the customers' (Langton, 1973, p. 32). Later, another precinct was built in a more central position and was fully let to traders. Langton's conclusion is that 'locating shopping (correctly) in relatively small towns is of paramount importance'.

Thus, the visible test of the correctness of the developer's decisions is the extent to which the shop units are let to traders. It is tempting to assume, as some writers do, that where developments remain partly unlet this is because of faulty locational or site assessment. But it seems likely also that the retail composition of a partly occupied centre can deter other retailers from occupying the vacant units (3.3.2).

There is really no way of knowing how well developers have been able to estimate the costs and revenues to be derived from redevelopment for retail purposes. The evidence discussed above suggests that methods of location and site assessment, and estimation of size of centre, are somewhat crude, and vary between one firm and another. However, it is clear that most precincts have been successful, to the extent that they are very substantially or completely let to retailers. There could be two main reasons for this apparent paradox. The first involves speculation that the most important single attribute of a precinct is its accessibility, particularly in terms of its siting on major pedestrian routes (in town centres). This virtually ensures the presence of many casual shoppers, which is necessary for comparison or 'shopping' goods shops, especially where those benefit from 'shared' business (4.2.1). This attribute is one easily measured for any prospective scheme: the only requirements are a map, and possibly a site visit and some discussion with local authority planners. If the scheme possesses good pedestrian access, then the other locational attributes (which are much more difficult to estimate) may in fact be unimportant, and mistakes in assessing them not fatal.

The second reason why developers can carry out poor assessments and yet perform successfully lies in the scope for profit which is inherent in their operations. The developer can justify uncertainty over methods of assessment as an aspect of 'risk' and thus expect a very substantial profit, with a large margin of possible error in his estimate. Thus his incompetence is partly subsidised by the landowner, who receives payment for his land at well below its value; and partly by the retailers renting the shop units who pay unnecessarily high levels of rent. This situation can occur because the developer can achieve local monopolies in new retail floorspace.

It is recognised that these conclusions may be somewhat controversial. Obviously there is a need for objective research into the performance of developers in providing new retail floorspace over the past 25 years in Britain, but such research will be made very difficult by the reluctance of those involved to give specific information on methodology of assessment, and on financial aspects of development. In the meantime it is worth stating that there are grounds to suspect the ability of many developers and local authorities to make rational decisions about the nature and scale of retail development, particularly in existing shopping centres. This theme will be returned to in Chapter 7.

3.3   DEVELOPERS' INTERACTION WITH PLANNERS AND RETAILERS

Having decided in principle to carry out retail development, the developer must negotiate with two sets of 'actors' in order to achieve successful development. These actors are local authority planners, whose approval is needed for any change of land use or new construction; and retailers, who are to occupy the new shopping space. This section reviews briefly some evidence of these processes of negotiation, and explores some of the implications for the eventual size and character of shopping precincts. A more detailed discussion of typical relationships between developer and local authority planner, with respect to town centre development, is given in Chapter 7.

3.3.1   Negotiation with planners

Any development of retail space carried out in Britain is legal only if planning permission has first been granted by the local planning authority. (3)   In most cases there are two stages: first, an 'outline' planning application is made in order to establish whether a shopping centre of a certain size and general layout may be built at a particular place; if permission for this is obtained, then a more detailed application is made which specifies the exact dimensions and appearance of the centre. The developer does not have to specify the exact types of shop that are intended to occupy the centre; but non retail uses, such as banks, have to be specified separately.

The decisions of a local planning authority are supposed to be guided by the relevant provisions of the approved development plan for the area concerned. Characteristics of development plans at various levels, and in particular their retail aspects, are discussed in Chapter 6. So far as the developer is concerned, any scheme for central area development may well lie within an area intended principally for retail purposes in the approved development plan. Thus there should be no dispute over the desirability of the scheme in principle, (4) although there may be scope for argument over its scale, or over details of layout and design. On the other hand, schemes for suburban centres are more likely to be in opposition to the development plan, especially where the proposal appears large enough to pose some threat to the nearest central shopping area. But smaller schemes, such as centres intended to serve new residential areas, are more likely to be acceptable to planners.

The model described so far as been of the developer presenting a detailed set of proposals to the local authority for permission or refusal. Proposals may also arise through the initiative of a local authority, who may wish to carry out central area renewal (3.2.1; 7.3), or see new suburban shopping facilities provided. In these instances, the local authority will specify the location and approximate scale of the scheme, but the developer may wish to negotiate details of finance, timing, layout or design.

3.3.2 Negotiation with retailers: major space users

One of the principal sources of uncertainty for the developer concerns the response of retailers to the completed scheme: will the demand be sufficient for all the retail space to be occupied ? Rent levels are normally high in new precincts when compared with older shopping areas; retailers may be reluctant to move to a new site, or set up a new branch, in a proposed development where the consumer response is unknown. So the developer has to demonstrate some positive advantages of the new centre in order to persuade retailers to move there.

One important step in this direction is to make agreements with a retail firm or firms concerning the space allocated for a major store or stores. This is normally done as early as possible in the development process (Table 3.2). The purpose of this is to demonstrate the viability of the scheme to other retail firms, and to suggest that customers will be attracted there by the presence of reputable major firms. For this latter reason, the term 'magnet stores' is often used to describe those premises which are let at an early stage. (5)

The magnet store is usually a department store, variety store or supermarket: the larger the centre, the more likely that there will be more than one magnet, and that at least one of them will be a department store (Marcus, 1978). Supermarkets are likely to be magnets in small city centre precincts, or in suburban developments. Care is usually taken to locate the magnet(s) such that a heavy pedestrian flow is established through the precinct: the American practice of placing magnets at each end of a pedestrian mall (for examples see Capital and Counties, 1970) has been applied in some of the larger British developments, such as Brent Cross (Blake, 1976). Further principles of precinct design are discussed in Darlow (1972) and Gosling and Maitland (1976).

The process of negotiation between developers and retailers concerning magnet stores is (not surprisingly) poorly documented. It appears that, since the developer is anxious to reach agreement as early as possible, the space is usually let at rents much lower (per unit floor space) than for the small shop premises, which are let subsequently.

It is clear that most developers believe that magnet stores are important in attracting other retailers, but little research has taken place in this area. Indirect evidence has been used by Marcus (1978) to suggest that supermarkets are less successful magnets than variety or department stores: in a sample survey of 40 precincts in England and Wales, it was found that precincts whose major space users are supermarkets tend to show the highest vacancy rates. It seems that British developers have taken little notice of advisors such as Nelson (1958), who used his experience of retail development in America to state clearly that, while there are advantages to food retailers in locating close to one another, there are virtually no advantages for the clothing or footwear retailer in locating next to a food store. This is because the two types of store generate separate types of shopping trips (4.2; 5.5.2).

3.3.3 Negotiation with retailers: minor space users

The types of shop and their locations within a precinct reflect the decisions of developer and retailer, and the results of negotiation between them. Information on these matters is available for a sample of British retail developments, from a report by the Centre for Advanced Land Use Studies (1975).

This report shows (pp. 15-16) that developers pay much attention to the selection of 'suitable' tenants for the development, and also to the location of such tenants within the centre. The developer's overall intentions for the centre are often made clear in his choice of 'magnet' store (3.3.2), but he is aware that the shops occupying the relatively small 'standard' units will add much to the centre's 'image' among consumers (7.1.3). Many developers try to achieve a wide variety of retail goods and services within the centre, so that it can provide fully for the shopper (Kaye, 1975, p. 54). Thus the precinct is seen as a complete centre rather than simply an addition to existing shopping facilities.

The choice of location within a precinct is strongly linked with the maximum level of rent that the retailer is willing to pay (see below). Thus, the firms willing to pay most are likely to obtain the more expensive central locations within the precinct, where the volume of pedestrians is highest. Other firms obtain inferior peripheral locations, but at lower rent. The developer may also discriminate between tenants, keeping incompatible neighbours well apart, and banishing 'dead frontages' (6) to the more remote corners of the centre.

The selection of tenants may also be affected by commitments on the part of developer or local authority to offer tenancies to retailers displaced by the prior clearance of old shop premises. It is not clear to what extent these offers are actually taken up: a large response has been reported in the Eldon Square Centre, Newcastle, where displaced traders were offered concessions on rent (CALUS, 1975, pp. 14, 17). But generally the rate of take up of new premises by displaced traders is very low (Smith and Gray, 1972). It appears that traders regard the rents in new precincts as being unreasonably high (Seeney, 1976). This view may be justified, since these premises are partly compensating for the low rents paid by magnet stores, and in some cases, helping provide excessive profits for the developer (3.2.4).

Processes that help determine rent levels themselves are also discussed in the CALUS report (pp. 5-14). The rent obtained for any shop unit will be an amount acceptable to both developer and retailer. The developer attempts to levy rents comparable either with those already charged in similar precincts elsewhere, or with those currently charged at 'prime' locations in the same town. Retailers normally attempt to estimate the likely levels of turnover and costs in the precinct, and allow the residual sum (excluding profit margins) to form an estimate of maximum rent to be offered. (7)   Some retailers, most typically those in footwear and clothing firms, are prepared to pay higher rents for the most central units (see above).   The CALUS report (Table 3) shows that, among a small sample of retailers in precincts, the rent paid was much higher for these firms (an average 9.6 per cent of turnover) than for other types of firm (for example, grocers 1.3 per cent; (8)   other food retailers 5.0 per cent).

An alternative method of assessing rent, much used in America, is to base the payments upon the turnover achieved by the retailer over the period concerned.   This bears advantages for the retailer where he is very uncertain about future turnover levels, and also for the developer, since his rental income can keep up with inflation, instead of remaining at the same level up to the date of rent review.   However, a number of problems, mainly legal and administrative, have precluded any widespread use of this system in Britain (Anon, 1973;   CALUS, 1975, pp. 8-9; Tisdall, 1976b).

One aspect of tenant selection which tends to be glossed over by developers and local authorities has been emphasised by McDougall et al (1974).   This concerns the position of the local independent retailer who wants to occupy space in a new precinct.   He may be deterred from so doing, in three ways.   Firstly, he is likely to be offered premises of between 1,000 and 4,000 square feet gross floor space, far larger than the average older single shop unit, and more than is needed for certain food and other types of trade.   Secondly, the rent demanded is likely to be far higher than for older premises, because the unit is larger and because rents per unit floor space are higher.   Thirdly, the developer will wish to seek assurances of the reliability of any potential tenant. This favours the established multiple firm rather than the local man who possesses just one shop, or who wants to start in retailing.

The result is that precincts tend to be dominated by multiple retail firms: 10 of the 14 centres surveyed by CALUS (1975, Table 12) had over 80 per cent of their total floor space (including vacant units) occupied by multiple traders. (9)   One centre - the Telford Shopping Centre (Phase I), financed and built entirely by a public sector authority, Telford Development Corporation - consisted entirely of branches of multiple firms.

3.3.4   The developer as landlord

The control of the developer over retail facilities extends beyond the period of planning, building and letting the shops.   This is because it is normal for developers of retail schemes to retain their ownership of the freehold or leasehold after development is complete.

Rents are normally subject to review at regular intervals, which have declined from a typical 21 years for schemes built in the 1950s,   to 5 or 7 years for more recent schemes.   This decline is clearly connected with increases in general rates of inflation.   At the time of review the new rent is likely to be set by comparative methods (3.3.3).

The advantages of centralised management of a precinct are explained by Kaye (1975):   apart from the services necessary to maintain cleanliness and a pleasant environment for customers and staff, these include promotional activity such as advertising the centre as a whole to the public.   The retailer does however face some restrictions on his freedom of choice.   These often include prohibition of sub letting of all or part of the premises to other retailers: a certain degree of control over advertising and window display, and even control over the types of goods sold. The latter control is designed to prevent serious competition between adjacent shops, and is probably found mainly in small suburban developments owned by public sector authorities.

Lastly, another situation should be mentioned in which the developer's decisions can have substantial impact. Many older shops in central and suburban shopping centres are run by tenants, often holding long leases at low rents and with no provision for rent review. When these leases expire, huge increases in rent may be demanded, since the landlord will now wish to charge rent at the 'market' value. Indeed, groups of shops are bought and sold on the expectation of 'realistic' rents being paid upon renegotiation of leases (Anon, 1972; Kerr, 1976). Alternatively, redevelopment of the site may promise bigger financial rewards. These changes can put a sudden end to hitherto successful shops, through no fault of the retailer.

3.4   SUMMARY AND CONCLUSIONS

This chapter has attempted to describe and explain sequences of decisions that are thought to be typical of the behaviour of property development firms and other agencies involved in shopping centre development. This rather cautious summary has to be given because there is little reliable evidence published about the decisions involved in retail development.

The developer provides new retail facilities which are let to several retailers. The location, scale, nature and timing of these facilities reflect decisions of the developer concerned and of other actors. The basic decision, to undertake development of a particular site, will be prompted both by the developer's estimate of profitability, and the local authority's desire to see development take place. Within this general rule, there are a number of different sequences of decisions and actions on the part of developer and local authority. In some cases the local authority may be the developer.

The local authority's wish to develop will be linked to several factors, some of which may be classified broadly as social or political, and therefore not quantifiable. The developer's assessment, on the other hand, is (or should be) based upon quantifiable financial criteria. He has to estimate the costs of development, and the revenues arising from the new space provided. Of these, the revenues are probably the more difficult to estimate, since they begin further in the future, and depend more upon factors over which the developer has no direct control. In effect one is attempting to forecast the behaviour of other actors (retailers), whose identity is uncertain.

In dealing with this situation developers do not appear to use the full array of techniques available to the 'normative' decision maker (2.2). It is more probable that developers generally make just one forecast of financial outcome, although a considerable degree of uncertainty (or 'margin of error') will be recognised in this process. Those who deal with developers have seemed to acknowledge this uncertainty, through their willingness to allow developers to make very substantial profits in many cases. It appears though that developers experienced in providing schemes with a large retail component become proficient at forecasting revenues, and hence build up a reputation for successful developments. In this, they are often helped by the nature of the commercial land market in Britain. The developer and local authority can usually combine to create local monopolies in new retail floorspace. Retail firms are obliged to pay rents at the levels stipulated by the developer, because of an absence of comparable alternative premises.

The detailed characteristics of pedestrian shopping precincts - the usual result of development - reflect qualities of the site, and also the results of negotiation between developer, local authority, and the retail occupiers. The developer will attempt to reduce uncertainty by making agreements at early stages with retail firms over the largest units in the scheme, albeit at the cost of some reduction in potential rent income.

It should be emphasised, lastly, that the success of the retail developer, evidenced by the addition of several hundred shopping precincts to existing town centre and suburban facilities, has itself been dependent upon certain conditions. The demand for new retail premises has arisen from growth in consumer disposable expenditure, and from the expansionary goals of many of the major retail firms (4.3.2). The policies of town planners have ensured that these new premises have been supplied in large clusters, and particularly in town centres (Chapter 7). The policies of financial investors in Britain have ensured that money has been available for speculative developments.

When these conditions are altered, the rationale for the developer's involvement may be severely weakened. In particular, the 'property collapse' of 1973-75, and changes in local authority attitudes, have led to a virtual cessation of proposals for central area development (7.3.6).

In general, some development of new retail space will obviously occur within the next decade, but probably at a rate rather lower than that of the 'boom' period of approximately 1955-1973. It seems likely that the main investors in new retail development will be financial institutions and major retail firms, both of which have substantial financial capital available for investment. Development itself may often be carried out by these agencies, and also by local authorities and development corporations. Until recently the role of the property developer appeared likely to become simply organisational, but with the probable repeal of the Community Land Act, new opportunities for development gains may occur. In any case, developers will continue to be important as landlords of existing precincts: thus the variety and quality of shops in many centres will continue to be affected by decisions outside the direct scope of the retailer or the consumer.

NOTES

(1) The term 'developer' may encompass financial institutions, retail firms, construction companies, and public sector agencies, as well as strict property development firms.
(2) The value of a site which has been cleared of buildings can be defined as: 'The present value of the stream of net annual incomes that can be earned by investing in the improvements necessary to put the land to its optimum use. The optimum or highest and best use is defined as that present use and programme of future use of a parcel of land which produces the highest present land value'. (Goodall, 1972, p. 76)
(3) The term 'local planning authority', and the relevant legislation, are explained in 6.1.
(4) Except in cases where the demolition of buildings of architectural or historic interest is involved (6.3.1; 7.3.5).
(5) A statement of the space requirements of several major multiple firms, for stores in new centres, is given in Northen & Haskoll (1977,

p. 45).
(6)   Premises with uninteresting window displays, such as building society offices.
(7)   This process is similar to that of the developer in estimating a maximum price to pay for land (3.1.3).
(8)   This figure presumably includes supermarkets, and thus partly reflects the favourable bargaining position of magnet stores.
(9)   Here defined as retail organisations having ten or more branches.

4 Attitudes to retail location: the retailer

This chapter examines typical decision processes of retail firms in Britain, and ways in which these processes affect typical geographical patterns of retail activity. Two important general points emerge: first, that locational decision making can only be understood satisfactorily with background knowledge of the full range of policies and decisions of retail firms; second, that the retailer's decisions are generally heavily constrained, either by social and financial factors, or by the decisions and policies of other actors in retailing. These other decisions and policies often have to be inferred or forecast by the retailer, especially consumers' decisions. Thus, the retailer's decisions are influenced by the way in which he attempts to deal with uncertainty.

No attempt is made in this chapter to describe typical geographical patterns of shops or shopping centres in terms of central place hierarchies or any other broad framework. Detailed classifications have been made by several geographers, of national hierarchical systems in Britain (Carruthers, 1967; Thorpe, 1968), and of regional or local systems (summarised by Scott, 1970, Chapter 7). Although these patterns represent the cumulative effects of past decisions by retailers, for our present purpose it is best to regard them simply as frameworks for the retailer's decisions. However, ways in which these patterns have been modified in recent years by retailers' decisions will be discussed.

Section 4.2 attempts to explore the complexity of retailers' decisions concerning location. Firstly, the rather simplistic normative advice published for prospective retailers is briefly described. It is shown then that locational decisions are conditional on decisions or policies concerning other aspects of retailing, themselves connected with the size and goals of the retail firm itself. This leads to discussions, in Sections 4.3 and 4.4 of the decisions and behaviour of large or 'multiple' retail firms, and then of small ('independent') firms. Finally, some recent trends in shopping centre growth and decline in Britain are related to the issues discussed in this and the previous chapter.

4.2 THE NATURE OF RETAIL LOCATION DECISIONS

4.2.1 Published advice for retailers

The prospective retailer will be able to consult several published sources of advice on methods of choosing a suitable location. General guides to retail management, such as Jensen (1963) or Fiber (1972) include chapters on this. The advice usually includes the following stages:
  i)   Choose the town or part of town in which the shop is
       to be located.
  ii) Search for available premises in this area, by reading
       the local press or trade sources, by contacting estate

agents and the local authority, and through personal contacts.
- iii) Examine each shop at first hand, assessing its general appearance, the nature of the shopping centre it lies in, and its location with respect to residential areas and to other shopping centres.
- iv) On finding an apparently suitable shop, make enquiries into its past trading performance.
- v) If satisfied, enter into negotiation for the price of the freehold or leasehold, and for the remaining stock (if any).

This type of advice is obviously suited to the individual wishing to start up one shop. Broadly speaking, he can do this in two ways. Firstly, he may take over a previously successful shop (a 'going concern'), selling much the same assortment of goods as the previous owner. In these cases much emphasis in the literature is given to the amount of custom that the shop already possesses, and to the price that the buyer should pay for the 'goodwill' of the shop. (1)   Location itself is given a largely negative emphasis, in that buyers are warned to avoid poor or deteriorating sites, which are evident where neighbouring premises are vacant, or occupied but of poor quality.

Secondly, the prospective shopkeeper may first choose the mix of goods to sell, and then will want to take over a vacant shop. This course of action is less expensive, since no payment need be made for remaining stock or 'goodwill'. However, there may be greater uncertainty attached to the decision, since existing levels of custom cannot be used as a guide to future performance. In these circumstances, more emphasis is placed upon the positive characteristics of location, and in particular, accessibility for consumers.

It is worth noting here that although this type of advice is by definition normative, it in fact suggests a model of behaviour close to Simon's 'Administrative Man' (1957b; see 2.3.3). Emphasis is given to methods of acquiring information; and it is implied that the shopkeeper can legitimately accept the first satisfactory opportunity. There is no discussion of methods of estimating the outcomes possible at different locations, and little explicit discussion of overall goals or of criteria for decision making. This is of course to be expected, since these books are written for a lay readership unversed in management techniques. More important though, there is an implication that the unexperienced retailer can easily find a suitable location, one which will allow him the opportunity to build up a successful business.

More detailed advice is of course available on the selection of retail location. Texts such as Nelson (1958) and Cox (1968) specialise in this: the target for advice may be the prospective independent retailer (as above), or the larger multiple firm wishing to open new branches. The methods outlined by Cox, whose book is written for the British market, are probably representative of those used by specialist consultants and estate agents, and reminiscent of those described by American 'marketing geographers' (2.5.4). Cox shows first how the retailer should judge whether a town centre or suburban location is most appropriate; then, how to measure the catchment area of any shopping centre; then, how to assess the strength of the existing competition within that catchment area, so that the share of the market for the proposed store can be calculated. In making these assessments the use of published statistics and special surveys is encouraged. Cox also emphasises the importance of town planning policies within the catchment area and within the shopping centre concerned.

This type of advice is clearly of value to the decision maker who wishes to compare the likely costs and revenues of a number of separate

locations. However, the critical comments made above (2.5.4) in respect
of marketing geographers' methods of assessment, apply here.

Nelson (1958) deals with those issues listed above, but also emphasises
the importance to the retailer of an appropriate site within a shopping
centre. This attention to siting stems both from the author's experience
and from consideration of consumer behaviour. Nelson distinguishes three
types of business that a shop can attract. Generative business is
produced by the store itself: its advantages for the consumer are
sufficient to warrant special trips there. Shared business is secured
by the store through the generative power of its neighbours; and
suscipient business is not generated by the store itself or its
neighbours, but by some other land use, a railway station for example.
This distinction leads to a more precise description of locational
requirements than that offered by the simpler texts.

Those shops relying mainly upon generative business should locate so
as to be easily accessible for consumers, but do not need to be adjacent
to other shops. On the other hand, those relying on shared business
must locate next to existing shops. Nelson also states that certain
types of shop may be compatible with other types, or with shops of the
same type, so that two shops sited next to one another will attract more
business than they would if sited well apart. This is because consumers
may be attracted to a group of shops where they can make useful
comparisons between them.

This type of advice is obviously important to retailers. It also
serves to illustrate a point which is not covered adequately in the
simpler accounts. If one assumes that retailers, in selecting locations,
compare costs and revenues at several locations, then it should be
recognised that for firms generating their own trade, revenues are less
likely to vary significantly between locations than for firms which rely
upon shared business. The former firm can choose from a large number of
potential locations, using criteria perhaps of cost rather than revenue
in making its decision. But the 'shared business' firm is restricted in
effect to certain sites within certain shopping centres, in which it is
likely to have appropriate neighbours. Such sites are also in demand
from other, similar firms. The firm therefore chooses a location using
criteria basically of maximising revenue, but it must also face
substantial costs in the form of high payments for land and buildings
('rent'). This point is illustrated in the comparison of relative
expenditures upon rent in modern pedestrian precincts (3.3.3). Here,
the 'comparison goods' retailers (5.5.2) of clothing and footwear pay
the highest rents, related to turnover. This is in order to secure the
most attractively located units within precincts. As well as generating
business collectively, these shops also benefit in a suscipient manner
from trade generated by the 'magnet' stores in the scheme (3.3.2).

Two points should now be clear. Firstly, for some retail firms, the
location of shops is crucial to success, but the choice available at any
point in time may be limited to a small number of suitable premises;
while, for other firms, many suitable locations may be available.
Secondly, the criteria which affect locational decisions are governed by
basic attributes of the firm. So far, this has been discussed in terms
of the 'type of business' the firm may attract. The following subsection
attempts to examine these attributes more directly, so that reasons for
variation in the nature and relative importance of locational decisions
among firms can more comprehensively be explained.

4.2.2 Policy areas and options for retail firms

Any retail firm will establish a number of policies about broad aspects of its operation, so that day to day decisions can more easily be made. In each of these policy areas, a number of options are available, but choice within any one area is likely to be constrained by choices already made in other areas. A classification of policy areas is tentatively suggested, as follows:

   i)   'Image' of the firm and its stores: this includes a consideration of the particular segment of the market (if any) that the firm wishes to appeal to, and also the extent to which it wishes to induce loyalty amongst its customers.

  ii)   The mix of goods and/or services to be provided.

 iii)   The relative importance of locational factors: this can be expressed as the level of 'rent' that the firm is prepared to pay.

  iv)   The relative importance of advertising.

   v)   The relative volume of sales, expressed as turnover per unit floor space or per employee.

  vi)   The level of mark-up: this is the relationship between the typical prices paid by the retail firm for its goods, and typical selling prices.

In this classification, the first two areas are of basic long or medium term policy, which cannot easily be altered and which affect all other policies. The other four areas may need almost continuous review, may not be applied consistently within the firm, and (as shown below) are strongly interrelated. Nevertheless they are clearly distinguishable in principle. They do not cover all aspects of the firm's policies, but concentrate on policies which include or relate to questions of location.

The choices in areas (iii) - (vi) can, at some risk of oversimplification, be expressed as high cost versus low cost. This treatment allows one to explore interrelationships between these areas. To begin with, no firm is likely to adopt policies of high costs in all four areas. Also, the apparently best combination of low costs throughout - low rent, low volume of advertising, high turnover and high mark up - is improbable, for reasons to be discussed. In practice, it is likely that any decision to adopt a low cost policy in one area will imply consequences of high costs in at least one other area.

Table 4.1   Policy areas and cost options for the retailer

		'Rent'	Advertising	Volume of sales	Mark up
			POLICY AREAS		
COST OPTIONS	High Cost	High	High	Low	Low
	Medium Cost	Medium	Medium	Medium	Medium
	Low Cost	Low	Low	High	High

Notes and Examples

'Rent' denotes costs paid by retailer for the shop premises, whether owned freehold or leasehold. High rents normally paid in town centre cores; medium in town centre fringe, larger suburban centres or new premises anywhere; low in older premises outside town centres.

Advertising denotes costs incurred by the retail firm and shop management, rather than on national scale by wholesale distributor or manufacturer. High includes extensive use of press, TV and radio, and/ or use of leaflets delivered door to door, and special events or promotions. Medium - occasional use of the above. Low - virtually no advertising.

Volume of Sales is relative to running costs, or possibly floor area. It is difficult to generalise: high volume would normally necessitate self selection by customers, and relatively small expenditure on staff and internal fittings. Low volume suggests attentive staff and expensive displays.

Mark up: No accurate information is available, but percentages would appear to vary with type of trade, more than with size or policy of the retail firm. In the grocery trade, 10 per cent average mark up would be regarded as low, and 30 per cent high: in most non food trades, typical percentages would be much higher than these figures. It is important to note that the price paid by different shops for the same article may itself vary considerably, often because larger firms can negotiate special terms with manufacturers or importing agents.

Table 4.1 presents the options in a standardised way. Low sales and low mark up are shown as high costs, since in each case the firm is (other things being equal) foregoing income by not selling more goods or not charging higher prices. No attempt is made here to quantify 'high', 'medium', and 'low', although qualitative descriptions are given. Also, no attempt is made to suggest relative costs involved in each policy area; the order in which they are presented is arbitrary.

Some typical relationships between policy areas can now be discussed. One such relationship is between 'rent' and advertising. Nelson (1958, Chapter 5) shows that stores generating their own business need not pay high rents, as discussed above (4.2.1), but must advertise extensively in order to attract consumers. Conversely, stores relying upon shared business need not advertise. This suggests some form of inverse ratio between rent and advertising expenditure. However, there are clear exceptions to this rule. Some of the largest retail firms in Britain occupy expensive sites in the most accessible parts of town centres, and yet advertise widely in the press or television. On the other hand, many small retail firms, especially those with only one shop, pay low rent and do not advertise at all.

An obvious relationship exists between turnover and mark up. Low prices (i.e. low mark up) will normally attract more custom, and lead to higher turnover. On the other hand, higher standards of service, involving relatively high staffing levels and/or expensive interior design, reduce the relative turnover, but profits can be restored by increasing the mark up. The choice of turnover/mark up levels is often linked with the firm's overall image which it presents to the consumer.

More complex relationships may exist between all four types of option. For example, the firm choosing to pay low levels of both rent and advertising must also expect relatively low levels of turnover, since it has no direct means of attracting consumers to the shop. It will be necessary then to charge relatively high mark up. Firms paying high levels both for rent and advertising will need to achieve a high turn-over, and may be able to do so at medium levels of mark up, by stocking a large variety of goods or through good display techniques.

In general the high advertising/low rent firms are likely to favour high turnover/low mark up. This is because the advertising is designed to make customers aware of the low prices. Conversely, high rent/low advertising firms are likely to favour low turnover/high mark up. This is because they intend to attract the customer either through apparent superiority over neighbouring shops, or through a reputation for high standards of service.

This discussion is continued below (4.3.4-6 and 4.4.3), where strategies appropriate for particular combinations of goods sold and size of firm are discussed. Some of these strategies are shown in Figure 4.1. It should be emphasised that these strategies are deduced from the general principles discussed above, and that evidence for their existence has to be sought from a general knowledge of retail firms and their policies. Comparative cost studies of British retail firms of various sizes and selling various combinations of goods do not appear to be available in a form which would help substantiate this treatment.

Figure 4.1   Policy options for hypothetical retail firms

(a) High quality department store

	R	A	V	M
HC	x			
MC		x	x	
LC				x

(b) Variety store

	R	A	V	M
HC	x	x		
MC				x
LC			x	

(c) Hypermarket

	R	A	V	M
HC		x		x
MC				
LC	x		x	

(d) Small food shop

	R	A	V	M
HC			x	
MC				x
LC	x	x		

(e) Fashion boutique

	R	A	V	M
HC	x		x	
MC				
LC		x		x

(f) Antique shop

	R	A	V	M
HC			x	
MC				
LC	x	x		x

Notes

The symbol 'x' indicates the most likely course of action of a firm in allocating resources (at high cost, medium cost, or low cost) to elements of its operation of a shop of the type indicated (the elements are rent, advertising, volume of sales, and mark up). For further details see Table 4.1.

4.2.3 Site requirements

One factor important to many firms is some specific site requirement which may act to narrow down their choice. Some firms need very large premises, because of their scale of operation, or the bulky nature of their goods. Such a firm may find few suitable existing shops available, and to widen its choice may consider either buying premises originally built for non retail purposes, or building its own premises.

Other firms that need substantial car parking space for their customers will also require either existing premises supplied with car parks, or again may seek land for purpose built premises. This type of firm is likely to have policies of low rent/high advertising/low mark up/high turnover, and examples will be given below (4.3.5).

Most firms will however restrict their search to existing retail premises. They may consider certain features, such as availability of off street servicing, to be especially important. Any such features required by many firms are likely to add to rent, and therefore the firm must decide whether they are worth paying for.

This section has attempted to explore retail location decisions in general terms. In order to pursue more detailed aspects, it is necessary to make a distinction between large (multiple) and small (independent) firms, and these will be discussed in the following two sections.

4.3 BEHAVIOUR OF MULTIPLE RETAIL FIRMS

4.3.1 The multiple retail firm

In examining the retail sector it is usual to distinguish 'multiple' and 'independent' retail firms. The multiple firm may in principle own any number of shops greater than one; but the term is often restricted to those owning ten shops or more, as in most of the Census of Distribution tables. Analyses of the structure of the retail sector in Britain show that nearly all retail firms may be described as 'very small' (owning only one shop); 'small' (owning between one and four shops); or 'not small' (owning ten or more shops) (Hall, 1971, pp 6-9). Thus the Census definition seems appropriate; it would appear to include firms for which the financial performance of an individual shop is unimportant compared with that of the firm as a whole.

In this section the main emphasis is on large firms operating at regional or national scale. This is partly because of their greater importance, and partly because it is among these firms that locational policies are likely to be most clearly formulated. After a brief discussion of recent trends in the multiple retail sector, two groups of firms are identified for discussion of locational policies, set in the context of policy options (4.2). These are 'traditional' and 'innovative' multiple firms: their locational policies, and the implications of these policies for patterns of retail activity in general, are discussed. An attempt is then made to review the methods of locational assessment and selection used typically by major firms. Finally, some general conclusions are drawn.

4.3.2 The multiple retail sector

The multiple sector has established an enormously strong position in British retailing, developing a 45 per cent share of total retail sales by 1975 (Table 4.2). This may be due partly to the relative inefficiency of cooperative and independent retailing, but this market share is much greater than in other West European countries (Davies, 1976a, p. 70).

The post war period has thus been dominated by the growth of multiple retailing. Some firms, such as Marks and Spencer or J. Sainsbury, have remained single entities unencumbered by other interests. Others, such as the Boots Company, have expanded partly through the take over of

Table 4.2   Percentage share of retail turnover in Britain,
            by type of organisation

	1961	1966	1971	1975
Independents	59	56	53	48
Multiples	29	34	38	45
Cooperatives	10	9	7	7

Source: Berry, 1978, p. 26 (original sources: Census of Distribution,
         1961, 1966, 1971; Economist Intelligence Unit, 1976).

---

other firms (Timothy Whites) selling similar products, but have still
remained retailers pure and simple. In other cases multiple retail
firms have merged or been taken over and now form small parts of vast
business empires. (2)   As a result, many decisions about the operation
of retail chains appear to be made from increasingly remote sources,
and locational policies may operate as much through default (as when a
chain of stores is acquired as an unintended result of a merger) as
through deliberation.

   For this and other reasons, problems exist in describing the
locational requirements and policies of multiple firms. This review
concentrates on the more visible policies - generally, those of firms
exhibiting rapid growth, or of established large firms which are still
exclusively retailers.

   As mentioned above, the goal of growth seems very common among major
retail firms, and can consist simply of a desire to increase retail
sales and/or a share of the market, or more complex goals partly
associated with diversification. Broadly speaking, increasing sales can
be achieved through opening new stores, and/or through making more
efficient use of existing stores. The former policy would appear to
have greater advantages in the long term, and increases the level of
fixed assets held by the firm. The latter may involve expansion or
modification of existing stores, and also changes in the range of goods
sold in them. It is possible of course for firms to achieve short term
growth through cutting prices or other promotional means, but most of
the large multiple firms have active growth policies involving store
building, expansion or acquisitions.

   Growth can be justified as it should lead to larger volumes of profits.
It seems also that investors expect growth, especially through the
acquisition or building of new stores, such that rapid growth can lead
to rapid increases in share values (Sullivan, 1976). These policies can
have important locational implications. Many firms are constantly
seeking new retail outlets, even in towns where increases in consumer
demand do not appear adequate to justify growth in shopping facilities.
Thus, new shopping facilities provided by developers can be taken up
quickly by multiple firms wishing to expand geographically into towns
where they have not hitherto been represented. An extreme example of
such policies was that of F.W. Woolworth in the 1930s. when an
objective of owning 1,000 stores apparently led to the building of
stores in unsuitable locations (Thorpe, 1966).

   It should not be forgotten that profitability remains a basic goal of
all firms. It has direct locational implications, since firms may
examine the financial performance of each of their shops, and alter or
close those which are least profitable.

4.3.3 Tradition and innovation in multiple retailing

An important model has been that of 'wheels of retailing' (McNair, 1958; Izraeli, 1973). This describes a process by which innovators in retailing begin by emphasising methods opposed to those used by established or 'traditional' firms, but gradually the innovators and established firms adopt elements of each other's methods and become more similar. Further innovation then occurs.

In British retailing one can distinguish three broad types of 'traditional' multiple retailer, which have been important during most of this century. The first has been the local or regionally based firm, typically selling food or other convenience goods in town and district centres from small shops. Many of these have long since closed or been acquired, while a few such as J. Sainsbury have grown and changed almost entirely their methods of retailing (J. Sainsbury, 1973).

A second type has been the regional chain selling comparison goods, such as clothing, footwear or jewellery, from small shops and almost exclusively in town centres. A number of these chains have successfully extended their operations to the national level through takeovers or a process of geographical growth (Scott, 1970, Chapter 3). Others have closed or become parts of huge combines such as the British Shoe Corporation, which in 1976 owned some 1,800 town centre shops still trading under the names of the six originally separate firms (Nuttall, 1976).

A third type has been the nationally based chain operating either clothing stores with or without other goods (C and A, Marks and Spencer), or a great variety of goods. The prime example of the latter is F.W. Woolworth, but other originally specialist firms such as the Boots Company and W.H. Smith appear to be approaching 'variety store' status. Department store chains (House of Fraser, Debenhams) also exist. These chains favour almost exclusively town centres and occupy very much larger premises than the other types of firm mentioned above, although Boots and W.H. Smith still possess a residue of small shop premises.

Against this background there have been two major waves of innovation in the multiple retail sector since the 1950s. The first was the development of self service techniques, pioneered in the grocery trade but later developed in variety and other stores. A direct result was the development of the supermarket, which allowed economies of scale through increased size and routinisation of day to day management. Supermarkets were however generally built in those locations already used by multiple grocers - town and district centres.

A second series of innovations have occurred since the mid 1960s and are still in progress: these involve firms which appeal to the public mainly on bases of reduced prices. As discussed below (4.3.5), these innovations have had important new locational implications which have led to a weakening of hierarchical systems of shopping centres. Some of the more successful innovations have influenced the policies of the 'traditional' retailers, although the locational effects of these changes remain to be worked out in full.

4.3.4 Locational policies of 'traditional' firms

Multiple firms operating small comparison goods shops, or larger clothing and variety stores, remain very strongly committed to locating in large shopping centres. This is because the presence of many shops selling similar goods draws a large volume of trade and aids the consumer's comparison processes, (4.2.1). Thus, general policies of high rent/low advertising are favoured (4.2.2).

Growth for specialist or comparison goods firms takes the form mainly of acquiring premises in towns where previously unrepresented: this process has been facilitated by the steady supply of new shops arising from town centre development. Those firms requiring much larger premises have tended instead to expand their own stores, which are more likely to be owned freehold or long leasehold, and Marks and Spencer in particular have been reluctant to expand their operation geographically since the war.

The multiple firms selling mainly comparison goods appear more and more to be dominating British town centres. The nature of the goods sold helps to ensure that they are relatively free from competition by price reducing firms locating in other types of shopping centre.

4.3.5 Locational policies of recent innovators

The major bases for innovation in retailing in recent years have been either the sale of new products or the sale of standardised goods at reduced prices. The former has tended to be pioneered by enthusiastic independent retailers who have rarely expanded into multiple firms, and much of their initiative has resulted in modification of product lines in variety stores. Innovation however on the basis of price cutting has been enormously important in multiple retailing.

This innovation has been successful in trades where branded goods dominate the market, because here a consumer's criterion for choice between shops is likely to be based, partly at least, upon price. This is particularly so in the grocery trade. Here, two major innovations have taken place in Britain since the mid 1960s. The first has been the development of very large 'superstores': purpose built single storey buildings of at least 50,000 square feet gross floor area and with special car parking facilities (8.1.1). One firm notable in this respect is Asda, a subsidiary of Associated Dairies, set up specifically to develop superstores. This firm's locational policy is catholic, involving conversion of old inner city factories or warehouses, or construction of new premises in inner city, suburban or edge of town locations. The main requirement appears to be existing premises or an undeveloped site sufficiently large for the purpose, and cheap in terms of 'rent' as described above. (3) Asda's success has been repeated by other firms, including more recently very large grocery firms such as Tesco and Sainsbury. However Asda's growth has been particularly rapid in this sector, due probably to its willingness to accept a wide variety of sites, and also to negotiate with local planning authorities.

The second type of innovation in grocery retailing has been the 'limited line discounter' of which the initiator is the firm of Kwik Save. As in the superstore, substantial price cuts are offered, but the stores are no larger than conventional supermarkets. Savings are effected, largely through reducing management staff numbers (and hence costs) within the store. This is achieved not only through the 'cardboard box' display of goods, but also through restricting goods to a limited number of brands, and dispensing with price labels on individual items. Prices are displayed in notices throughout the store, and are memorised by the staff at the check out tills. These features lead to reductions in the number of staff necessary, and relatively fast throughput of customers at the tills. Thus the firm can achieve a very high level of turnover relative to costs.

The number of Kwik Save stores has grown at a rapid rate since the early 1970s. Their stores occupy purpose built or existing premises, and are often in suburban shopping centres. This type of store can fit into the conventional shopping centre much more easily than the superstore; but, because of reliance upon price cutting and advertising, the firm is not restricted to any one type of location.

This type of innovation has also spread to other more established firms: for example the 'Key Discount' stores set up by Key Markets, a firm which also owns superstores and small conventional supermarkets (the 'David Greig' stores). Locational policies in such firms appear to involve use of stores owned already by the firm, in contrast with Kwik Save which has had to build stores or purchase them from other firms.

Innovation in non food retailing, where based upon price cutting, has had somewhat different locational implications. An important innovation has been the 'retail warehouse', in which goods are sold to the public direct from storage, and display facilities or customer service are minimal. Many firms have developed in this way since the late 1960s, of which electrical goods firms such as Comet Radiovision are predominant. This firm began by selling hi fi equipment through mail order from one warehouse. It found that customers were willing to buy equipment directly from the warehouse in order to save money, and so expanded its scale of operation geographically, and also product wise to a wide range of household electrical goods, heating appliances, etc. Its stores are similar to warehouses in appearance, with minimal expense devoted to display or service in the store. Prices and locations are advertised in local newspapers and specialist magazines. The stores typically are former warehouses or industrial buildings, which offer suitable storage facilities for bulky goods, and adequate car parking facilities. They are usually located outside recognised shopping centres. Comet have recently taken on some characteristics of the more established retail firms, emphasising such qualities as variety of merchandise and quality of after sales service. Since the early 1970s the firm has expanded its operations mainly through the acquisition of smaller competitors selling similar goods in similar locations.

Retail warehouses, in locations similar to those used by Comet, are also commonly found in most towns for sale of frozen foods, furniture and carpets, and building or do it yourself materials and equipment. Again, good delivery access and customer parking facilities are essential: locations and prices are advertised to the public.

Price cutting firms can however operate from ordinary suburban retail premises: a good example is the off licence firm of Augustus Barnett. As with the firms mentioned above, contact with the public is made through extensive advertising. The shops need only be small because of the high value for weight ratios of wines, spirits and cigarettes. The premises chosen by this firm tend to be fairly old, presumably low rent, shops located on major roads almost anywhere in the urban area. This particular locational innovation has spread much less to other firms than in the other cases mentioned above.

The firms discussed above all base their appeal to the public upon price reductions, which are achieved through combinations of cost reduction and high turnover. The locational policies of these firms show certain features in common, but also some important contrasts. The common feature is reluctance to pay high 'rent': this is to be expected, given the heavy expenditure upon advertising. Thus, these firms tend to avoid town centres and the more important district centres in their selection of locations, and instead choose relatively cheap sites or cheap premises with adequate car parking facilities. Differences between price cutting firms' typical locations reflect differences in size of store and type of goods sold.

These firms are of great potential importance in British retailing. As innovators, their influence extends to older established firms, particularly in a general climate of increased price consciousness among consumers. They are also important in proving that firms can prosper while ignoring relationships between size of shopping centre and size of catchment area, which derive from central place theory and which have dominated British town planners' concepts of retail systems (6.2.1).

4.3.6 Location and site selection for multiple firms

So far the policy a firm may operate in respect of store development has been explained broadly, emphasising its relationship with the firm's basic policies. Locational decisions themselves can now be examined. These should, in principle, involve certain procedures, firstly for selecting the geographical area concerned; secondly, for assessing the probable costs and benefits associated with each potential site.

In reviewing the processes of location and site selection used by multiple firms, one faces difficulties caused by the variety of locational policies involved, and by the lack of reliable information on techniques of locational or site assessment. For reasons already discussed, it is unlikely that the methods suggested by Cox (1968) are typical of all firms (4.2.1). Thorpe has suggested that some firms attempt to estimate the expenditure likely to derive from the catchment area of a shopping centre, and then make allowance for the competitive effect of other firms, as recommended by Cox. But other firms simply assume that sales are proportional to the population of the catchment area, using ratios found to exist for other stores owned by the firm (Thorpe, 1974b). Although the latter method would appear less rational than the former, it is capable of more rapid application, and may in fact give more reliable results for certain firms, especially if no direct competitors appear to exist, selling similar goods and providing similar standards of service.

Davies (1973a) emphasises that in evaluating possible new sites the retail firm relies a great deal upon past experience:

'Many companies use certain yardsticks or rules of thumb
to estimate the sales potential of new or existing stores.
These often take the form of a ratio between some measure
of population size and the floorspace and rents of the store,
further weighted by a proportional factor which may seem
arbitrary but has usually been arrived at through trial and
error and several years of experience'.

These conclusions are echoed, in a more critical manner, by Heald (1972):

'Every year millions of pounds are invested in the
retail field on the development of new stores, yet the
majority of decisions regarding the siting of new stores
are still based on a combination of hunch, experience and
a few rudimentary calculations'.

Heald also points out that location decisions often have to be made under pressure:

'A major problem facing retail groups is the decision to
accept or reject a property put forward by a developer.
Typically ten new sites a week (4) are up for consideration
all of which must be assessed correctly, otherwise the

54

investment may turn out to be unprofitable or the company may
lose a valuable site to its competitors'.
This suggests that some firms do not decide in advance which towns they
are interested in, and then search themselves for suitable sites, as
suggested above; instead they tend to wait upon information supplied by
developers and estate agents. This contrast in methods is also mentioned
by Thorpe (1974b).

Thus, one may summarise locational decisions as being made under
conditions of uncertainty and under pressure of time. It is not
surprising then if multiple retail firms have evolved relatively simple
and imprecise methods of locational assessment.

4.3.7 Locational assessment methods

A good account of typical methods used in locational assessment, both in
America and in Britain, is given by Davies (1976a,Chapter 9). This
account draws mainly on the work of American marketing geographers
(2.5.4). Attention is also given here to methods involving multi variate
analysis, which have been developed by Davies himself (1973a, 1977a) and
Heald (1972); for critical comment see Doyle (1973). These methods are
described in articles which clearly have a normative rather than
descriptive function, as they describe new methodology and discuss its
advantages.

It would be unreasonable to assume that sophisticated statistical
methods or mathematical models are used by many firms in locational
assessment. More typical perhaps is the method used by the Boots
Company, and outlined by Pope (1975). Forecasts are made of the future
level of trade of the centre in which a new store is being considered,
and then the performance of the store is estimated through comparison
with existing stores owned by the company in similar shopping centres.
This method clearly makes full use of the most reliable source of
information available to the company: detailed records of costs and
turnover in existing stores. But the use of this type of comparative
method ignores the possible effects of competition from other firms upon
either existing stores, or the proposed store. The process of making
analogies between stores in different locations, and extrapolating
existing performance to future situations, seems to involve some dubious
assumptions.

The extent to which this method, or the conventional marketing
geography methods based upon central place theory, or other methods, are
used by British multiple retail firms is impossible to judge. It is
probable that methods are generally derived in order to present quick
results, and to make full use of the information available to the firm,
particularly on the performance of its own stores. This would represent
the best type of response of 'administrative man' to stimuli which
require urgent decisions. There is clearly a need for the release of
more information by major firms on their methods of locational assessment,
and the ways in which these relate to their more general policies. This
information would not be solely of academic interest. It would aid the
process of improvement of methods, and would also aid the decision
making processes of both developers and town planners, who are dependent
upon multiple retail firms for the achievement of many of their policies.

4.3.8 Locational decision making in multiple firms: conclusions

The evidence reviewed in this section indicates that multiple firms are
collectively able to make considerable impact upon British patterns of

retail location. This impact is partly exercised in the selection of
locations for new stores, an area in which geographers have contributed
to methodology and hence have tended to concentrate their interest. It
may be however that policies of closure or alteration of existing stores
by multiple firms have a greater impact today. This topic has received
little academic attention.

It appears also that an understanding of retail location decisions must
involve an appreciation of the overall policies of a firm. Locational
decisions are intimately bound up with decisions on type of image for
the firm, advertising expenditure, rate of mark up, adoption of new
retailing methods, and criteria for profitability. These considerations
must also be understood by planners if they are to anticipate future
requirements of multiple retailers. This is important, as many firms
are applying pressure to develop new stores in hitherto improbable
locations, and withdrawing investment from the established town and
district centres. These possible conflicts of interest between
retailers and planners are to be discussed in Chapters 7-9.

4.4 BEHAVIOUR OF INDEPENDENT RETAIL FIRMS

4.4.1 The independent retail firm

The independent retail firm is defined as one owning less than a
specified number of shops, ten in the Census of Distribution tables.
The great majority of independent firms can also be classified as 'small':
these have been defined by Hall (1971) as owning fewer than five shops,
and having an average turnover per shop of under £50,000 per annum (at
1971 prices). This section attempts to describe and explain broad
aspects of the locational behaviour of 'small shopkeepers'.

Severe problems are involved in carrying out this task. Independently
owned shops as defined above, numbered some 391,000 in 1971 and were
present in all types of retail trade: clearly any generalisations will
be of limited value. Problems exist in attempting to describe decision
processes of small shopkeepers involving store location: as elsewhere
in this chapter, there is a lack of published information, although some
useful sample surveys of small shopkeepers have been made recently
(Bates, 1976; Berry, 1977).

This section adopts therefore a largely deductive approach, drawing
upon evidence of small shopkeeper behaviour in general rather than
locational decisions in particular. Firstly a brief description is
given of recent trends in the independent retail sector. Then, typical
goals and attitudes of small shopkeepers are examined. This leads on
to a discussion of locational choice in the context of policy options
for the firm as developed above (4.2). It is shown that the small
shopkeeper is normally in a disadvantageous position, which can be
remedied to some extent by the adoption of one or more 'strategies',
each of which have locational implications. Finally, some evidence of
locational decision making by small shopkeepers is reviewed: decisions
concerning closure or alteration of existing premises are included in
this discussion.

4.4.2 The independent retail sector

In 1971 the independent sector owned about 83 per cent of all shops but
commanded only about 53 per cent of total retail sales. Numbers of
shops and share of trade have both probably continued to decline in the

56

1970s. The decline has been rapid for independent shops selling
groceries and other convenience goods (see Table 9.5 and sub section
9.3.2), but this decline has partly been compensated by increases in
numbers of independent shops selling comparison and specialty goods
(for definitions, see 5.5.2).

The sector includes a majority of 'traditional' convenience goods
retailers, and a minority of 'progressive' or 'innovative' retailers,
mainly selling goods for which demand is increasing. However there is
insufficient evidence available to warrant a special discussion of
innovative firms, as in the previous section.

4.4.3 Goals and attitudes of small shopkeepers

Those factors which cause small shopkeepers to set up in business, and
which control their subsequent decision making, are likely to be
similar to those found in studies of 'small' businessmen in general.
The following findings emerged from discussions with small businessmen,
organised by the Bolton Committee on Small Firms:
   'The underlying motivation of these respondents can best be
   summarised as 'the need to attain and preserve independence'.
   This need for 'independence' sums up a wide range of highly
   personal gratifications provided by working for oneself and
   not for anybody else. It embraces many important satisfactions
   which running a small business provided - the personal
   supervision and control of staff, direct contact with customers,
   the opportunity to develop one's own ideas, a strong feeling of
   personal challenge and an almost egotistical sense of personal
   achievement and pride - psychological satisfactions which
   appeared to be much more powerful motivators than money or the
   possibility of large financial gains'   (Golby and Johns, 1971, p.5).
Along with this desire for independence and responsibility, there was
a strong dislike for any suggestion of control or intervention by
outside agencies. This is exemplified by an apparently universal
dislike for Value Added Tax, because of the paperwork required and the
possibility of government inspection. But this dislike also extends to
advice on business methods or offers of financial help. 'Big business'
is disliked almost as much as government.

Most of the businessmen who took part in the Bolton Committee
discussions were torn between the desire to remain small, and the feeling
that they should be interested in growth. The reasons for remaining
small - a wish to continue to participate actively in the business,
instead of simply 'managing' it, was perhaps the most important - were
consistent with their original motivations for starting the business.
Therefore the majority had decided not to attempt any major expansion
of trade.

Few studies have examined the motivations and attitudes of small shop
keepers in Britain. The most comprehensive study is probably that of
Bechhofer and associates (1971; 1974a; 1974b), who interviewed about
400 small shopkeepers in Edinburgh in 1969. The results confirm the
more general findings of the Bolton Committee. When asked why they had
gone into retailing, 81 per cent of the sample said that 'independence'
was an important or very important reason. At the same time 'money'
and 'getting ahead' were also highly rated (by 72 per cent and 62 per
cent respectively). These latter reasons seem however to have been more
important in theory than in practice, since the survey shows firstly
that incomes from shopkeeping were generally low. Secondly, few shop
keepers appeared really to want to 'get ahead', since 77 per cent of the

sample expressed no interest in changing the ways in which they carried on their trade. Most of the respondents had started their businesses from a financial basis of personal savings or loans from members of the family. Few were willing to seek financial help from banks or other institutions, or to seek professional advice on shop management or location.

The picture that emerges is one of satisficing behaviour (2.3.3). Setting up a shop tends to be a response to problems of employment or health rather than a way of making a fortune. Once established, the shopkeeper tends to adopt a strict routine for making decisions on everyday matters. Consideration of any possibilities of improving income other than by purely incremental means is unlikely, except when pressure is applied from outside sources. Alternative solutions to a problem are unlikely to be considered in full.

4.4.4 Policy options and strategies for the small shopkeeper

The analysis of cost options described above (Table 4.1) can be applied to small shopkeepers as well as to large firms. The fact that a retailer owns one shop, or a small number of shops, tells us nothing about financial constraints or style of retailing. However we might expect most retailers of this type to have limited funds available for purchase or rent of premises, for fitting and staff costs, and for advertising. This means that he cannot expect a high turnover, as many potential customers will be unaware of his presence. At low levels of sales he must employ a high mark up in order to meet his costs and make some profit, but the high mark up will deter customers. However, three strategies are open to the retailer to remedy this situation.

The first strategy that would follow from the analysis of cost options would be simultaneously to increase advertising and reduce the mark up: in other words to cut prices and advertise the fact. (This assumes that in the short term it is not feasible to increase 'rent' by moving to a better located shop). The purpose is to attract many more customers, thereby increasing volume of sales. But this can be a risky strategy, because costs are certainly increased and the rise in sales may not materialise immediately, or at all.

A second strategy is to ensure that the high mark up is not resented by customers, by selling goods of a specialised nature for which the customer cannot compare prices amongst shops. This strategy is exemplified by the antique trade, where virtually all goods offered are unique in some way, and prices reflect the trader's knowledge and the buyer's degree of commitment to the purchase (or perhaps his gullibility). Many other retailers of comparison or specialist goods can also achieve rates of mark up much higher than in the grocery trade, because of lack of immediate competition.

The third strategy for maintaining a reasonable turnover against cut price competition is to provide other benefits to customers, which induce their loyalty. One such 'benefit' is to be closer to home than any other similar store: this means that the retailer may perceive an advantage in being the only one of his kind in a particular residential area. This privilege may be worth paying a higher than normal rent for, in a new shopping parade to serve a council housing estate for example. Another 'benefit' for customers may be a high standard of service: this means that the retailer has to devote personal attention to the customer, offering advice, reassurance, deference, or even a form of friendship, according to the wishes of the customer concerned. Discussion with food retailers has shown that they are clearly aware of these matters (Sofer,

1965), and that they tend to categorise their regular customers and
behave appropriately towards them. In more general terms, the retailers
in that survey, and in that carried out by Golby and Johns (1971),
realised that this type of personal service was the best way to retain
their customers in the face of price competition. These factors
probably apply most strongly in trades such as butchery and greengrocery,
where there can be considerable variation in quality of produce, so that
customers need to be reassured that they are buying wisely for their
families. General grocers are most susceptible to price competition,
because of the standardised nature of their goods, and it is not
surprising that outlets of this type have been closing in recent years
far more often than in any other trade.

Perhaps the most important general point about small shopkeepers in
the present context is that their running costs ('rent', staff and
maintenance) are generally small, and their expectations are often small,
compared with multiple firms. This means that the small retailer can
survive at much lower levels of custom than the larger firm would need
at each of its shops. So the small independently owned shop is typically
found in suburban shopping centres or in isolated positions, where it can
aspire to a fairly small but regular clientele. An exception to this
rule is provided by the small specialist shop (such as the antique
dealer, discussed above), which does not depend upon local residential
areas for its custom, but can attract from a wider area, largely by
reputation. These shops are often found in areas where competition for
sites from multiple retailers or genuine local shopkeepers is minimal:
for example, in ribbons of old shops close to town centres.

Many independent retailers are of course located in town centres.
Some of these, such as owners of fashion shops, should expect to
correspond with the stereotype discussed for comparison goods multiple
retailers above (4.3.4): high 'rent' and high mark up being justified
by the attraction of many casual customers. Others, particularly food
retailers, may occupy older premises in the town centre and pay lower
rents than the average (although probably higher than those to be paid
outside the town centre).

4.4.5 Locational decisions of small shopkeepers

It should be clear from the above discussion that while location per se
may have a relatively small effect upon the small shopkeeper's degree
of success, there are strong constraints upon his choice of location.
A general constraint is likely to be one of cost, such that new premises
in city centres, for example, are widely regarded as being too expensive
for new independent retailers to rent (Seeney, 1976). More subtle
constraints also exist. Many prospective retailers will consider only
those properties in areas already familiar to them. Those who inherit
or acquire a particular shop from relatives are the most constrained of
all.

Nevertheless, for most new retailers, there is probably a genuine
choice to be made between a number of available shop premises. There is
very little direct evidence about ways in which these choices are
typically made. One can however make some inferences from survey results
relating to other aspects of entry into retailing, and also from informed
opinion in this field.

It appears that relatively few small shopkeepers start simply through
taking over an existing business from a relative. For example, of the
808 small shopkeepers interviewed in a survey carried out in eight
English towns in 1974-75 by the Manchester Business School, only about

59

six per cent inherited their shop (Bates, 1976, p. 49). The great majority appear to make a free decision to enter retailing.

Locational choice is often constrained by personal circumstances. Bechhofer et al (1974b) consider that many are almost 'forced' into retailing through family pressures, unemployment or even poor health. In these circumstances the attractions are in being able to work 'at home' and at one's own pace. It seems reasonable to suppose that this type who is 'escaping' into retailing will be likely to be strongly influenced by opportunities that present themselves, such as the offer of retail premises by a relative or friend. Otherwise the principal aim may well be to minimise the initial cost of the venture: this will take the form of choosing the cheapest premises available (presumably a vacant shop in an off centre location), and/or a type of trade where costs of shop fitting and buying stock are low (e.g. greengrocery).

Bechhofer et al (1974b) also found that in Edinburgh a proportion of the small shops (perhaps 20 per cent of the total) seemed likely to be 'failures' almost irrespective of the circumstances of ownership. These were the shops in very poor locations, and/or with bad histories, and tended to change hands frequently (at least once a year) or remain vacant for long periods. These shops would attract the new retailer with insufficient financial resources to start a business properly. In addition, the shops' history and poor location would mean that they had virtually no regular custom. On the other hand, the remaining 80 per cent of the small shops were 'stable' and tended to be run by the same retailer for very long periods, up to his retirement or death. It follows that at any one time relatively few of these stable shops with a good reputation would be available for the new retailer. Those that were available would probably command a high premium for the 'goodwill' of the shop. (5)

The difficulties to be found in starting up a new shop, and the high failure rate resulting, have been emphasised by other writers. Gornall (1954), in a paper based upon personal knowledge of greengrocery, shows how easy it is to set up a shop in this trade, and how difficult it is to make any profit in the first year or so. A.Smith(1971, p. 36) quotes several sources with similar opinions, although stating that 'quantitative evidence is hard to come by'. It appears that in general the new entrant should not expect to make a reasonable living from his shop for the first two to three years, since it will take him this long to attract a sufficient number of regular customers, no matter what merits the location may have. So the most important single requirement for the prospective retailer seems to be that he should have sufficient financial resources: (i) to be able to buy a reasonably good shop in a reasonably good location, preferably as a going concern; (ii) to be able to buy sufficient fittings and stock for the new shop; (iii) to be able to survive until the shop begins to be reasonably profitable. It will be evident that locational factors are only of moderate importance in this context.

These conclusions would apply most strongly to retailers selling convenience goods. In this area of retailing, consumers are very conscious both of price and quality variation, and the numbers of shops are declining. It would seem that a new entrant to retailing would do better to sell goods for which the demand is rising rapidly. The snag here is that these types of goods are not likely to be sufficiently in demand yet for a shop to rely entirely on local customers, unless the location is chosen very carefully. It follows that the retailer should choose a conspicuous location, to attract 'passing trade', and/or advertise widely. However we should not assume that the retailer is entirely aware of these requirements: the author has observed a number of instances of shops selling non food goods (e.g. toys, records) in ordinary suburban shopping centres, that have apparently had little custom, and have opened and closed within a few months.

Decisions by retailers to close down shops also have impacts upon patterns of location. It is as well to remember that shops may close for institutional reasons (expiry of lease, or compulsory purchase), or personal reasons (retirement, ill health, or death), as well as financial reasons (bankruptcy or declining income). No information appears to be available on the relative importance of these types of reason. Bechhofer et al (1975) managed to interview a small number of retailers who had closed down in Edinburgh. About a quarter of these had been able to sell their shops as going concerns, and retire in reasonable security. In most of the remaining cases the personal and financial reasons mentioned above had interacted over a period, often of several years, during which the shop had become less profitable and more of a burden. They had found difficulty in disposing of the shop, and when it was eventually sold at bargain price, the money had to be devoted to paying off debts. Most of these shops would probably go to inexpert new retailers, themselves making precarious financial arrangements and quite likely to close after a short period (see above).

It is important to gain some idea of the relative numbers of shops that are likely to close because of the owner's retirement: this is a reason for closing that is not affected by the location of a shop or its competitors, and this type of shop is most likely to be offered as a going concern. In the Manchester Business School survey, only about 16 per cent of the 731 small shopkeepers who gave valid replies were aged 60 or over, but a further 24 per cent were aged 50-59 (Bates, 1976, p. 32). In answer to another question, 78 per cent said that if they retired from retailing, they thought that the shop would continue to trade, under a new owner (not a relative). This is similar to the proportion who bought their shop as a going concern (79 per cent) (Bates, 1976, pp. 49, 85).

4.4.6 Conclusions

These concluding remarks are designed first, to draw some important general points from the material already discussed, and secondly, to relate these findings to the theoretical stance adopted in Chapter 2.

This section has suggested that small shopkeeping in Britain today is a precarious means of earning a living, and that the failure rate is high within a general downward trend in the number of small independently owned shops. The most successful small shops seem to be those that establish a substantial and/or loyal clientele, usually from the surrounding residential area; and those that can offer specialist goods and/or services, attracting customers on merit. In each of these cases, location per se is unlikely to be the decisive influence on success or failure; but a bad location (particularly one in a blighted area) may prejudice the chances of success. There is no information on the extent to which prospective retailers consider locational factors, but it does appear that the most badly located shops are likely to be taken up by the most ill prepared shopkeepers. Furthermore, the merits of a particular location are usually reflected in its price or rent; and one would expect a well prepared retailer to know the level of rent he can afford to pay, and the type of location he will need. It is then a question of waiting for a suitable shop to become available at a suitable price.

To sum up, the small shopkeeper's decisions on location are influenced by 'chance' factors of availability of suitable shops, and personal finance. Having acquired a shop, its locational attributes become rather less important than the abilities of the retailer himself in the struggle to achieve reasonable profits. Retailing seems to attract large numbers of inexperienced and incompetent businessmen, but there are powerful forces that ensure that most of the incompetents do not survive for very long. Efficient shopkeepers in reasonable locations can on the other hand survive comfortably, and lend some stability to a rapidly changing pattern of small shops.

It appears then that 'normative' decision making is rare in the independent retail sector. Locational decisions are inevitably involved in setting up a shop, but it is unlikely that even the simplistic advice discussed above (4.2.1) is generally observed. After starting the shop, locational decisions are likely to become necessary again only under considerable stress. (6)   The small shopkeeper, unlike the multiple firm, does not build up any experience of locational decision making, and thus does not know which methods of assessment to adopt, or which criteria to use in choosing between alternatives. He is also unlikely to seek or heed the advice of professionals in this field. Thus, the locational decisions of small shopkeepers are likely to seem irrational and unpredictable, although considered en masse one would expect a degree of response to changing locational costs and benefits.

4.5   AN ASSESSMENT OF RECENT CHANGES IN THE RETAIL ENVIRONMENT

This chapter can be concluded with a brief examination of relationships between the processes of decision making already described, and broad changes in typical patterns of retail location. A number of postwar changes in the retail environment have been mentioned in Chapter 1. These include   (i) changing attitudes of consumers to questions of value for money and standards of service;   (ii) the growth, then decline, in importance of the property developer in providing new retail facilities; (iii) the introduction of planning controls on retail development;   and (iv) changes in manufacturing and wholesale distribution. All of these have had very significant effects upon numbers, types, sizes, and locations of shops. These effects have taken place in two ways: through providing constraints upon decision making about size and location of shops, and through modifying patterns of income and expenditure.

These changes have generally favoured the large retail firm, and told against the small independent. So far as changes in income and expenditure are concerned, the large firms have benefited from economies of scale in both buying goods for resale, especially since the abolition of resale price maintenance in 1956 and 1964;   and in building new premises. The small firm has generally not had the financial resources to increase its activity to a level at which economies of scale begin to occur. This has meant that consumers have increasingly tended to buy standard branded goods - particularly groceries - in the larger stores, where prices are generally lower. This theme will be examined further in Chapter 9.

Locational choices of all retailers have become subject to constraints, particularly those imposed by town planning policies, which have generally restricted new retail development to specified locations, and imposed control over redevelopment or expansion of existing shops. Small retailers have thus lost their pre war freedom to convert ordinary houses into shops – probably the cheapest way to start a shop. Large retailers have not been able to have complete freedom of choice in selecting new locations: planning policies have often forced them to compete with other firms for expensive city centre sites (6.2.5). However the largest firms have often been able to benefit (relatively) through negotiation with developers and planners, for example in providing 'magnets' for new precincts (3.3.2).

So it appears broadly that the large firm has been able to cope successfully with post war changes in the retail environment. This is despite the fact that the policies of developers and planners have imposed constraints upon locational decision making, and may have added to operating costs, through inflation of rent. Until the mid 1960s, almost all major retail firms were equally affected by these constraints, and so any competition between firms would be mainly in respect of the goods they sold. Since then, price competition appears to have become more important, and many firms have tried to respond by increasing store sizes in order to reduce unit costs. This has forced them to seek non central sites, and the most successful firms may well have been those which have found means of acquiring such sites despite the generally negative attitudes of planners in this respect. The firms of Comet and Asda, described above (4.3.5) have both achieved rapid growth by converting existing non central and non retail properties to retail use. An alternative means of coping with the need for larger premises, open only to the largest firms such as Marks and Spencer (4.3.4) has been to use their bargaining power with planners and developers to increase the size of central area stores.

For the small retailer, either entering the profession or seeking new outlets for expansion, the choice of locations continues to be constrained largely by factors of cost. The decline in demand for premises in areas subject to declining trade levels (Table 1.1) does not assist existing traders in such areas, but it does allow a supply of cheap premises to become available for new users. The policy of Augustus Barnett (4.3.5) shows that profitable use can be found for small premises in apparently unpromising locations. But generally, it appears that unsuccessful retail businesses often succeed each other in badly located shops.

Two final conclusions emerge from this chapter, which are similar to those from Chapter 3. First, there is a lack of reliable detailed information upon the decision making processes of retail firms, especially with regard to location. This applies almost as much for the large and powerful multiple firm as for the small independent. This review has thus been exploratory, attempting to relate locational to other policies of the firm, and drawing contrasts between various types of firm. In this way any future research findings can be put into some overall context.

The second conclusion, which appears clearly despite the paucity of empirical evidence, is that most retail firms are forced into situations of having to make rapid locational decisions in response to opportunities. The large firm copes with this problem by formulating simple procedures for choosing between locations, within some agreed overall policy for expansion or change. The small firm tends to regard locational decisions as characterised by uncertainty, and therefore prefers not to make them at all. In making the initial sequence of decisions involved in starting the shop, a location may be chosen largely by default, because for example the shop is particularly cheap, or has a good reputation, and not because the location itself appears optimal. Henceforth, any changes in advantages or disadvantages of the location tend to be ignored, unless

the situation becomes intolerable. Normative procedures for appraisal
of locations, and for decision making generally, seem remote from the
real world of the small shopkeeper.

NOTES

(1) The right to continue trading under the same name, using the same
suppliers, etc.
(2) A good example is Allied Suppliers,formed by merger of several
grocery firms and now part of the Cavenham empire, itself part of
Generale Occidentale S.A., operated from France and Hong Kong (Benwell
Community Project, 1979, p. 46).
(3) This can be inferred from statements by Asda spokesmen, for example
Ridgway (1976).
(4) A firm as large as the Boots Company may have to consider between
40 and 50 opportunities per week (Pope, 1975).
(5) It is not clear whether this finding is typical. In the Manchester
Business School survey it was found that 46 per cent of 802 grocery
shops surveyed had operated under current ownership for less than five
years, and only 32 per cent for ten years or more (Bates, 1976, p. 47).
(6) For a discussion of current sources of stress for small shopkeepers,
and their reactions to stress, see below (9.3.5).

5 Attitudes to retail location: the consumer

5.1 INTRODUCTION

The previous two chapters have attempted to explain why developers and retailers set up shops of certain kinds in certain locations. The results of these decisions are the gradual readjustment of existing geographical patterns of shops and centres. In this chapter the decision processes of consumers are reviewed, with particular emphasis on choice of shop. The theoretical material examined is drawn from several disciplines, while the empirical evidence discussed is mainly taken from studies of shopping behaviour in Britain.

For a number of reasons, not least the importance of marketing as an applied academic discipline, there is far more published material on consumer behaviour than on developer or retailer behaviour. It is possible therefore to organise this material rather more systematically, and to provide better empirical justification for theoretical propositions, than in earlier chapters. Section 5.2 draws largely upon psychological material in considering individual consumer decision making, with respect to retail goods. This treatment is then extended in 5.3 to cover the activity of shopping: that is, choosing which shop to visit as well as which good or service to purchase. The next section reviews some empirical material of shopping behaviour in Britain, which is interpreted with reference to conclusions from previous sections. Lastly, some more general conclusions are drawn about consumers' attitudes to retail location, and an attempt is made to establish broad relationships between shopping behaviour and the whole spectra of retail goods and shopping centres. The validity of normative and descriptive decision theory (Chapter 2) is finally discussed with reference to consumer behaviour, particularly the selection of destinations for shopping trips.

5.2 CONSUMER DECISION MAKING

5.2.1 Motivation and frame of reference

In this section a descriptive model of purchasing as a series of decisions is proposed and discussed. As a prelude, it is worth examining briefly some of the broad motivations behind the processes of choosing and buying retail goods and services. There are two reasons why this is important in the present context: first, that the choice of product often determines the choice of shop; second, that the processes involved in choosing goods to buy may well be similar in part to those involved in choosing a shop to visit.

A great deal has been written about possible motives for consumer behaviour, based upon theory or observation. The theory has been summarised by Kotler (1965) (1) as follows:

    i)   The Marshallian Economic Model. 'Purchasing decisions are the result of largely 'rational' and conscious economic calculations. The individual buyer seeks to spend his income on those goods that will deliver the most utility (satisfaction) according to his tastes and relative prices'.

ii)   The Pavlovian Learning Model. Derived from experimental
      psychology, the model nowadays is based upon four central
      concepts: Drive, Cue, Response and Reinforcement. Drive
      (or needs or motives) 'refers to strong stimuli internal
      to the individual which impel action'. A cue is a weaker
      stimulus which 'determines when, where or how the subject
      responds'. The response is the subject's reaction to any
      cue or cues, and depends partly upon the extent to which
      the experience is rewarding, i.e. drive reducing.
      Reinforcement occurs when the experience is rewarding;
      there is a tendency for the response to be repeated on
      future occasions.

iii) The Freudian Psychoanalytic Model. Man feels guilty
      about some of his basic urges - especially sexual - and
      tries to repress these from his consciousness. These
      urges are denied, or become transmuted into socially
      approved expressions. Therefore the individual's
      behaviour in purchasing goods is never simple, and
      frequently is not comprehensible in depth by an outsider
      or even himself. The original Freudian theories have
      now been modified, and the urge for power (Adler) is an
      important development.

iv)   The Veblenian Social psychological Model. Veblen saw
      man principally as a social animal - 'conforming to the
      general forms and norms of his larger culture and to the
      more specific standards of the subcultures and face to face
      groupings to which his life is bound. His wants and
      behaviour are largely moulded by his present group
      memberships and his aspired group memberships'. Kotler goes
      on to say that a person's behaviour and attitudes can be
      shaped by the influence of his culture, subculture, social
      class, reference group, face to face group (family or peer
      group), and finally by personal factors.

It is noticeable that textbooks written for students of marketing (e.g.
Kassarjian and Robertson, 1973; Foxall, 1977) tend to dismiss the
economic model as unrealistic, and concentrate on the approaches derived
from psychology or social psychology. This may seem surprising, since
American studies (e.g. Myers and Mount, 1973) have demonstrated that
household income levels are important predictors of the frequency with
which certain goods are bought. Marketers appear to dismiss the economic
model for two main reasons. First, actual models of consumer demand
devised by economists (Brown and Deaton, 1973; Green, 1976) are
difficult to test empirically, as with many other branches of micro
economic theory. Second, marketers exist to influence purchasing
behaviour, and will expect to achieve greater success through
manipulating consumers' 'irrational' psychological processes than their
'rational' economic calculations. This is because rival branded goods
are usually similar in objective terms and thus will possess similar
levels of marginal utility to the consumer.

Market researchers emphasise that each individual perceives retail
goods and services within his own frame of reference. This can include
the effects of knowledge and past experience of goods and services
(Pavlovian model); the effects of subconscious motives and early
upbringing (Freudian); and the effects of the social environment
(Veblenian). The various psychological and social psychological theories
that have been applied in market research all seek to explain aspects of
consumers' frames of reference, and where possible relate them to more

easily observed attributes such as income level or standard of education. Schewe (1973) reviews applications of four theories in social psychology to marketing research - achievement motivation (McClelland, 1961); role theory (Goffman, 1959); direction theory (Riesman et al, 1961); and cognitive dissonance theory (Festinger, 1957). These theories all help to explain ways in which individuals will perceive certain types of goods, although it would be unwise to adopt any one theory in isolation to predict an individual's purchasing behaviour. (2)

5.2.2 The purchase process

The theories mentioned above are given attention because they can be applied to the analysis of decisions by consumers to choose particular goods and services from the whole range available. It is worth examining briefly the types of decision involved in a typical purchase process (Figure 5.1). (3)

   i)   Formation of need: the well known 'hierarchy of human needs' model (Maslow, 1943) suggests that while food, clothing and shelter are basic needs, the higher level needs tend to be felt by a minority of consumers, and are very susceptible to social and psychological influences.

   ii) Intention to buy: the need is recognised and a decision is made in principle to buy a good or service to fulfil that need.

   iii) Consideration: this stage and the next may not occur, if the decision to buy immediately implies the purchase of a specific product, as would probably be the case with routine food shopping. For other intended purchases, it is often necessary to gather information about the good in question, and to assess the economic and social implications of the purchase. This period of consideration will be followed either by the formation of an evoked set, or by a postponement of the purchase.

   iv) Formation of evoked set: there is evidence to show that when the prospective buyer is faced with a large number of alternatives, he reduces these to a shorter list - the 'evoked set' (Campbell, 1969). (4) This is likely to include between one and about seven possible choices (Miller, 1956).

   v)   Choice decision: this is the decision to buy a specific branded good. It may be made as a matter of routine (see above), or after evaluation of those items in the evoked set. The latter course normally involves the seeking of information: Cox (1963) distinguishes between (a) marketer dominated information (e.g. advertisements; (b) consumer dominated (word of mouth); and (c) neutral information (e.g. consumer group reports).

   vi) Purchase and no purchase: one of these will follow, depending on availability of the good.

   vii) Post purchase effects: these indicate the consumer's degree of satisfaction with the good or service in question. Three feedback loops are shown in Figure 5.1 which suggest that the effects may be favourable, in which case a repeat purchase of the same brand is likely at some future date; or less favourable, in which case the effects of the purchase lead to the formation of need

Figure 5.1   The purchasing process

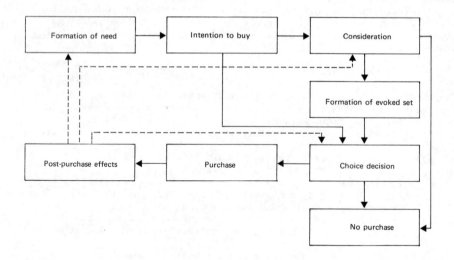

Figure 5.2   Methods of purchasing

	PATH I	PATH II	PATH III
Influence	Marketer / self	Social	Self / social
Need	Desire	Obligation	Necessity
Degree of information	High	Low-medium	Low
Source of information	Marketers	Consumers	Various
Interest	High	Low	Low
Perceived risk	Medium-low	Medium-high	Low
Size of evoked set	High-medium	Low-medium	Low
Brand Loyalty	Low	High	High

(perhaps for a replacement) or influence the consideration
stage. Marketers are keen to encourage brand loyalty
(the first loop mentioned), and use the theory of cognitive
dissonance to recommend that firms do their utmost to
reassure customers that they have made a wise decision
(e.g. Kaish, 1967). (5)

5.2.3 Attitudes to purchasing

It has been assumed so far that sequences of decisions made by all
consumers have common elements. However, a number of studies (e.g.
Gronhaug, 1972; Gronhaug, 1973; Wood, 1972) have shown that consumers
vary in their attitudes towards a prospective purchase. The central
concept is of perceived risk: Bauer (1960) argues that consumer
behaviour involves risk in the sense that any action of a consumer will
produce social and economic consequences that he cannot anticipate with
certainty. Consumers thus develop 'strategies' to enable them to act
with relative confidence when making purchasing decisions. Brand
loyalty, or the seeking of information from an appropriate source, are
common strategies. The degree of risk perceived in any purchase depends
upon characteristics of the consumer and the product involved (Taylor,
1974). The consumer affects the process through his frame of reference
(5.2.1) and thereby, the degree of social significance perceived in the
possession of the product. Goods and services can themselves be
classified according to the degree of economic risk and social risk that
their purchase would normally entail (e.g. Prasad, 1975, Fig.1).
 The degree of perceived risk appears to affect the purchasing process
in that where risk is high, the decision to buy at all may be made only
reluctantly and the size of the evoked set is small. Further differences
between high risk (Path I) and low risk (Path II) sequences are explored
in Figure 5.2, which is highly speculative since there appears to be
relatively little published empirical analysis of actual purchasing
decisions. Path III represents a common attitude to unimportant,
routine purchases, and is added partly to suggest that the social and
psychological influences much emphasised by market researchers are often
of minor importance when the need for the product is immediate.
 This point leads to a reminder of the warning posed by the work of
writers such as Ehrenberg (1969; see 5.2.2 above). For large groups of
consumers, regularities in behaviour may be more important than
differences between individuals. Ehrenberg (1972) and Massy et al (1970)
have been able to formulate comprehensive models of brand purchasing
behaviour which require few assumptions and in which variation between
individuals is regarded as a stochastic effect whose extent and
direction can be forecast. The investigation of differences between
individuals in their response to opportunities to purchase goods will,
in the context of retail studies, be worth while only if at least some
of these differences are shown to be systematically predictable from
measurable characteristics. This is a theme that is discussed again in
Sections 5.4 and 5.5.

5.3 THE SHOPPING TRIP

5.3.1 The shopping process

In this section the attempt is made to extend the decision sequence
described above to the activity of shopping - buying certain goods in

certain shops. While this is fairly easy in a descriptive sense, the discussion of factors influencing the decisions becomes more complex. Each shop possesses characteristics which attract or repel consumers; among them, a location. Thus, the section ends by discussing geographical research on shoppers' perceptions of retail location, and the effects of these perceptions upon certain aspects of shopping behaviour.

First, we can attempt to place the shopping trip within the purchasing process, as described in Figure 5.1. A simple treatment would be that the consumer decides precisely which good to buy (the choice decision), then forms an evoked set of stores. One store is chosen as a destination for the trip, and the purchase is made there. The purchasing act reinforces that store's inclusion in future evoked sets (Figure 5.3).

This treatment would not be realistic in many instances. The consumer has to use information in assembling an evoked set of stores; the 'consideration' stage in Figure 5.1 extends to stores as well as goods. Another possibility is that the consumer will decide first to visit a certain store, and then will form an evoked set (goods) in the store itself, from those goods on display. He may decide to buy other goods not originally on the shopping list. So the choice decision (stores) can influence the formation of an evoked set (goods) or even the decision to buy. Or, a visit to a chosen store to buy chosen goods may end in no purchase being made there because the goods are not available, or available but unsuitable in some way. The consumer will then either (i) abandon the purchasing attempt; or (ii) buy a different good at the same store; or (iii) go to another store and try to buy the chosen good there. The acts of purchasing or not purchasing both affect consideration of other items in the future; it seems best to term these effects 'post trip' rather than 'post purchase'. The whole process of buying goods in shops is evidently quite complex, and as described here necessitates a diagram (Figure 5.4) which is more complex than Figure 5.1, the purchasing process considered in isolation.

Of course the situation would normally be more complex than this, because consumers are likely to buy more than one good, and visit more than one store in one trip. In fact many products will be grouped by the consumer into bundles, for example 'groceries' or 'hardware', and he will know which shops are associated with which bundles. His shopping trip may be stimulated in the first place by a need to buy specific goods, or a bundle of goods. Having decided to make the trip for this purpose, he may decide (either in advance, or during the trip) to buy other products. Many goods may be needed, but not urgently. They can be bought at a convenient time, during a trip made for some other purpose.

There is evidence that in Britain, three housewives out of four plan their food shopping trips in advance, with a slightly smaller number making a shopping list. However, nine out of ten who make the list will then add to it while shopping (IPC, 1970, p.24). The same survey showed that few housewives (the exact percentage is not given in the report) do all their shopping at one store in any one trip (p.18). This is presumably because, while 'food' is considered to be one bundle of goods, different types of food (especially meat, vegetables and bread) are normally bought in different specialist shops. This is not the same as visiting several shops before deciding where to buy a particular product ('comparison' shopping). The latter is unlikely to be common in the purchase of routine goods such as foodstuffs, for two reasons. First, most housewives will have accumulated knowledge of where products may be bought most economically or most satisfactorily according to other criteria. Second, the time spent in making such comparisons is unlikely

Figure 5.3   The shopping process (I)

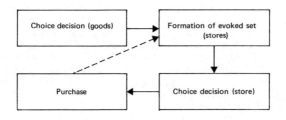

Figure 5.4   The shopping process (II)

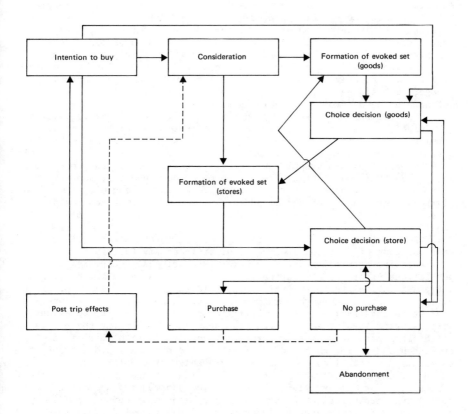

to be compensated by the extra value gained by making the best possible purchases. The housewife may however use information sources, such as word of mouth, or posters in supermarket windows, in deciding where to buy certain products. The design of some shopping centres (particularly markets) facilitates this.

Information on non food shopping in Britain similar to that presented in IPC (1970) does not seem to be available. In an American city, Dommermuth and Cundiff (1967) found that even in shopping for items of clothing (for which 'comparison' between shops is usually said to be important), the majority of housewives only visit one store before making a purchase. Averaged over a number of clothing and hardware goods, only 29 per cent of the purchases involved visiting more than one store, and 15 per cent visiting more than two. However, comparison by 'window shopping' may occur without one actually entering more than one shop. Also, one can make a purchase on the basis of information stored from previous visits to that or other shops. In fact, part of the shopping trip may be devoted deliberately to securing information about goods with little intention of buying.

5.3.2   Images of retail stores

At this point it is necessary to examine the criteria that the consumer uses to select one or more particular stores in which to make the desired purchases. This selection process involves two important influences: characteristics of the stores from which the selection is made, and characteristics of the consumer, which affects his perception of the satisfaction to be derived from shopping in each store. This subsection will examine briefly the first of these influences, and the next two the second, emphasising both attitudes to shopping in general, and the learning process involved in gaining knowledge of specific stores.

It has been stated above (4.2) that retail firms endeavour to cultivate an 'image' of their stores in the minds of customers. Market research studies have enquired into the images of stores or retail chains held by a sample of consumers, and have attempted to relate these with measurable socio-economic or demographic characteristics (e.g. Doyle and Fenwick, 1974). Berry (1969) distinguishes five major components of store image: location, design, product assortment, services and personnel, to which a sixth – price range – should be added. The consumer's perception of these features may of course be different from that of the firm itself. (6)

Three important points should be emphasised at this stage: first, that location of a store is only one of at least six factors that influence its attraction for consumers; second, that consumers' perceptions of stores may be inaccurate, or at least affected by social and psychological factors; third, that visiting a particular store is often a matter of habit rather than conscious assessment. This suggests that store loyalty may be an important attribute in shopping behaviour, just as brand loyalty is in purchasing behaviour. (7)   But the process of choosing between stores is not really comparable with that of choosing between brands. The number of different types of retail product bought by a family within (say) one month is probably far greater than the number of separate stores visited in that time. Since the range of stores is relatively smaller, there is more opportunity, and reason, for collecting information about stores. This means that consumers' perceptions of stores and knowledge of the local retail system are important factors in their shopping behaviour.

5.3.3 Attitudes to shopping

The set of images that a shopper holds of a set of stores will be a manifestation of a more general attitude to shopping. Shopping must be considered as an important activity in itself, rather than simply as a means of acquiring certain goods and services. Tauber (1972) suggests that

> 'peoples' motives for shopping are a function of many variables, some of which are unrelated to the actual buying of products ... an understanding of shopping motives requires the consideration of satisfactions which shopping activities provide, as well as the utility obtained from the merchandise that may be purchased'.

He goes on to characterise motives as 'personal' and 'social'. Many of these in fact are similar to the motivations considered earlier under the titles 'Freudian' and 'Veblenian'. But Tauber also emphasises that shopping is an opportunity for exercise, and an interesting diversion from household routine. The sample of housewives (from various parts of Britain) surveyed in IPC (1970) generally supported the view that 'shopping is more of a pleasure than a chore'. Shopping for clothes emerged as the second most popular of nine listed activities (second to preparing meals), while shopping for food came fifth. However, shopping for food was generally seen as a more skilful and important activity than shopping for clothes; the latter was pleasant in itself, but shopping for food brought some reward by increasing the housewife's self esteem. (8)

Every consumer will have to some extent a general frame of reference (5.2) for all of his decisions and activities as a consumer. Part of this frame of reference which we are concerned with here can be termed his 'attitude to shopping'. In a well known article Stone (1954) identified four types of consumer in suburban Chicago:

(a) The economic (33 per cent of the sample), who preferred stores which offered efficient service and low prices;
(b) The personalising (28 per cent), who wanted to be treated in a personal and friendly manner by store personnel;
(c) The ethical (18 per cent), who felt an obligation to shop + hedonistic (?) in certain types of store;
(d) The apathetic (17 per cent), who were not interested in shopping and wanted to minimise the effort involved.

The first two types were more common among those who had recently moved to the area: the economic were mainly young housewives in socially mobile families. This type would be the nearest equivalent to the 'rational' consumer usually described in the economic oriented literature. The personalising tended to be older and have smaller families; they would feel insecure in a new district, and would want to be reassured by the friendly attitude of store personnel. This type of consumer is much less likely to shop in the most 'rational' places, or to carry out long searches. The last two types were found mainly among long established residents. The ethical were of higher social status than the apathetic; the former felt they were entitled to deferential treatment from shop assistants, whereas the latter were more likely to be unsuccessful socially. Both of these attitudes would imply loyalty to certain stores, the ethical for obvious reasons, and the apathetic because this type of consumer would often simply shop at the most accessible store.

There is evidence from studies carried out in Britain that attitudes to shopping are clearly expressed in terms of preferences for certain

types of shop. A survey of British housewives (IPC 1970) contrasts
attitudes towards supermarkets and counter service food shops. One
would hypothesise from Stone's work that a substantial minority of
housewives would be unwilling to use supermarkets, from personalising
or ethical motives. In fact this is not the case, since 72 per cent of
the sample used supermarkets regularly, and a further 19 per cent
occasionally. In the over 55 age group, 20 per cent never used
supermarkets, but part of this is probably due to problems of access to
supermarkets rather than dislike of them. Among reasons given for
liking supermarkets were, as well as 'economic' ones such as 'range of
goods' and 'lower prices', reasons connected with the shopping process
itself. The supermarket gave them the opportunity to make their own
choice at their leisure from a variety of products. This is to some
extent an 'economic' motivation but it also helps the housewife feel
that she is serving the family in the best possible way (Sofer, 1965).
A survey of shoppers in Watford (Daws and Bruce, 1971) provides other
information on attitudes to shopping. 61 per cent of the sample agreed
that 'supermarkets are the ideal way to get family shopping'. Only 25
per cent agreed with the 'ethical' statement that 'the 'small man' type
of shop is usually better than a branch shop of a big organisation'.
Similar results were obtained by Bowlby (1979).   Attitudes of British
shoppers to hypermarkets and local shops are discussed further in 8.1.4
and 9.2.
  These survey findings apply mainly to 'convenience' shopping in which
pre purchase decision making is limited in extent, and one would expect
shoppers to be loyal to certain stores. Goods which are bought
infrequently, and especially those which have high value (economic or
social) to the buyer, will probably require more extended processes of
choice, both of brand and store. Studies have shown that in these
circumstances the choice of store appears to be affected by the
consumer's perception of the amount of risk involved in the purchase.
In one survey, buyers of hi fi equipment were found to be more likely to
patronise department stores than specialist shops if they felt that their
knowledge about the equipment was slight (Dash et al, 1976). Another
survey found that consumers in the upper social classes disliked buying
goods in discount stores if these goods carried 'social' risk – that is,
possession of them was likely to indicate one's social status (Prasad,
1975).

5.3.4 Searching and learning

A consumer will be able to make the most appropriate choice of store for
his purchases if he has prior knowledge of the set of stores accessible
to him. The 'search', in its fullest sense, should include all behaviour
which is directed towards obtaining the most utility from a proposed
purchase. Search can occur at home (in the processes of gathering
information about products and stores), and in the shopping centre
(through window shopping or enquiring within stores). Schneider (1975)
uses the terms 'informational search' for the former method and 'spatial
search' for the latter. The method and amount of search involved in any
purchasing process depends upon the consumer, the product, and the nature
of the retail system used by him. It will depend upon the consumer
because different consumers will take up different attitudes towards
consideration and forming an evoked set. Also, attitudes to shopping
may be important. It will depend upon the product; search will be
unnecessary or wasteful in the case of goods bought frequently, but will
be needed for goods bought infrequently through ignorance of their

characteristics and of the points at which they are sold. Nelson (1970) points out that for many products (e.g. canned food, paint) the best way to acquire knowledge of them is to use them; one cannot assess their worth just by inspecting them in the shop. These he terms 'experience' goods: those that can be assessed visually are 'search' goods. However it is possible (and often necessary) to devote informational search to experience goods. Generally speaking, for expensive products it becomes worth while devoting considerable time and energy towards making the most rational purchase possible (although one should not suppose that consumers always do). Also, infrequent and expensive purchases are unlikely to be as urgent as most of those made as a matter of routine. One can delay these until the information required has been gathered in full.

Bucklin (1967) summarises these points in a threefold classification of search. Full search occurs when 'it is of extreme importance to the consumer that multiple store visits be made to satisfy her shopping task'. He gives as an example the woman, conscious of her social status, who needs to keep up with fashions and impress others. But it would apply equally to a consumer who is very interested in a proposed purchase, and wants to buy exactly the right product (Path I in Figure 5.2).

The second type is called directed search. This 'connotes the consumer's concern for the purchase, particularly with respect to price, but that considerable ... search would not be worthwhile'. The consumer will decide fairly quickly what type of good he requires, and will know in which type of store it is likely to be found. He may or may not have a precise product or precise store in mind. This process may apply to rarely purchased goods in which the consumer is not really interested (Path II in Figure 5.2) but more probably to goods required fairly often, which are widely available.

The third type, casual search, applies where 'there are no compelling social or economic reasons that motivate the shopper' to carry out an exhaustive search (Path III in Figure 5.2). This pattern of search 'is likely to prevail for many everyday needs of the household'. Strategies to avoid searching include brand loyalty and store loyalty; another would be buy the first brand seen in the first store visited. The extent to which casual search is used by a consumer will probably reflect his attitude towards shopping and his valuation of time.

The purpose of a trip may also influence search processes. Several unconnected purchases may be made in one trip; the need to carry out all the purchases may restrict the opportunity for physical search. If the requirements of one particular purchase have led the shopper to a relatively unfamiliar locality, then the need for search in buying other goods on the shopping list is greater than normal. The resulting stress could cause abandonment of some purchases, or post purchase dissonance. This and similar problems seem to have been neglected by researchers.

The individual's attitude towards search, and indeed his purchasing habits generally, are likely to change over time. Apart from the effects of changes in family circumstances, he is going to have to adjust to changes in the pattern of retail outlets. The closing of a favourite store forces a degree of search upon the consumer, but the opening of a new outlet does not. The ability of the new store to advertise itself may be very important, at least in the short term, in altering patterns of expenditure. But even then, many consumers will perceive risk in patronising a new store in an unfamiliar place.

The topic of changes over time in shopping activity, and its relationships with theories of search and learning behaviour, has been of interest to several geographers in recent years. Golledge and Brown (1967) hypothesised that 'search activity' (the visiting of several destinations in succession, followed by repeat visits for further comparison) is eventually replaced by a stable 'habitual response' stage. In the present context this would relate particularly to consumers who had recently moved home. Horton and Reynolds (1971) used similar concepts in discussing the development of an individual's 'action space' – the set of locations with which he is familiar. More recently Burnett (1973; 1977; 1978) has tested a number of learning models against shopping trip data from Sydney, Australia and Uppsala, Sweden. In both cases patterns of destination choice appeared to alter and become more consistent over time. Lloyd (1977) found that consumers who had moved within an urban area were more likely to choose new destinations for low order (convenience) goods and services than for high order (shopping and specialty, see 5.5.2). This may partly reflect the more dispersed pattern of opportunities for purchase of low order goods rather than any contrast in store loyalty. A British study (Nader, 1968) has found that on a housing estate in County Durham, those who had moved there from Sunderland carried out twice as much shopping in Sunderland as those who had moved from elsewhere. However in another study, no statistical association was found between length of residence and any trip characteristic (Davies, 1973b, p.47).

5.3.5 Consumers' perceptions of retail opportunities

At this point some recent studies with a more clear geographical interest should be mentioned (for an introduction to recent geographical research, see 2.5.3). Thomas (1976) in a useful review article shows that geographical theory – especially central place theory – did not allow for variation in behaviour between consumers faced with a similar choice of shopping centres. Empirical discoveries that many consumers were not using their nearest shopping centre, even for food shopping (e.g. Clark, 1968; Ambrose, 1968), helped to encourage the development of new theories of spatial consumer behaviour, such as that of revealed space preference (Rushton, 1969).

Rushton distinguishes between 'spatial behaviour' and 'behaviour in space'. The former describes the manner in which the consumer will evaluate alternative destinations for the shopping trip, and choose from them; the latter describes 'the actual spatial choices made in a particular system'. The former exists independently of any particular geographical pattern of shopping centres, but the latter is strongly influenced by this pattern. Revealed preference theory is used by Rushton to analyse spatial behaviour: this analysis derives indifference curves from postulates of the way in which consumers trade off accessibility and attraction, in choosing between retail opportunities. The centre chosen for any particular trip lies on a higher indifference curve than any other centre. Thus the size of centre, and its location relative to the consumer, influences the likelihood of a visit there, as is the case with central place theory and spatial interaction theory. But the consumer's basic preferences are not determined by the actual pattern of shopping centres available to him.

Thomas (1976, p.44) points out that in its applications by Rushton (1969) and Clark and Rushton (1970), the theory was not very successful in predicting destinations for shopping trips. This lack of success is ascribed to an averaging of indifference curves over all consumers, which seems fallacious, given the variation in preferences and behaviour that can be recognised between consumers, irrespective of their location.

Examination of such variations should also therefore be a necessary task for geographers attempting to explain patterns of behaviour. To date this examination has largely taken two forms: the first is the association of measurable aspects of behaviour with measurable demographic or socio economic characteristics (to be discussed in 5.4). The second is the study of consumers' perceptions of retail opportunities and the ways in which these vary, both with consumer characteristics and consumer location.

The study of consumers' images of stores is well established in market research (see above). Some geographers have attempted to investigate a related but different topic - the extent to which consumers possess information about the complete set of stores in a district. Empirical work (e.g. Smith, 1976; Bowlby, 1972) has shown that the extent of knowledge of frequently patronised shops such as grocery stores varies with both social status of the consumer, and his length of residence in the district. This may not be very helpful in the examination of consumer behaviour, since the consumer's information held about alternative retail opportunities (termed his 'action space' by Horton and Reynolds (1971)), (9) and 'information field' by Potter (1979), is normally greater than the set of stores that he habitually uses. In this respect the geographical research should again be criticised for overemphasis on variation caused by the location of the consumer, and underemphasis on variations among individuals in their perception of opportunities (Thomas, 1976, p.56). An exception to this criticism lies in the work of Hudson (1974; 1976), who investigated the personal constructs (Kelly, 1955) held of various shops and shopping centres in Bristol, by a sample of students, and then attempted to relate these perceptual elements to aspects of spatial shopping behaviour. The attempt was only moderately successful, but investigation of this type could possibly be used in combination with revealed space preference analysis (see above) to explore the influences of both personal and locational characteristics upon behaviour in space. Potter (1979) has also demonstrated variations in size and shape of information field (see above) with consumer characteristics.

There is evidence to show that consumers' perceptions of whole shopping centres can also vary, and that these perceptions can help explain patterns of spatial behaviour. Hudson (1976) found that a model of shopping centre choice explained aggregate behaviour more closely than one of shop choice. Downs (1970) used semantic differential scales to investigate the images held by consumers in Bristol of various shopping centres. His sample found no difficulty in responding to questions on the main shopping centre in Bristol (Broadmead), and some consistency in the answers was revealed by factor analysis, suggesting that many consumers shared some elements of a generally clear image of this centre. However, when asked about smaller 'centres' close to the home, the respondents could not express any opinions about each centre as a whole, and this part of the interview was abandoned. Downs suggests that the shoppers possessed no images of these small centres, but only of certain shops within them.

5.3.6 Conclusions

It has been shown that the shopping trip can be viewed as a sequence of decisions, in which choice of destination is affected by many factors. These include the nature of the goods required, the degree of search felt to be necessary, and a host of other factors which vary among shoppers, partly according to demographic or socio economic characteristics, and partly according to more personal attitudes to the activity of shopping. Choice of destination is also constrained by the geographical disposition of shopping centres in the shopper's locality, and by his or her means of access to them. In addition, shoppers do not necessarily behave consistently over time.

The complexity of this situation renders analysis of observed shopping trips extremely difficult, although in aggregate terms a fair degree of correspondence with spatial interaction model predictions (Batty, 1976) is often found to occur. However, these models are poor at predicting aggregate behaviour in situations where their parameters are not fully known. This seems to be due to their weak theoretical content and explanatory power (Sheppard, 1979). Hence the considerable recent research into disaggregate models of store choice and other aspects of shopping behaviour (2.5.3; 5.3.5).

The next section extends this discussion, concentrating on areas where behaviour has been found to vary fairly systematically with measurable characteristics of the shopper. This by no means offers a complete answer to the problems discussed above, but it does suggest some relationships which planners should be aware of when formulating policies for the retail sector.

5.4 SYSTEMATIC VARIATIONS IN CONSUMER BEHAVIOUR

5.4.1 Attributes of consumers

Many studies in marketing attempt to show that markets may or may not be 'segmented' for certain products, or types of retail activity. They may show, for example, that demand for a product is strongest from a particular income or socio economic group, or within a particular type of residential area. The value of this finding to marketers is that they can then obtain more profitable results by appealing to the most rewarding segment of the market. If this segment is easily identifiable from Census or other readily obtainable data, so much the better. Our interest is principally in attitudes to retail location; the value of any positive findings in this section should be that it becomes easier to deduce some features of shopping behaviour in an area, from such data sources.

The 'groups' that any consumer will belong to vary in size from the household to the nation (or even political bloc). The groups that are usually defined at scales between these two limits do not really encompass homogenous blocs of people all of whom behave in roughly the same manner. It is more that most of their members share certain characteristics and attitudes, which are not held to such an extent by members of the other groups in that set. But in some classifications, for example by household income, it is unreasonable to expect very much uniformity within the 'group'. A household earning £2,500 per annum could be a large family living in poverty, an affluent retired couple, or a very affluent single student. It is best not to rely too much upon arbitrarily defined groups of this kind, but to consider income in a more general sense as an important attribute of a household. One can then look at the ways in which variations in this attribute affect shopping behaviour.

One can identify at least seven attributes of the individual consumer. The last two are geographical attributes which reflect the influences of the first five, but cannot adequately be dealt with under those headings. The attributes are:

A. Household size, and position of buyer in household.
B. Age - sex.
C. Household income.
D. Socio economic group; lifestyle; standard of education.
E. Racial or cultural group.
F. Use of car.
G. Area of residence.

To give this discussion some degree of structure, one can examine some effects of these attributes upon a number of stages in the shopping process, and two more general features of shopping behaviour. These are:
a. Formation of need.
b. Use made of information.
c. Degree of physical search.
d. Attitude to shops and shopping.
e. Nature and frequency of shopping trips.

Figure 5.5 is a matrix including all possible interactions between personal attributes (A-G) and characteristics of shopping behaviour (a-e). In the cells of the matrix an indication of the importance of the importance of the interaction is given, with a threefold classification: strong, moderate, and weak or uncertain. The values shown here are based on results of surveys, or derived from earlier discussions in this chapter. Throughout they should be regarded as very tentative and open to argument.

Figure 5.5 Consumer attributes and shopping behaviour

Attributes	Aspects of behaviour				
	Need formation	Information usage	Search behaviour	Attitude to shopping	Trip characteristics
Household type	X		x	x	x
Age and sex	X	x	x	X	x
Income	X	x	x		x
Social	x	x	x	X	X
Racial	x	x		x	
Use of car	x		x		X
Area of residence		x	x		X

X   strong interaction
x   moderate interaction
(blank) weak or unpredictable interaction

It should be recognised firstly that the strength of any such interaction will vary with the type of product involved in the purchase. Frank (1967), from a survey of Chicago households concluded that characteristics of grocery purchases, such as total demand, average price paid per item, and brand loyalty, show little or no relationship with any measurable demographic or socio economic features. Routine food and other shopping seems for most households not only to be a matter of habit, but also quite likely to be similar in nature to that of other households with very different attributes.

5.4.2 Demographic, social and economic influences

In this sub section the 'effects' of the first five attributes of a household (Figure 5.5) are considered in turn using results from several British surveys. The first of these is the size of the buyer's household. This will obviously affect the demand for goods and services, although probably not in a regular fashion, since demand is also influenced by income and other factors, and some goods are only required once in each household (e.g. washing machines). Effects upon information seeking, degree of search and attitudes to shopping are not clear. There is some evidence (e.g. in Byron, 1967; Ambrose, 1968) that larger families generate more frequent shopping trips than smaller ones, and also tend to visit centres nearer to the home. Families which include children of under five years may also generate more trips than average (Daws and Bruce, 1971, Table 5).

Second, the buyer's sex and age group. The relationship with need formation is very strong, since many goods and services are sold to members of particular age groups or sexes. Similarly, use of information sources, especially magazines, will vary. There is evidence that elderly people have a weaker knowledge of retail opportunities (Potter, 1979) and are inclined to search less than younger shoppers. Attitudes to shopping may also differ, for example in dislike of supermarkets (IPC, 1970), and other attitudes to grocery shopping (Bowlby, 1979, p.316). There is a problem here in distinguishing changes in attitude and behaviour over time, from the retention of attitudes and behaviour from earlier stages in life. Differences between old and young may reflect the latter process rather than the former.

Marked differences occur between the sexes in respect of frequency and type of shopping trip, mainly because of the housewife's role as provider of household goods for the family. Differences also occur between age groups, but it is difficult to separate these from effects of income, car ownership and family size. One characteristic of the elderly in Britain is that they are far less likely than other groups to go shopping by car. They are also less likely to make one main food shopping trip per week, but nevertheless carry out slightly fewer trips altogether than do younger shoppers (Bradley and Fenwick, 1975, Tables 9 and 30).

The third attribute, household income, undoubtedly has very important impact on the ability to buy many of the less 'essential' goods and services, and therefore on shopping trips for these items. Analysis carried out by the author (Guy, 1975, pp 30, 51-54) illustrates variation in British consumption of a number of goods and services with household income.

The influence of income per se on facets of shopping behaviour is almost impossible to determine, because income levels are strongly correlated with levels of education, social class, car ownership, and area of residence (weaker associations also exist with age, sex and household size). Because of contrasts in data availability, many American but few British studies attempt to associate some aspect of shopping behaviour with variation in income. In the British context it is best to concentrate analysis on the other attributes mentioned above.

The fourth attribute, 'social' characteristics, include perceptual elements (e.g. status) as well as those measurable objectively (e.g. socio economic group). In Britain, studies of shopping behaviour tend to use the latter (or 'social class' as defined for official purposes) as an explanatory variable, but again this can lead to confusion with the effects of household income, and to a lesser extent, car ownership.

The social and psychological characteristics and environment of an individual will certainly have some effect on need formation; this may be accentuated by the tactics of marketers through the use of specialised information sources. Bucklin (1969) found that 'liberated' housewives in California carried out less spatial and informational search (5.3.4) when purchasing routine household goods than the more conventional type of housewife: the effort involved was presumably thought not to be worthwhile. No other variable representing income or attitude to shopping explained behaviour as well as this characteristic. On the other hand, there is evidence (summarised by Schiller 1972) that middle class shoppers in Britain make longer shopping trips to more centres than average. This seems to be partly because such shoppers (who are likely to use cars for shopping) have greater knowledge of the system of shops and shopping centres, and partly because they buy a wider range of goods. Schiller, and Davies (1973b) also found that some middle class shoppers dislike large town centres with their rather standardised range of multiple stores, and like smaller towns with attractive visual features and atmosphere. But this attraction is also due to the location of certain high quality or specialist shops and services there (Schiller, 1971).

The fifth attribute - racial and cultural - has been studied little in this country in terms of effects on consumer behaviour. The statement by Sexton (1972) that differences between black and white in America simply reflect income differences may also be a valid hypothesis for investigation in Britain. Davies (1973b, p.60) reports that in Coventry, the behaviour of coloured immigrants seems to be similar to that of the working class white population, except that Saturday shopping expeditions seem to be more strongly a social occasion involving the whole family.

5.4.3 Car ownership and trip characteristics

The use of a car in shopping has a number of important effects upon behaviour. The car itself, its accessories and its maintenance are responsible for heavy expenditure in car owning households. Family Expenditure Survey data for 1971 (Department of Employment, 1972, Tables 28, 29) show that these households spent on average £7.18 per week on transport and vehicles; households without a car spent only £1.20. The use of a car is certainly beneficial to the searching process: it enables one to visit centres that are inaccessible by public transport, and makes it easy to visit more than one centre in one shopping trip. Its main effects are to be seen in the nature of shopping trips and fall into two categories. First, the car itself can transport a greater volume of goods than one could possibly carry any distance. Second, as intimated above, it gives the shopper a wider choice of local centres at which to shop.

One can draw some broad conclusions about car use in shopping in Britain, and then discuss how its use affects choice of shopping centre and other features of shopping trips.

In 1976 some 56 per cent of households in Great Britain owned one or more cars (Department of Transport, 1978, Table 52). A much smaller proportion, perhaps around 20 per cent have a car continuously available for shopping. (10)   In many households the car is used by the husband, for work trips, and therefore is available only on weekday evenings or Saturdays, on which day well over 60 per cent of households have a car available for shopping (Bruce and Delworth, 1976, p.6). This figure may include households without cars who are offered lifts in other cars.

Use of cars for shopping in Britain is not as high as these figures might suggest, although contrasts appear to exist between convenience and comparison shopping. For grocery shopping trips, even those with full car availability do not exclusively use cars: Bowlby (1979) found that only 56 per cent of such shoppers in her Oxford sample used cars 'very frequently'. Only 29 per cent of those with limited car availability used cars very frequently for grocery trips: walking (45 per cent) was more popular. A distinction can also be made between 'main' and 'non main' grocery trips: the former are at least twice as likely to be made by car (Bradley and Fenwick, 1975, Tables 14, 25; Hillman et al, 1976, p.79).

Variations in the use of cars for personal or comparison shopping are poorly documented in the literature. In the Watford survey, the percentage using cars to travel to the town centre for shopping rose from 27 (weekdays) to 45 on Saturdays: the Saturday trips were associated mainly with non food purchases (Daws and Bruce, 1971, Table 19). Over 80 per cent of trips from one outlying area were made by car. Thus the use of cars may be much higher for non food than food purchasing trips, largely because of the greater distances which normally have to be travelled.

In discussing any effects of car usage upon shopping behaviour, several difficulties occur. Car ownership and availability tend to be strongly associated with income and social class, and car owning households represented most strongly in outer suburban and rural areas, where accessibility to local shops is often poor (Bowlby, 1979; Guy, 1976a; Hillman et al, 1973). Car availability itself may have two types of effect. Firstly, it enables access to shops which would otherwise be inaccessible. This can be observed with respect to hypermarkets and superstores, which have catchment areas far larger than a conventional supermarket or small shopping centre (8.1.3). For comparison or specialist shopping the car makes possible the 'social class' effects noted above (5.4.2), including patronage of centres with visual attractiveness or snob appeal.

A second effect of car use is where car parking facilities become a determinant of shopping centre choice. For food shopping, 29 per cent of respondents to the Building Research Establishment survey in four towns stated that a centre's parking facilities were 'taken into account a great deal' in choosing where to shop (Bruce and Delworth, 1976, p.36): this factor ranked seventh out of 17. In the Oxford survey, 37 per cent agreed that 'given a choice between good shops and good parking facilities, I would choose to shop where there is better parking' (Bowlby, 1979, p.310). It does not follow however that actual choices are determined by car parking facilities to the extent suggested by these results, since for many households a centre chosen on other grounds (such as quality of goods, choice of shops, prices) will also possess good parking facilities.

For comparison or specialist goods, there is little evidence of any independent effect of car parking facilities. In the Watford survey, although over 30 per cent of car users said that parking was a 'difficulty' in shopping in Watford town centre, (Daws and Bruce, 1971, Figure 11), only one per cent of those who shopped in other towns gave 'easier parking' as their main reason (p.75). Similarly, in the Sunderland Corporation (1971) survey, less than two per cent of those respondents who disliked their present shopping facilities for any reason quoted car parking problems. Car parking facilities will probably help determine choice of centre where several large centres are accessible, as in the suburbs of a conurbation.

Generally then it is clear that several systematic variations in shopping behaviour, such as distance travelled, frequency of trips, etc., are related to variations in car availability. Much of this variation

82

can also be explained in terms of household size, income, or social class. Use of the car itself in shopping seems largely to be an effect of attitudes to shopping rather than a cause: this is clearly shown by the non use of cars by many households in situations where cars are available.

5.4.4 Area of residence and trip characteristics

In Section 5.3 an attempt was made to set out ways in which the effects of a geographical pattern of shopping centres on the shopping behaviour of local residents could be analysed. In this sub section, a more pragmatic approach is taken, related to typical circumstances in Britain. Shopping behaviour varies considerably between residential areas in respect of indicators such as frequency of trips or mean distance travelled in food shopping trips (e.g. Daws and Bruce, 1971, Table 13). These contrasts appear to be due both to the association of type of residential area with social class, income group, and car ownership; and to variations in patterns of retail opportunities available to consumers. The influence of the latter, particularly on trips for food and household goods, can be explored through consideration of the behaviour of shoppers living in two types of urban area (Thomas, 1976, p.29): the inner city, and the outer suburbs. The former is generally characterised by large numbers of isolated 'corner shops' or small groups of shops, together with ribbon development of shops along major roads. Most residents have a wide choice of shops within walking distance. The outer suburbs in contrast contain mainly purpose built shopping centres spaced well apart.

There is likely to be some interaction between area of residence and use of information, in that the inner city residents have the opportunity to acquire a detailed knowledge of which shops sell which products, while shopping or on other business in their home area. Outer suburban residents have to make specific shopping trips over some distance and will not always have the time for window shopping as well. Therefore they will have to use more information, either published or word of mouth. In the same way inner city residents have more opportunity for search; Bowlby (1972) shows that in Evanston, Illinois, people living in areas with closely spaced shops searched more widely than those living in lower density areas (when variations in social class and age had been accounted for). Middle class consumers, and those who use their cars in shopping, often tend to live in low density areas; but that it is these groups who seem likely to want to search the most (5.3; 5.4.2). So there can be some conflict between the desire to search and the level of opportunity to do so without too much effort. People living in rural areas are quite likely to be inhibited in their shopping behaviour, and to search less than urban consumers, as has been demonstrated in Sweden (Swedner, 1962).

Characteristics of shopping trips may thus be expected to differ somewhat with the type of residential area, even when other influences on behaviour are held constant. Inner city residents who are able to use cars for shopping appear to use them somewhat less than suburban or rural dwellers (e.g. Hillman et al, 1973, Table 3.14). This may arise from the ease of access by foot to local shops in inner city areas, or from the problems of parking at shopping centres. More information on influences of this kind must await the production of more clearly disaggregated data from surveys of shopping behaviour.

The discussion has now covered all of the relationships shown in Figure 5.5. Probably the main conclusion to be drawn from this treatment is that the five facets of shopping behaviour (a-e) are strongly linked to each other, but they seem to be unequally affected by any given attribute. This is important because it means that behaviour in general cannot easily be predicted for any set of households, by examining just one attribute. Advertisers, retailers and town planners will be interested in different facets, and therefore each one of these groups may be advised to use a particular set of attributes in trying to predict behaviour. The planners will be most interested in facet (e) - the nature, frequency (and destination) of shopping trips, but unfortunately this is affected by almost every attribute. Since the attributes themselves are also strongly interrelated, it may be possible to use just one or two of them to make 'satisfactory' predictions. But this is not the same as understanding shopping behaviour, which has been the concern in this chapter.

5.5   RETAIL LOCATION AND THE CONSUMER

This section draws together a number of points made in earlier sections, and attempts to set out some broad relationships between shopping behaviour and classifications of retail goods and services, and of shopping centres. The chapter is concluded with a brief discussion of the relevance of the decision theory discussed in Chapter 2.

5.5.1   Retail models and shopping behaviour

In this chapter the emphasis has been on the individual consumer, the way in which he makes decisions, and the influences behind these decisions. This is a relevant consideration for geographers and planners investigating shopping behaviour, because as Thompson (1966) pointed out: 'the fundamental factor affecting the geographic distribution of retail trade is the manner in which consumers organise their perceptions of the external environment with which they are faced'. In this respect the postulates of consumer behaviour involved in central place theory or spatial interaction theory are inadequate, since they do not allow any variation in behaviour between consumers apart from that which responds in a wholly predictable manner to the pattern of location of shopping centres.
   The work reviewed in this chapter has indicated three broad sets of reasons why the use made by any particular consumer of any particular shopping centre is not wholly predictable. First, his demand for the goods available in that centre reflects a variety of observable and unobservable influences (5.2). Second, the location of a store or centre is only one of several qualities that a consumer will take into account, when deciding what to buy and where. There are at least five other important attributes of a store which are likely to influence its degree of patronage (5.3). Bucklin (1967) shows how this 'image' component of a centre's attraction can be inferred from trip data and assessed for its relationship with measurable attributes of the shopper. Third, the shopper's knowledge of shopping centres, the stores and goods or services available in them, is not perfect. Methods of information seeking, and searching, can both affect the perception of location. The more search (mental and physical) that is carried out, the more the consumer will be aware of alternative retail sources of a product or service. This gaining of experience of the retail system takes time, so the behaviour of a newcomer to an area is likely to be different from that of longer established residents. Whether the shopper wants to

acquire this knowledge at all will depend upon his attitude to shopping: the personalising or apathetic shopper will not want to, so he will ignore parts of the retail system that others living in the same area would use.

5.5.2 Towards an explanation of shopping behaviour

These conclusions about the perception of location lead into some general concepts about shopping trips, shopping centres, and retail goods and services. These are far from original, but it may be of interest to see them derived from the descriptions of behaviour presented here, rather than from a more abstract basis such as central place theory (e.g. Berry, 1967, Chapter 2).

The first concept is that shopping is an activity which necessitates the taking of decisions. In theory, each purchase requires at least two decisions: the choice of product and the choice of store (not always in that order). Taking these decisions can lead to stress, before or after the purchase. Consumers will adopt strategies to avoid this stress - a particular strategy is often part of an attitude to shopping in general. Two important strategies, which almost all consumers will use at times, are, first, the acquisition of knowledge about retail products and stores; and second, the cultivation of shopping habits, so that the two decisions, or at least the second one (where to shop) are often made without detailed consideration. The first strategy may precede the second one, so that the consumer feels he is making an informed habitual response. Acquisition of knowledge is carried out by seeking information about products and stores, and by searching in stores and shopping centres. We should remember that among consumers there are very wide variations in the amount of importance attached to knowledge of products and stores; and widely differing degrees of habitual response.

The second concept is that shopping trips themselves consume time and money, irrespective of the cost of goods purchased. Again there are two main strategies available for dealing with this problem. The first is to carry out a purchase in such a way as to minimise the cost of the trip. This means that normally the consumer would choose to buy the product in the nearest shop that sells it (subject to his knowledge of local shops and his correct perception of distance). The second strategy is to buy as many goods as possible in a single trip, thus reducing the number of trips required over a given period. Of course these two strategies are not entirely compatible: it is likely that the multi purchase trip will involve some goods being bought further away from home than they need be (Bacon, 1971). One way around this problem is for the consumer to classify goods into bundles, and associate one bundle with one trip to one centre. This would be a habitual response, as discussed above.

Three more points about the first strategy (distance minimisation) should be noted. First, the consumer may decide that this objective is less important than others, such as saving money on the purchase itself, or trying to enjoy the trip more by choosing a pleasant store. In this case he may not shop at the nearest appropriate store. Second, the distance to be minimised may not be that between home and shop - the purchase may be carried out in course of another type of trip, such as journey to work. Third, the value of minimising distance increases directly with the frequency with which the product is bought. Therefore we should expect the location of a store to be more important to the consumer if it sells goods that are bought frequently.

The <u>third</u> broad concept is that retail goods and services can be classified in response to the consumer's shopping behaviour with respect to them. In doing this we are glossing over a great deal of variation in consumer behaviour, in time by one consumer, and in space by many. Nevertheless, some sort of classification is useful provided it is not applied rigidly to actual products and stores. That devised by Copeland (1924) is appropriate here since it refers essentially to consumer behaviour rather than to properties of the products themselves. As redefined by the American Marketing Association (1948), it consists of:

(a) Convenience goods: these are 'consumers' goods which the consumer usually purchases frequently, immediately, and with a minimum of effort';

(b) Shopping goods: these are 'consumers' goods which the consumer in the process of selection and purchase characteristically compares on such bases as suitability, quality, price and style';

(c) Specialty goods: these are 'consumers' goods on which a significant group of buyers is habitually willing to make a special purchasing effort'.

The main contrast is between convenience goods, on the one hand, and shopping and specialty goods on the other. Convenience goods are bought frequently: they have been termed 'routine' purchases at earlier stages in this chapter. Therefore the consumer gains much by minimising the average trip length for convenience goods; being able to buy these within walking distance of the home is advantageous in saving money, and in reducing one's dependence upon the vagaries of cars or buses. Buying these goods with a minimum of effort also implies the achievement of habits, to reduce stress and to save time by shopping regularly in the same store or stores.

Shopping and specialty goods can be regarded as similar because they both require far more pre purchase consideration than do convenience goods. The consideration for shopping goods takes the form of search during the trip; that for specialty goods largely takes place before the trip is carried out. The distinction between the two would probably in real life be difficult to draw, but as stereotypes they are valuable in suggesting different types of shopping behaviour. Shopping goods are held to give rise to 'comparison shopping', which seems to be a blend of 'full search' (Bucklin, 1967) and shopping for enjoyment (Tauber, 1972). But the acquisition of knowledge can reduce the stress of shopping and the amount of time spent, leading to the 'directed search'. The method used will often depend upon attitudes to shopping and other facets of behaviour. The comparison shopper will prefer a large shopping centre with good opportunities to compare similar goods in different stores. Those wishing to buy shopping goods without going through the comparison process will attach more importance to the cost and time spent on the trip itself. Lastly, those buying specialty goods are presumably willing to travel to wherever the product can be bought; or if this is impossible then they can have it delivered. So location of the store selling the chosen object is not important. (11)

5.5.3 Conclusions

This chapter has reviewed a considerable amount of theoretical and empirical material on consumer behaviour in space. A simple descriptive model of sequential decisions involved in purchasing goods has been extended to the more complex process of organising a shopping trip. This treatment has allowed a structured explanation to be made of consistent variations in observable shopping behaviour. There is far more published evidence to draw upon than in previous chapters, although much empirical work remains to be carried out.

A broad issue which runs through this chapter is the extent to which variations in aspects of shopping behaviour do in fact correspond with variations in family, social and economic characteristics of consumers. Although the studies reviewed in 5.4 seem to suggest regularities in aspects of behaviour, other work such as that of Frank (1967) and Bucklin (1969) suggests that there is little connection between aspects of behaviour and measurable characteristics. A recent study by Howe (1978), which performed factor analysis upon data from a large sample survey of shopping trips in north west London (Mann, 1977) also found virtually no systematic relationship between variables describing characteristics of shopping trips, for both convenience and shopping goods, and socio economic characteristics.

One reason for this dichotomy may be that the studies reported in 5.4 have generally focussed attention on contrasts between mean values of trip length, frequency, etc., for various groups of the population. Insufficient attention has been given to variation among the constituents of each group. Thus, means may be different but not significantly different. Even where significance tests are used (e.g. Daws and Bruce, 1971), the proportion of the total variation in behaviour explained by segmentation of shoppers is not analysed. Clearly a more rigorous statistical approach to the analysis of shopping behaviour is needed in British studies.

In examining consumer behaviour, particularly with respect to choice of shop or shopping centre, it seems necessary to resort to both normative and descriptive decision theory (Chapter 2). Normative concepts are involved in most of the models of consumer trip making: the shopper is supposed to possess perfect information about all accessible shopping centres, and to make a 'rational' assessment of them. This information includes their distance from home and selection of goods (central place theory); or the travel cost involved and a measure of 'size' (spatial interaction theory). The more recent 'choice' models, in which 'utilities' are assigned to centres on the bases of several attraction and impedance variables, are also normative in generally assuming perfect information and choice of that centre which maximises utility (e.g. Rushton, 1969; Pipkin, 1977; Schuler, 1979). The apparent corollary that shoppers will always visit the same centre for a particular type of trip, does not necessarily occur, since the 'rational' consumer can organise trips to several centres to minimise effort over a period of time (Bacon, 1971; Evans, 1972). Also, the 'attraction' stimuli, such as comparative prices at a supermarket, vary over time, thus creating apparent inconsistency of choice (Hay and Johnston, 1979).

Unfortunately the formulations mentioned above, where empirically tested, have not proved fully successful in predicting destinations for shopping trips. A descriptive theoretical approach, as used in this chapter, is also necessary. It shows that shoppers do not have perfect information about shopping opportunities, and that their choices are not fully 'rational', or consistent over time. The descriptive approach relies heavily on social and psychological theories which emphasise individuals and their differences, and is thus difficult to integrate with the normative theory, which relies largely on economic concepts of rationality, which render all consumers the same in their choice mechanisms. Links between the two exist in Simon's concepts of 'bounded rationality' (2.3.3) and in the geographical application of learning

theory (5.3.4). These concepts need however to be related more clearly
to empirical evidence of variation in shopping behaviour. At present it
must be concluded that, although a reasonable understanding exists of
such variation, accurate prediction of shopping trips in any situation
where parameters are likely to change is not yet possible.

NOTES

(1) See also Golledge (1970).

(2) For a more detailed discussion see Guy (1975, pp.4-7).

(3) The following model of the purchase process is highly simplified:
more complex models have been suggested by several writers (e.g. Nicosia,
1966; Howard and Sheth, 1969).

(4) It has also been suggested that consumers may allocate alternative
items into an evoked set (from which the final choice is made), an inert
set (which is ignored), and an inept set (which is immediately rejected)
(Narayana and Markin, 1975).

(5) One should add a note of caution here. Extensive studies
(summarised in Ehrenberg, 1969) have shown that both brand loyalty, and
the incidence of repeat purchasing of any brand, are usually
proportional simply to the brand's share of the total market for the
product involved. Systematic variations from this rule are confined
to situations where the brand is being introduced to or withdrawn from
the market. It appears that while advertising and marketing strategies
may influence a brand's share of the total market for the product, they
are unlikely to have any separate influence on the likelihood of repeat
purchases. This finding suggests that psychological theories such as
that of cognitive dissonance may be of little relevance.

(6) Market researchers such as Grubb and Grathwohl (1967), and Lessig
(1973) have attempted to relate consumers' images of stores to their
images of themselves.

(7) Wrigley (1979) has shown that stochastic models of brand purchasing
behaviour (5.2.3) can successfully be extended to the analysis of store
choice.

(8) In a more recent survey in Oxford, 73 per cent agreed with the
proposition that 'The way a person shops for the household groceries is
a good indication of how capable they are all round' (Bowlby, 1979,
p.311).

(9) The action space itself is likely to be perceived in a distorted
manner, and behaviour may be influenced by the dimensions of the
'cognitive map' rather than by true locational relationships (Mackay
et al, 1975).

(10) This unofficial estimate includes two (or more) car households
(11 per cent in 1976), plus households where the car is not used for
work trips.

(11) For further discussion of location of specialty goods stores, see
4.4.3.

6   Attitudes to retail location: the planner

6.1   TOWN AND COUNTRY PLANNING IN BRITAIN

6.1.1 Introduction

This chapter examines the role of the town and country planning system
in Britain in influencing retail location decisions and spatial
patterns. Ways in which the planning system has reacted to the policies
of developers and retailers, and has modified their decisions on retail
location, are discussed. This leads to some conclusions about the
effects of past planning policies, intended or unintended, thus setting
a framework for the more detailed examination of retail planning issues
in later chapters.
    The chapter deals almost exclusively with the statutory town and
country planning system in Britain, set up by the Town and Country
Planning Act 1947 and subsequently modified several times. (1)   This
system was set up basically to control rates and means of growth and
change in the built environment, and its operation is vested in local
authorities, with some guidance and control from central government.
Other aspects of central and local government intervention in the retail
sector, such as the maintenance of trading standards, are not dealt with
here, since they affect the routine management of shop premises, rather
than locational decisions of retail firms.
    This introductory section is concerned with the purposes of planning
intervention in decision-making processes in retailing. Later sections
deal with the methods of intervention, their relationships with the
purposes, and the results of such intervention.

6.1.2 Planning traditions, attitudes and policies

Planning policies in Britain have developed from a number of attitudes
held by the early members of the planning profession. These attitudes
are still held by many planners and local authority councillors, and
help to determine typical responses to initiatives from the retail trade,
as discussed later in this chapter.
    Accounts of the development of the planning profession in Britain
(e.g. Cherry, 1974; Hall et al, 1973, Volume II) show that the main
beliefs of the early planners arose essentially from a reaction against
the more harmful aspects of urban growth in the nineteenth century.
The earliest types of public intervention in Victorian towns were
intended to improve the quality of life by ensuring adequate water
supply, drainage, refuse collection and street lighting. It became
clear also that many problems of health could be avoided by better
design of houses and residential areas. The provision of better roads,
public buildings and parks would also bring advantages to town dwellers.
There arose thus a need for specialists in the design of whole areas of
new development: these specialists in 'town planning' were influenced
by engineering ideals of efficiency, and architectural ideals of beauty
in the physical environment. They believed that the fulfilment of these
ideals would have highly beneficial effects upon urban populations.

A principal concept which emerged was that of 'good design'. This applied to individual buildings, to parts of towns and to whole towns. Buildings should not only be designed efficiently for their purpose, but should be intrinsically attractive visually, and should also complement their surroundings. Residential areas should be clearly delimited; they should contain adequate services for their population, and should be served efficiently by a road network. Towns should also be clearly delimited, and should not be allowed to 'sprawl' over rural land, especially good agricultural land. Within towns, industrial and commercial areas, which tended to pollute through noise and smoke emissions, and attract large volumes of traffic, should be kept well away from residential areas. The whole town should be designed also to ensure that all parts had good access to the town centre, parks and countryside by both private and public transport. Roads should be adequate to permit reasonably free movement in all parts of the town.

Another important concept, implicit in planners' attitudes to society, was that the planner possessed a unique understanding of towns and town design, and was hence an 'expert' whose views should be respected by society. The planner's decisions and policies would benefit everyone in the long term, and thus the process of planning should not be corrupted by the short term requirements of either business firms or politicians. Indeed, it appeared evident that the effects of uncontrolled residential, industrial and commercial development would be so bad that a highly organised system of control over new development was necessary. This was eventually provided in the 1947 Town and Country Planning Act, which, with later modifications, forms the basis of the present planning system (Cullingworth, 1976, Chapter V).

6.1.3 The statutory system of town and country planning

This system, updated by the 1971 Town and Country Planning Act and the 1972 Local Government Act, consists basically of two interconnected types of activity. First, the local planning authority (2) must prepare development plans, which indicate in broad terms policies for controlling the pattern of land uses within its area. The second activity is of development control: any proposal to erect a new building, alter a building, or effect a change in land use must be submitted to the planning authority, who may approve the application, with or without conditions attached, or may reject it. Such development control decisions should have regard to provisions of the approved development plan or plans for the area concerned.

Since 1968 development plans have existed at two levels. The structure plan is prepared by a county or metropolitan county council, and one plan will cover the whole county, or a substantial part of it. It will set out broad policies for the extent and location of population change, housing development and major types of economic activity within the area. In contrast, local plans are usually prepared by district authorities, cover much smaller geographical areas, and usually contain detailed proposals for land use and development. In some respects they are similar to the development plans prepared for all areas before 1968. (3) Structure plans must be submitted to central government (4) for approval: local plans are formally 'adopted' by the district councils that prepare them, after the approval of a structure plan which includes the area concerned. (5)

In later sections typical policies for development and land use which affect the retail sector (6.2) and the detailed operation of planning control at the local level (6.3) will be discussed.

6.1.4 Modern attitudes to planning intervention

By claiming the right to approve or refuse any application for
development or change of land use, planners involve themselves in
processes of economic change at the local level. A convenient model is
of the 'market' (composed of private businesses and their customers)
making decisions in principle, and then the planners 'intervening' to
modify these decisions. This model is too simple to be fully realistic,
but it does allow one to consider broadly the rationale for intervention
in the market.

Most writers in the field of planning would probably agree that the
uncontrolled operation by private enterprise of markets in land and
labour, especially within urban areas, is likely to lead to inequitable
distributions of opportunities and resources, and to various types of
negative externality (e.g. Broadbent, 1977). Planning intervention is
justifiable in order to reduce the extent of these inequalities and
externalities. Debate within the planning profession has focused on
two issues here: the extent to which intervention is necessary, and
the methodology that should be used in order to intervene to the best
effect. Clearly, the two issues are related. For purposes of
simplification one may contrast three attitudes to these questions.

First, the view (A) can be taken that planning should seek only
marginal adjustments to market decisions and trends, in the general
interest of improving the efficiency of the market as a whole. At the
same time, some of the severest negative externalities can be reduced
through internalising their costs to the firms that are responsible for
them. In addition, certain goods which the market does not supply to
required standards may have to be provided or subsidised by the public
sector. For example, Stewart (1974) suggests that if planners can
understand the detailed working of sub markets at the local level, and
the 'philosophy' and 'nature' of the market in general, then they will
be able to improve the performance of the market, while continuing to
set limits on its field of operation.

A second attitude (B) is that planners should take a more positive
role in pursuing the achievement of certain social and economic goals,
which can be inferred from knowledge of the opinions and values held by
the population of the area concerned. Within this approach the market
may be seen as a tool for the achievement of certain goals, but also as
preventing the achievement of others. Therefore, it has to work within
quite severe limitations imposed by planners. This view underlies the
'rational comprehensive' model of the planning process and especially
the 'systems approach' to planning (McLoughlin, 1969; Chadwick, 1971).

A third view (C) is that the market economy inevitably leads to
unacceptable levels of inequity in society. It follows that all means
of production, and all resources of labour and land, should be owned or
controlled directly by the State. A modified version of this view is
that land should be owned by the public sector but that some aspects of
the market economy would continue to apply (e.g. Broadbent, 1977).

Three broad points should be made in discussing these three stereotypes. Firstly, none of them derive directly from the traditional
criteria of the planner as described above (6.1.2). These were largely
concerned with visual qualities of the environment, or with simple
spatial relationships. Intervention in the market was thought to be
necessary, but no clear attitude was adopted, and indeed economic and
social concepts were given little consideration. It follows that,
secondly, planners are divided amongst themselves between the three
attitudes, since none of them follow directly from the planning

tradition. Also, most planners cannot or do not wish to hold consistently to any one of the three attitudes. Thirdly, each attitude should be considered in the light of the powers available to planners to carry out their policies. As Broadbent (1977) has shown, power remains strictly limited at both national and local level in a mixed economy such as the British system. The state has comparatively little resources available for direct action in fulfilment of economic and social goals. It must therefore seek the cooperation of the private sector in order to fulfil these goals; but this is not always obtainable. It follows that views (B) and (C) described above are, in the present political and financial climate in Britain, unrealistic. View (A) therefore appears, if only by default, to offer a role that planners should adopt in intervening in market decisions.

This view implies that intervention should take place only if it is necessary. Any policies of intervention should have clear justification under one of the following reasons: (i) that intervention improves the performance of the market as a whole; (ii) that the market cannot adequately meet the requirements of consumers; and (iii) that the uncontrolled operation of the market produces unacceptable negative externalities, either in the retail sector, or for other activities.

These principles in fact underlie much of the current intervention in retailing of the state at national and local level. At national level, for example, the collection of Census of Distribution data is justified for reason (i); provision of certain goods and services, such as library facilities, for reason (ii); and control of trading standards for reason (iii). At local level we find justification for much of the town planning intervention to be discussed in this chapter: in particular, the forward planning of housing development and economic activity, mainly for reason (i); and the operation of detailed development control, mainly for reason (iii).

Questions of appropriate limits to, and methods of, intervention are highly contentious. One cannot establish definitive general rules. However it should be noted that circumstances have occurred in which intervention has had significant negative effects, on that market in which intervention has occurred, or elsewhere. This is not surprising, since, as already discussed, planners have not generally studied the social and economic effects of their land use policies.

The major task of this chapter then is to isolate the main effects of planning intervention, in the form of town planning policies, upon the retail sector and upon locational patterns. The next two sections include description of recent and current planning policies at various levels, and discussion of their impact upon decision making in the retail sector. This will enable some conclusions to be drawn in the final section about the attitudes which planners have tended to adopt towards the retail sector, and their relationship with the traditional concerns of the British land use planning profession.

6.2 PLANNING POLICIES FOR RETAIL ACTIVITY

This section examines typical policies for the location and scale of retail activity, formulated in plans adopted by local authorities since 1947. The section is structured according to formal types of plan, as described in 6.1.3, and there is also a brief discussion of retail policies in new towns. As well as describing typical policies, an attempt is made to explain these in terms of underlying principles of land use planning.

6.2.1 Policies in pre 1968 development plans

Until the passing of the Town and Country Planning Act, 1968, there was one system of comprehensive land use plans to cover the whole of England and Wales. The essence of this system was that the planned land use for any site was depicted in statutory 'Town Maps' or 'County Maps' (Cullingworth, 1976, pp.77-80). Thus the development plan provided exact rather than general guidance for planning responses to applications for development (6.3.1). It had been intended in the 1947 Town and Country Planning Act that the local planning authority (6) should carry out comprehensive surveys every five years, and if necessary submit new versions of development plans. This process did not generally occur in fact, largely because of long delays in obtaining government approval for the first run of development plans. In some counties or county boroughs the original development plan, produced in the early 1950s, would not be approved until the end of the decade: it would then remain in force, although increasingly subject to amendments, for the 1960s and 1970s. In other cases one 'review' plan would be prepared and approved, probably around 1960. After about 1964 the government was intent on developing a new system of two tier development plans, and was thus not prepared to consider further reviews to development plans.

Thus, the pre 1968 development plan policies remained in effect for far longer than had been the intention in the 1947 Act. Policies which reflected the methods and ideals of the 1940s had an enormous effect upon planning decisions involving all sectors of the economy, including the retail sector, in all parts of the country. For this reason, it is important to examine these methods and ideals.

The ideals of the planning profession in the late 1940s were those described above (6.1.2), dominated by a belief in the value of planning intervention in order to carry out policies for improving amenity and preventing urban sprawl. The recommended method of plan preparation had been devised by Patrick Geddes at the beginning of this century, and was generally described in three stages: survey - analysis - plan. This method has been described in the following manner:

'First the planner made a survey, in which he collected all the relevant information about the development of his city or region. Then he analysed these data, seeking to project them as far as possible into the future to discover how the area was changing and developing. And thirdly, he planned: that is, he made a plan which took into account the facts and interpretations revealed in his survey and analysis, and which sought to harness and control the trends according to principles of sound planning'. (Hall, 1974, p.12).

The implications of this method for the retail sector can be examined more closely through the medium of a well known book much used in the 1950s and 1960s in planning schools and local authority planning offices: Lewis Keeble's 'Principles and Practice of Town and Country Planning' (1959). (7) He states that:

'The objectives of Town Planning ... may be summarised as the provision of the right amount of land for each use in the right place and on sites physically suitable for each use. This includes the proper spatial relationship... of homes and shopping places of various levels' (p.88).

It followed from this that the planner, through use of the survey-analysis-plan method, could discover faults in the existing arrangement of homes and shopping centres, and rectify these by appropriate action. Furthermore, he could ensure that the 'right' size and location of

shopping centre were created to serve areas of new residential
development. A strong theme throughout this book, although implicit
rather than explicit, was that the planner could identify and implement
the 'best' plan for a particular area, the 'best' solution to a
particular problem. This was to be achieved through careful survey and
analysis, and the application of fairly simple principles of town design
and space standards. The former type of principle ensured that land
uses were 'correctly' related to one another; the latter that the
'right amount' of land was devoted to each use. The 'analysis' stage
would then simply be the comparison of survey results with preconceived
ideal patterns of the location and provision of facilities. Relatively
little attention was given to any need to consider a number of possible
solutions to any planning problem, and to use evaluative methods to
help choose the 'best'. No attention at all was given to ways in which
the needs of members of the public (for example, consumers and
retailers) could be elicited, or how this information might help the
planner in his work.

Keeble (1959, Chapters 7, 8) then described the types of survey that
he considered the planner should carry out in preparing a development
plan. At 'regional' (i.e. county) level, surveys to establish the
catchment areas of the more important service centres were recommended,
using methods common among British geographers of the time. The purpose
of this was to assist in the choice of locations and sizes for new
schools and other public facilities, rather than influence policies for
retailing. Keeble (1959, p.54) held that: '... the Planner is not in
a position to influence directly the choice of settlements by banks,
insurance companies, shopkeepers and other suppliers of services'.

However, there is little doubt that in many urban areas planners did
base their policies for individual shopping centres upon their supposed
place in a hierarchy of tertiary activity centres. Davies (1976a,
pp.124-8) shows how American classifications of business centres within
large urban areas (e.g. Berry, 1963) were adapted by British planners.
It became common for four or five levels of centre to be discerned:
these were often termed 'central area', 'regional centres' (only in
conurbations), 'district centres', 'neighbourhood centres', and 'local
centres'. Each level would serve up to a certain population, and it
was presumed therefore that shopping facilities serving greater
catchments would be inappropriate at that level of centre. This meant
in turn that facilities designed to serve the whole urban area should
only be placed in the town centre. Thus, a deductive model of shopping
and service centres in an agricultural area (Christaller, 1966) gave
rise to a normative system of directives for the location of retail
development within urban areas.

Keeble's recommendations for surveys within urban areas were concerned
mainly with the physical manifestations of retail and other land uses:
these included surveys of land use, floor space, and age and condition
of buildings. The latter two would be particularly necessary in town
centres, and would help planners choose the most suitable areas for
redevelopment, and also the size and type of new facilities that should
be provided to replace buildings cleared for road construction or other
purposes.

Keeble also suggested that surveys of catchment areas for district
and neighbourhood centres should be carried out. One reason for this
was so that gaps in the pattern could be identified, and appropriate
proposals made either for entirely new centres, or for enlargements of
existing centres. He felt that, in general, some local shops should
always be available within a quarter of a mile of all houses, while

'larger local centres' should be provided within half a mile (Keeble, 1959, p.104).

In preparing proposals for retail uses in a development plan, the method recommended was: (i) calculate the total amount of retail floorspace needed in the town; (ii) deduct existing floorspace to reach a total of new floorspace needed; (iii) allocate this extra floorspace between shopping centres (most simply, between the central area and all other centres combined). This method, which survives in many structure plans, will be discussed below (6.2.4).

The discussion so far has been of methods recommended to planners in one well known text book. Since published evidence about processes of plan making during the 1950s does not appear to exist, one is forced to use this type of source. It should be noted however that published retail planning policies (in, for example, statements relating to Town Maps) were generally extremely brief. This suggests that the amount of attention devoted to the 'analysis' stage in many planning offices was very small. This was partly because town planning staff were small in number and often untrained, and partly because the processes of survey required in the 1947 Act - particularly land use surveys - were very time consuming. Therefore it seems unlikely that methods any more sophisticated than Keeble's were used: in fact, his methods may often have been used partially or wrongly.

It appears then that most Town Maps of the early 1950s were closely similar to maps of existing land uses, altered by a few proposals for housing redevelopment and new extensions of the urban area. For retail as for other types of land use, the Town Map would portray the existing system of shopping centres, modified in a few respects for various reasons which reflected either urgent necessity or broader planning principles.

These modifications to the existing pattern of retail outlets might include:

   i)   some extension to central area commercial uses

   ii)   removal of some central area or other commercial uses because of road proposals (8)

   iii)   removal of parts of 'ribbon' shopping uses in the inner parts of towns (continuous ribbons along major radial routes were considered undesirable)

   iv)   provision of new neighbourhood centres in existing residential areas (usually provided only that suitable land was available for this purpose).

Apart from these possible modifications, it would follow that the pattern of shopping centres which happened to exist shortly after World War II would henceforth become that which the planners appeared to regard as the most desirable for the town in question. The plan, once approved, would become a firm basis for development control. Thus, any proposal by a retailer or developer to establish some form of shopping use, in an area not zoned for this use, would be 'contrary to the provisions of the development plan' and would probably be rejected. The only general exception was that shopping provision on a small scale within residential areas ('corner shops') was normally held to be acceptable.

To conclude, the policies embodied in the typical development plan must be criticised on two major counts. First, they gave the retailer or developer little or no positive guidance about the opportunities for development and expansion in a particular area. This resulted from the emphasis on land use zoning instead of economic analysis and forecasting. Second, they tended to result in the fossilisation of patterns of shopping centres and restriction upon the innovation of new forms of retailing, particularly in suburban areas.

6.2.2 Amendments to development plan policies

It would be wrong to claim that the 1950 style development plan is still totally adhered to in any part of Britain, even where this forms the only statutory planning document. These plans have in many instances been partly or wholly replaced, by formal or informal expressions of policy, or by some combination of the two.

Formal amendment to an approved development plan was allowed in the Town and Country Planning Acts. The local planning authority could at any time submit 'alterations or additions' to the Secretary of State, who would consider these and decide whether to amend the approved plan accordingly. Alternatively, the process of amendment could be initiated by the Secretary of State himself. An important type of amendment that was frequently submitted during the 1950s and 1960s was the Comprehensive Development Area plan for all or part of a town centre. It became clear to many planning authorities that the proposals for the town centre, embodied in the original development plan, were quite inadequate: in particular, radical alterations to the road system appeared necessary. Such proposals were likely to be combined with proposals for increasing the area devoted to commercial uses, particularly offices and shopping. This topic is discussed in detail in Chapter 7.

Many other formal amendments were submitted and approved during this period, but it is difficult to make any generalisations about their impact upon retail location decisions.

Informal plans and statements of planning policy have become more and more important since the virtual ending of formal development plan or amendment submissions, in the late 1960s. Some of these have statutory significance in that they can legitimately form the basis for development control, but do not need government approval (for example, conservation area policies). More often the plan or statement has simply been adopted by the local planning authority despite the lack of statutory approval. Some of these informal plans will have been the outcome of detailed analysis, testing of alternatives, and public participation; on the other hand some will have been prepared in an ad hoc manner within the planning office, so that the public is largely unaware of their existence, let alone content. Where these informal plans are used as justification for development control refusals, the central government departments tend to confirm such refusals on appeal (6.3.1), but this is not always the case.

Again, it is impossible to generalise about the retail content of informal plans and policy statements. Some of the largest local planning authorities have prepared specific policies for retailing; otherwise, informal town centre or district centre policies will be relevant. These are likely to be concerned with principles of vehicle and pedestrian access, and design and layout of the centre, as much as with any more general guidance on opportunities for retail development. It appears that the rather limited views of planning intervention discussed above (6.2.1) are still held in many quarters.

6.2.3 Retail planning policies in New Towns

Important differences exist between new towns and established urban areas so far as planning policies are concerned (Cullingworth, 1976, Chapter XI). These have led to quite different results in retail planning terms which can be summarised briefly.

New towns were authorised under the New Towns Act 1946, which gave them a special status in two ways. First, each town was to be designed and built by a special non elected body (a Development Corporation). This was to ensure a more rapid and efficient programme of construction and management. Second, the Development Corporations were given powers to acquire any land within their areas by compulsory purchase if necessary. This facilitated the assembly of large sites for town centre and other major developments.

These two special conditions enabled the planning of shopping provision to be carried out in a much more radical way than was generally the case in other areas. (9)   The Development Corporation staff, or their advisors, were able to choose locations for shopping centres without direct responsibility to local political and commercial interests. This has meant that in almost all cases the main shopping and business centre of a new town has been an entirely new construction, usually located at some point of near optimum access for the inhabitants of the town as a whole. (10)   Had existing political interests dominated, it is possible that in some cases, existing town centres would have been expanded, probably with unsatisfactory results. Even in new towns where the existing main shopping centre is being expanded (e.g. Peterborough, Northampton), major district centres have already been provided, including superstores and vast car parking areas. Again it is reasonable to argue that this would probably not have occurred under conventional local government.

The number, size and location of smaller shopping centres has also been planned in a more thorough way than would be the case with the typical local authority. This reflects not only the greater opportunities for free choice in this matter, as explained above, but also the greater number and expertise of planning staff typically working in or on behalf of new town management. The basic disposition of centres is usually set out in the Master Plan for the town concerned; this plan has generally been prepared by firms of consultants possessing some expertise in matters of forecasting retail demand. Subsequently the Development Corporation will normally acquire the land needed for these 'neighbour-hood' centres, will build them and let them to retailers.

Thus there is generally little scope for the developer or retailer to take the initiative in the typical new town; he must accept the opportunities provided by the Development Corporation. However, the Corporation will generally have taken a great deal of care to ensure that these opportunities are suited to the needs of the parties concerned.

6.2.4 Structure plans: forecasting, evaluation and policy formulation

The system of structure plans and local plans was established in the 1968 Town and Country Planning Act, and modified by the Local Government Act 1972. At the time of writing, some 29 county structure plans have been approved in England and Wales, a further 28 have been submitted and are awaiting approval, and 21 are still being prepared. (11) Virtually all parts of England and Wales are now covered by approved or draft structure plan policies. It is possible thus to draw some conclusions about the scope, content and importance of structure plan policies for the retail sector.

The formulation of structure plan policies for the retail sector should be considered within the context of structure planning as a whole. The structure plan was intended as a 'strategic' framework within which detailed 'tactical' local planning policies could be formulated (Solesbury, 1975): its purpose was to ensure that these local policies were consistent with broad planning aims for a county or metropolitan area, and also with established regional policies. The structure plan was intended to be broad in outline, and its policies subject to revision in the light of experience.

Despite these intentions, the programme of initial structure plans in England and Wales is still not completed, some eleven years after the inception of the system. This is due partly to administrative delays caused by the reorganisation of local government in 1974. It appears also that structure plans themselves have required far longer periods for preparation and approval than was originally intended. This is not the place for a full discussion of this phenomenon (see Drake et al, 1975; Dunlop, 1976). However, two important types of influence on structure planning methodology should be identified.

The first influence has been the 'advice' emanating from central government in respect of structure plan preparation, and two important documents setting out advice on structure planning need to be mentioned here. The first of these, the 'Development Plans Manual' (Ministry of Housing and Local Government, 1970), gave detailed advice on the form and content of structure plans and local plans. Some of this advice was so detailed that it seemed to leave the local authority little room for discretion. An example is given below (Table 6.1) of the analyses and policies recommended for retailing in county structure plans.

The second source of advice was issued within a Department of the Environment Circular in 1974, subsequently reissued with amendments in 1977 and 1979. The circular states that the structure plan should 'provide guidance for development and development control on matters of structural importance'. Structural matters 'affect the whole or a substantial part of the structure plan area; or influence the development of the area in a significant way' (Department of the Environment, 1979, para 2.1). This means in effect that structure plans should adopt a selective rather than comprehensive treatment of planning problems and issues. An emphasis on relating the depth of treatment to the importance of the issue concerned is clearly established here and elsewhere in the Circular (e.g. paras 2.10 - 2.12).

This advice, while consistent with original intentions for structure plans, has never been reconciled with the very detailed specification of methods in the earlier Development Plans Manual. Unfortunately, planners have generally appeared to favour the Manual's approach and have devoted considerable resources to the analysis and forecasting of relatively trivial phenomena, while neglecting the development of methods of policy analysis and formulation and of monitoring of policies (Haynes, 1974; Drake et al, 1975).

The second influence lay in an emerging attention to quantitative techniques of forecasting and evaluation, within a cybernetic conceptual framework (McLoughlin, 1969; Chadwick, 1971). Following a number of specially commissioned sub regional planning studies, which formed a 'test bed' for new methods, the new structure plans appeared as an opportunity for the further development of scientific method in plan policy formulation (Batey and Breheny, 1978). The main emphasis lay in the explicit production or 'generation' of several 'alternative' plans for the spatial disposition of population and economic activity in the geographical area concerned; followed by the evaluation of these plans with reference to the goals and objectives which the plan was intended to fulfil. (12) An important emphasis also lay on the need for cyclical thought processes, such that an exploratory evaluation

Table 6.1   Central government advice on structure planning policies
            for shopping

A. Policies and general proposals

1. General policy: (e.g.)   - foster growth in town centres
                               - develop district centres
                               - etc

2. Quantity of floorspace at certain future dates

3. Distribution of floorspace - in main centres
                               - elsewhere

4. Criteria and policies for   - location of new development
                               - local planning & development control
                               - existing development

5. Priorities and phasing of planning action

6. Implementation: (e.g.)   - promotion and assistance by local
                                  authorities
                               - assembly of sites by local
                                  authorities
                               - scope of private development

B. Supporting information

1. Survey

   a. Existing situation (e.g.) - floorspace by centres
                                 - turnover by trade and centre
                                 - accessibility of centres
                                 - prosperity of centres

   b. Recent trends (e.g.)   - retailing methods
                                 - customers' habits
                                 - changes in transportation

   c. Commitments (e.g.)   - new shopping centres
                                 - new pedestrian precincts

2. Estimates

   a. Future changes (e.g.)   - increases in expenditure
                                 - changes in retailing methods

   b. Future needs (e.g.)   - more out of town centres
                                 - less shops in main centres
                                 - more district centres

   c. Constraints (e.g.)   - access problems
                                 - land availability

   d. Assumptions affecting a - c above

   e. Alternative policies (e.g.) - strengthening suburban facilities
                                  - growth in central area

   f. Conclusions relating to e, leading to policies and general
      proposals

   g. Programme for planning action

Source: Summarised from Ministry of Housing and Local Government,
         1970, p.73.

99

procedure would lead 'back' to refinement in the plan generation process, and so on.

This approach, while clearly an improvement upon previous approaches in terms of consistency and comprehensiveness, turned out to be rather less than ideal for the purpose of structure planning. The necessity for comprehensive information assembly and modelling of the urban or regional 'system', for thorough specification of alternative plans, and for complex evaluation procedures, conflicted with the 'broad brush' concepts in structure planning outlined above. In the 1970s, economic and social problems became more evident and planners began to view the structure plan as a vehicle for combatting urban decline rather than one for controlling urban growth (Drake et al, 1975; Massey and Meegan, 1978).

These shifts in emphasis were reflected in a lack of agreement over the purposes of policies for retailing in structure plans. To begin with, the central government 'advice' in the Development Plans Manual was not reconcilable with that in the later Circulars. These did not specify 'retailing' or 'shopping' to be a matter of 'structural importance', and it was not made clear whether new policies for retailing were necessary at all. Almost all structure plans have in fact included policies for shopping centres of various types and sizes; but one feels that retailing has been regarded by most structure planners as a secondary concern. As a result, shopping policies have not been formulated in a manner consistent with the methodological advances discussed above.

The Manual recommended in effect a continuation of 'survey-analysis-plan' methods for the formulation of shopping policies (Table 6.1). The 'plan' stage would consist firstly, of allocating increases in shopping floor space to each of the important shopping centres in the area concerned; and secondly, in specifying policies for the control of new development. The allocation of floorspace 'requirements' is a feature of many structure plans. As shown in Figure 6.1, a common method of analysis attempts to forecast separately, and then adjust, the probable levels of supply and demand for floorspace in each centre at some future date. Measurement of 'demand' usually involves assumptions about the position of the centres in some central place hierarchy. The detailed stages of the analysis recall the 'step by step' method used for many years by consultants to local authorities (Diamond and Gibb, 1962; Distributive Trades E.D.C., 1970, Chapter 5). It is possible also to use spatial interaction models for this process, by regarding the projected floorspace 'supply' in the centres as attraction indices. Sales at each centre can be predicted, and the attraction indices then adjusted so that after several runs of the model some consistent relationship between floorspace and sales emerges. Both of these methods thus attempt to establish an equilibrium in which supply and demand appear to be in mutual adjustment. (13)

An alternative approach is to use a spatial interaction model to test the effects of several alternative policies of shopping centre development (Figure 6.2). For example, a conventional policy emphasising growth in town centres, can be compared with policies which allow development of out of town centres or hypermarkets at various locations (e.g. Berkshire County Council, 1976, Chapter 7). Evaluation of alternative policies takes place with respect to selected outputs of the interaction models, such as changes over time in sales in certain centres, or indices of accessibility which are derived from predictions of trips. This approach is clearly in keeping with a general emphasis upon explicit processes of generating and evaluating alternative plans,

Figure 6.1 Estimation of floorspace 'requirements' by simplified central place hierarchy method

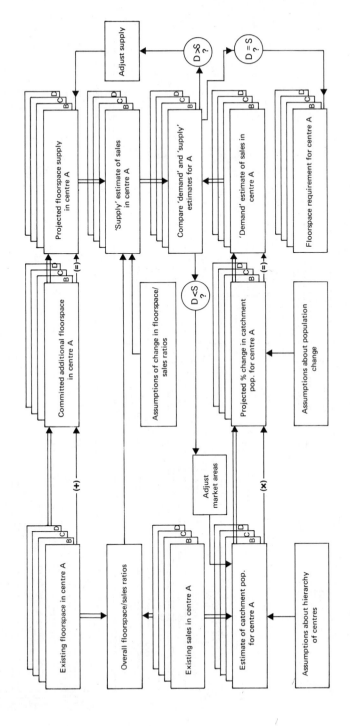

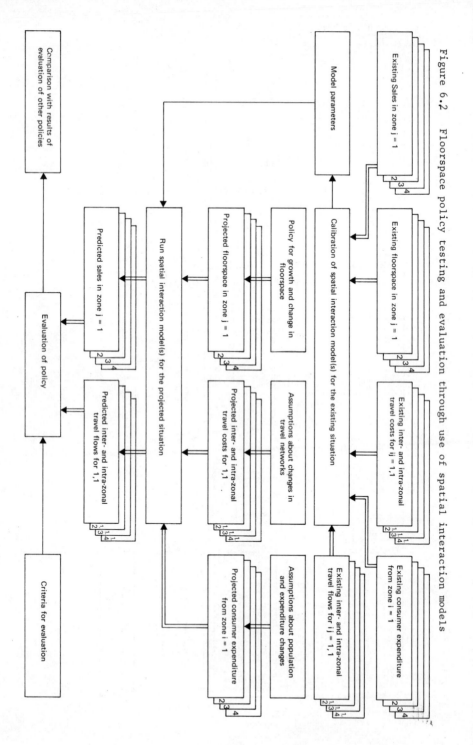

Figure 6.2   Floorspace policy testing and evaluation through use of spatial interaction models

which has characterised much of the structure planning effort.

These methods are however liable to criticism. The 'step by step' method relies entirely on invalid assumptions of a stable system of central places and market areas. The spatial interaction method dispenses with these assumptions, and allows one to test 'non trend' policies, such as the encouragement of out of town shopping centres. Its major disadvantages are firstly, its requirements for massive data sets needed in realistic disaggregate modelling formulations (Moseley, 1975); and secondly, the difficulty of forecasting changes in parameter values consequent upon changes in the system of shopping centres (see also 2.5.5; 5.3.6).

Policies which specify targets for retail floorspace in shopping centres have met substantial criticism, irrespective of the method used (Thorpe, 1975a; 1975b; Williams and Arnott, 1977). Firstly, they tend to rely upon the extrapolation of past data of retail floorspace and expenditure, which are often unreliable. Secondly, aggregate forecasting of floorspace needs of retailers is difficult, because of uncertainty about the future changes in demand and costs, themselves subject to changes in the national economy. Thirdly, the assignment of floorspace increases to particular shopping centres is made more difficult by lack of knowledge about the efficiency of retailing in existing shops. Fourthly, the whole approach tends to lead to policies in which small increments of retail floorspace are proposed for each of several centres. This is unlikely to match the requirements of those retail firms that prefer to develop very large new stores. In addition, the wishes of developers and retailers to provide new centres or large stores in entirely new locations cannot be met by policies of incremental growth in existing centres.

Despite these criticisms, many planners have attempted to forecast floorspace requirements in structure plans, and these forecasts have then - perhaps after some modifications - become targets whose achievement is to be aimed at as part of the structure plan. This attitude is clearly derived from basic beliefs in the validity of existing systems of centres, particularly central areas in towns, for the fulfilment of demand by consumers for retail goods in the 1980s and beyond. These beliefs would seem unreasonable in the light of evidence of considerable changes in consumer behaviour in recent years, particularly the increase in the use of cars for shopping trips.

Further problems arise in evaluating the effects of alternative policies so that a choice of policy can be made. Where a spatial interaction model is in use, certain outputs assist evaluation (see above). More generally, only one method has been used extensively in structure plans: the 'goals achievement matrix' or similar techniques (Lichfield et al, 1975, Chapter 5). This method assesses the extent to which alternative plans fulfil the goals and objectives determined at the outset of the plan making process. Value judgments are needed to determine which objectives are most important. The original method (Hill, 1968) allowed analysis with respect to separate groups in the population, but in most structure plan applications the distributional effects of policies are neither measured nor evaluated (Booth and Jaffe, 1978).

This or other methods are commonly used to evaluate alternative land use plans as a whole: evaluation of alternative <u>retail</u> policies according to specific objectives is uncommon. Since a set of policies for shopping is usually produced, one must conclude that the <u>implicit</u> evaluation of alternative policies has occurred. The nature of the objectives and of the evaluation criteria used in such choices is obscure.

Thus, it appears that shopping policies in structure plans have not generally been prepared in a rational manner. Much of the work has relied upon outdated and unsatisfactory concepts, whether descriptive (central place theory) or methodological (survey-analysis-plan). The more rational methods commonly used in the generation and evaluation of entire land use plans have not been applied generally in the formulation of shopping policies. Furthermore, some detailed and competent analyses of shopping behaviour have apparently had little influence upon policy formation. This reflects both a lack of interest in objective discussion of shopping policies, and a more general lack of attention to policy analysis in structure planning.

6.2.5 Structure plan policies

As discussed above, structure plans usually contain policies for retailing, whether this is regarded as a 'key issue' or not. At the time of writing there is no comprehensive review available of structure plan policies for retailing, but the comments of Thorpe (1975b) and Moor (1975) on draft structure plan policies of certain county authorities are useful.

These policies can be summarised under two headings. First, policies for existing shopping centres. These are usually presented for various sizes of centre: for example, 'Town Centres' (considered individually), 'District' or 'Neighbourhood' centres, and 'Local' centres and shops. This type of division may be indicative of beliefs of central place hierarchies, or may simply be regarded as a practical system of classification. It can though impose uniform policies on centres which possess contrasting features.

Policies for town centres almost invariably emphasise their importance for shopping and other commercial, social and cultural purposes. Their importance should, it is suggested, be maintained or enhanced, often through redevelopment or new development if appropriate. This may involve the setting of floorspace targets (6.2.4). Policies often support the provision of extra car parking in town centres, and traffic management and pedestrianisation schemes which are intended to make conditions safer and more convenient for the shopper.

Policies for district centres appear to vary much more, partly because the number and status of such centres will vary with size of town and other factors. Some policies assume district centres to have fairly distinct market areas, which limit their potential for growth: others allow that these centres compete for the shopper's custom. The former attitude is likely to lead to policies of restricting growth or change, except in response to population change in the surrounding area. The latter type of attitude may lead to policies in which certain centres are allowed to grow, possibly through the addition of superstores, as in Leeds (Finney and Robinson, 1976). A structure plan would not normally specify which centres were to grow, as this would be considered a matter for the district authority to attend to.

Policies for local centres, if expressed at all, are likely to be broad in nature. Such policies emphasise their importance for convenience trading in residential areas, but may discourage further growth to 'district centre' level. Where new residential areas are proposed in the structure plan, local or district centres may be proposed for them, but exact sizes or locations are not discussed.

The other main type of structure plan policy is that which deals with 'new types of trading' (Thorpe, 1975b). This theme is dealt with in more detail in Chapter 8 below. In summary it can be stated that there

104

are broadly three attitudes in published structure plans: firstly, a complete ban on hypermarkets, superstores and out of town shopping centres. This may extend even to a ban on any retail development outside existing centres. Secondly, some policies recommend a more open minded or 'flexible' approach, in which applications for new large stores will be considered on their own merits. A number of conditions are then stated which each application must satisfy: these may be so stringent as to disqualify almost any possible scheme. Finally, a more genuine acceptance may be found, which recognises that large new stores are appropriate in certain circumstances. Suitable locations are then suggested, usually in areas of rapid population growth.

This brief summary of retail policies in structure plans demonstrates four main points. First, as emphasised above, policies tend to reflect the traditional concerns and methods of planners in dealing with the retail sector since 1947. Second, it appears that many planners either do not understand or are not prepared to contemplate the requirements of certain retail firms in the 1970s, particularly those which prefer, for economic reasons, to build very large stores in edge of town locations. Third, there is little explicit attention paid to the wishes of consumers, or recognition that consumers possess a variety of attitudes to shopping and also vary considerably in their shopping trip behaviour.

The fourth conclusion concerns the purpose of structure plan policies. Structure plans cannot provide specific proposals for any exact area of land, and are intended to provide a framework for the development of detailed and site specific policies in local plans. County authorities do however have responsibility for important planning applications, according to the details of 'development control schemes' (Cullingworth, 1976, pp.117-120). So, some aspects of structure plan policy (such as a ban on new shopping centres) may be implemented by the county authority, whilst others (such as the encouragement of neighbourhood centres in new residential areas) are not. (14)   A further problem at present is that formal local plans hardly exist; and in their absence, structure plans may include detailed policies more appropriate to local plans. These points have been discussed by Stocks (1976), who recommends that the structure plan should concentrate on 'issues that are truly strategic for the county as a whole', thus echoing the Department of the Environment Circulars on structure planning (6.2.4). In his opinion such issues would normally include the following:

  i)   the role of the dominant centre in the county;
 ii)   minimum levels of convenience trade to be safeguarded
        within urban areas;
iii)   circumstances in which large new stores, and/or new
        durable goods centres, should be encouraged, if any,
        and positive suggestions for their location;
 iv)   policies for 'clearing and remodelling areas of
        shopping obsolescence';
  v)   other issues only at the request of districts.

It would follow from this that the allocation of floorspace to centres within the county would be regarded as unnecessary, or as a function which district councils should perform in preparing local plans. This is a sensible conclusion in view of the critical comments made above. There is little sign however that Stocks' ideas have been heeded by county planners.

6.2.6 Policies for retailing in local plans

The formal local plan is intended to provide detailed planning policies and a basis for development control, set within the more broad policies of the approved structure plan (Department of the Environment, 1979, para 3.1). The local plan will normally be prepared by a district authority, but occasionally by the county. Since local government reorganisation, counties and districts have prepared 'development plan schemes' (Mabey and Craig, 1976) which set out programmes of preparation of local plans: the areas to be covered by each plan, the type of plan, and the authority responsible for preparation./

Local plans fall into three categories: district plan, subject plan, and action area plan. The district plan appears likely to be the most common type to be produced in the next few years. It is defined as 'the comprehensive planning of relatively large areas, usually where change will take place in a piecemeal fashion over a long period' (MHLG, 1970, p.39). Of the three categories it bears the closest correspondence with the development plan 'town map' produced under the former system; but district plans are unlikely to be as comprehensive as town maps. There is no general intention to cover all built up parts of the country with district plans, as was the intention with the former development plans. It may also occur that the typical district plan does not adopt precise land use zoning in the old style.

The subject plan is intended to deal with 'particular planning aspects in advance of the preparation of a comprehensive plan or where a comprehensive plan is not needed' (MHLG, ibid). There would seem to be an opportunity for counties or districts to produce 'shopping' subject plans, in which proposals for modifying existing patterns of shopping centres could be made in the light of the requirements of retail and consumer interests. Formal central government advice on appropriate topics for subject plans is at present conspicuous by its absence, but informal indications are that subject plans are regarded as being of low priority. It is considered inappropriate to treat a subject such as shopping in isolation from other planning issues.

The action area plan involves 'the comprehensive planning of the area indicated in the structure plan for improvement, redevelopment or new development' (MHLG, ibid). It seems likely that action area plans will be prepared mainly for town centres, new residential areas, and areas of residential redevelopment. This will amount to a continuation of much of the local planning work carried out at present: plans for all of these types of area will need some statement of policies for retail development.

Since the local government reorganisation in 1974, district councils have put considerable effort into the preparation of local plans (Fudge, 1976). In many cases plans are complete, but they can only be 'adopted' and thus have statutory authority, after approval of the county structure plan. At the time of writing it is not possible to provide any comprehensive review of policies for the retail sector in local plans.

An insight into planning policies at the district council level is however provided by Thorpe's (1975b) review, although this deals only with metropolitan districts. The authorities surveyed usually had firm policies for town centres, and for some of the more important district centres. These policies would normally be concerned with the physical limits of the centre and proposals for new development or redevelopment, and with improvements to traffic flow, vehicular access to shops and pedestrian movement. Policies which recommended specific limits on floorspace or turnover in particular centres were not at that time as common as in county level planning policies.

Policies for specific local or other small centres were uncommon, although there was a general attitude that new retail development should not occur either in shopping 'ribbons' or in locations isolated from existing shops. In some cases detailed attention was being given to standards of local shopping provision in general. Here, Thorpe shows that contrasting policies were formulated for the inner parts of towns (generally built before 1914) and outer areas (post 1914). In the outer city it would be proposed that 'essential' retail facilities were provided within walking distance of all homes (cf. Keeble, 1959; see 6.2.1). In the inner city there might be some question of providing new retail facilities in areas of housing redevelopment, but a more important issue was that of the decline in numbers of existing shops. This matter will be discussed in more detail in Chapter 9.

The policies reviewed by Thorpe were generally 'informal' statements designed to supplement approved development plan policies. The current round of formal local plans may be expected to take a rather more fundamental look at problems and opportunities in the retail sector. One would hope that where appropriate, alternative policies will be examined and that the views of retailers and consumers will be sought. However there is little indication that local plans, of any of the three types, will involve   significant methodological advances upon existing development plans and informal statements.

6.2.7 Conclusions

This section has summarised and attempted to explain both the formal bases for planning policies concerning the retail sector and the general nature of these policies themselves. Despite the diversity of policies and methods of formulating them, it is possible to draw some general conclusions.

First, one is hampered, as elsewhere in this book, by a paucity of recorded information. While the volume of writing on methodology in planning is very large, particularly in the very different fields of urban models and civic design, there is much less writing on planning policies, and less still of a critical nature. Much of the writing by planners themselves has tended to be biased and unincisive.

The second broad conclusion is about the nature of policy formulation in land use planning. Those policies affecting retailing have generally been framed with very broad aims: for example, to contain urban development, or to improve urban amenity. There has been little awareness of the nature, purposes and limitations of planning intervention in the workings of the retail sector. Thus, economic and social effects upon retailers and consumers have often arisen as unintended side effects of policies based largely upon physical or aesthetic criteria.

This leads to a third conclusion: that planning policies are usually conservative in nature. (15)   In the retail sector, this is evident in the reliance upon outdated central place concepts, and in the frequent refusal to consider the merits of large new stores in suburban or out of town locations.

These rather gloomy conclusions should be tempered by the realisation that many planners are aware of the nature of retailers' and consumers' requirements, and have attempted to produce policies to help meet these requirements. So far they have often been frustrated by the decisions of local politicians, or by the sheer difficulty of making positive use of the existing legal and administrative system of land use planning. Some examples of these problems will be discussed in later chapters.

6.3 PLANNING POLICIES, PLANNING DECISIONS AND RETAILING

The purpose of this section is to discuss ways in which the British planning system affects the decisions that property developers and retailers make with regard to retail provision. Firstly, the extent of planners' control is described through a brief summary of relevant planning law. Secondly, the relationships between planning decisions affecting retail development, and the broad planning policies already discussed, are examined. Finally, some conclusions about the long term effects of the planning system on changes in the location of retail activity are presented.

6.3.1 Development control and retailing

In order to understand the limitations upon the scope of planning policies at local level, it is necessary to consider the effects that planners have on specific retailing decisions. This sub section describes briefly the present nature of development control and other such powers available to local authority planners. More complete reviews can be found in planning textbooks such as Cullingworth (1976); Telling (1977).
    The scope of the planner's development control powers hinge on the meaning of the term 'development'. This is defined in the Town and Country Planning Act 1971 as:
        'the carrying out of building, engineering, mining or other
        operations in, on, over or under land, or the making of
        any material change in the use of any buildings or other
        land' (Part III, Section 22).
Any new retailing venture, or modification of an existing business, would seem to require building or engineering operations, and possibly a change of use. But many operations or changes of use, generally of a trivial nature, are exempt from planning permission, through the provisions of the General Development Order (1973). It may be useful at this stage to indicate, in Tables 6.2 - 6.4 broad types of action in retailing which are subject to planning control; and some which normally are not.
    The tables suggest that planners' legal powers over the retail sector have limited effect. They can prevent growth of retail floorspace in any area, but cannot prevent decline (through vacancies or demolitions), or changes in type of shop or in retailing methods within the existing physical fabric.
    These rules are applied by planning authorities through procedures of 'development control'. A developer, retailer, landowner or any other person wishing to carry out any of the actions listed in Table 6.2 is legally obliged to apply for planning permission to do so. His application must then be considered by the local planning authority within a certain period of time: the authority may grant or deny permission as it sees fit, although its decision should conform to approved planning policies for the area concerned. The person making the application may then appeal to the Minister (16) against refusal of permission: appeals are decided by the Minister (in reality, by an Inspector appointed by him, or by civil servants in his Ministry).

Table 6.2   Courses of action in retailing which are normally subject
              to planning control

   i) Erection of a new building for retail purposes (the design of
the building has to be approved by planners, even if it is accepted that
the site should be used for retail purposes. The amount of floorspace
proposed is also subject to control).

   ii) Extension or major external alteration of an existing building
already used for retail purposes.

   iii) Complete or partial demolition of a building which is listed
as being of architectural or historic interest, or which lies in a
conservation area. Minor external or internal alterations may also be
subject to control in these circumstances.

   iv) Change of use of an existing building to retail purpose. (i.e.
from some other use such as residential, office, industrial or
warehousing). Change of use from retailing to one of these categories
is also subject to control. 'Uses' are defined in the Use Classes Order
(Table 6.4).

   v) Change of use of part of an existing building, or an area
adjacent to the building, to retail purposes or any associated use.
(Examples would be of the change in an upper floor from residential use
to storage of retail goods; or the provision of car parking space on
adjacent land).

   vi) Display of advertisements, under certain circumstances.

Table 6.3   Courses of action in retailing which are not normally
              subject to planning control

   i) Demolition of a building (except as under (iii) in Table 6.2).

   ii) Closure of a shop, so that the premises become vacant.

   iii) Change of type of shop. (Changes of use are generally not
deemed as 'material' unless they involve a change from one broad class
to another: see Table 6.4).

   iv) Intensification of use within existing space devoted to
retailing (e.g. the introduction of self service).

Table 6.4   The Use Classes Order

   The Use Classes Order specifies 'classes' for the purpose of
Section 22(2)(f) of the Town and Country Planning Act 1971. Any change
of use of buildings or an area of land to another use within the same
class does not constitute 'development' within the meaning of the Act,
and thus does not of itself require planning permission.

   The definitions given below are taken from the Town and Country
Planning (Use Classes) Order 1972 (Statutory Instrument 1972 No.1385).

Use Classes relevant to this discussion include:

'Class I. - Use as a shop for any purpose except as:

   i)   a shop for the sale of hot food;
   ii)   a tripe shop;
   iii) a shop for the sale of pet animals or birds;

iv) a cats-meat shop;

v) a shop for the sale of motor vehicles.

Class II. - Use as an office for any purpose'.

'Shop' is defined as follows:

'a building used for the carrying on of any retail trade or retail
business wherein the primary purpose is the selling of goods by retail,
and includes a building used for the purposes of a hairdresser,
undertaker, travel agency, ticket agency or post office or for the
reception of goods to be washed, cleaned or repaired, or for any other
purpose appropriate to a shopping area, but does not include a building
used as a fun fair, amusement arcade, pin table saloon, garage,
launderette, petrol filling station, office, betting office, hotel,
restaurant, snackbar or cafe or premises licensed for the sale of
intoxicating liquors for consumption on the premises'.

'Office' is defined as follows:

'"office" includes a bank and premises occupied by an estate agency,
building society or employment agency, or (for office purposes only)
for the business of car hire or driving instruction but does not include
a post office or betting office'.

'Post office','betting office', and 'launderette' are also defined.

Notes:

1. Any change from a shop of the type named under Class I (i.e. selling
    hot food, etc.) to a normal shop is given automatic planning
    permission under the General Development Order (Cullingworth, 1976,
    p.101).

2. Planning authorities in granting permission for any development
    can attach conditions, and these may forbid certain changes
    normally allowed within Use Classes (Cullingworth,.ibid.).

6.3.2 Development control and planning policies

The nature of typical relationships between planning policies and
development control decisions is by no means clear. McLoughlin (1973)
has found that development control planners tend to respect, as far as
possible, land use zoning established in approved development plans and
subsequent amendments. They often ignore planning policies which do not
relate to specific parcels of land or which are not framed simply in
terms of land uses: for example, a policy for the restriction of
floorspace in a particular class of shopping centre. When faced with an
application for which there seems to be no relevant planning policy,
development control officers tend to use the criteria which they
themselves regard as important. These criteria reflect established
principles of local planning, such as the promotion of good design and
the avoidance of 'visual intrusion', generated by heavy traffic flows
through residential areas. These criteria would normally outweigh any
commercial or social reasons in favour of the proposed course of action.

A further cause of these somewhat conservative attitudes - or perhaps
manifestation - is the fear of creating 'precedent'. An application
may be made for a scheme which does not appear to correspond with
approved planning policy, but which nevertheless appears desirable to
the planners on social or other grounds. The application may yet be

refused, because it is felt that, if allowed, it will create precedent for other similar applications which cannot then logically be refused. It is held that one such development may be desirable but several are not. These arguments often ignore any rational assessment of the likelihood of further applications being made at all. Similarly, much notice is taken of previous planning decisions for the site concerned, or similar sites nearby (McLoughlin, 1973, p.93).

These arguments force one to question the extent to which structure plan policies can successfully be implemented through the present system of development control. Firstly, control takes place mainly at district level while structure plans are prepared by county planners. Secondly, as suggested above, development control officers are likely to find certain aspects of structure plan policy difficult to apply to specific cases. The vast majority of proposals for development in the retail sector are unlikely to engage the attention of county planners. For these cases, draft or approved local plans may form a basis for decisions; otherwise, the long established criteria of good design (etc) may still apply.

6.3.3 The effects of planning control on retail change

The discussion above indicates that the British system of planning control has little impact upon decline or gradual change in retailing, but may have substantial influence upon innovation and rapid change, especially where this leads to demand for new types of retail premises. Planning control decisions usually respond to physical criteria, rather than economic or social. These principles have meant that the planning system has facilitated certain types of change in retailing, hindered others, and had little overall effect in some cases.

It is clear that in most cases change and growth in town centres has been facilitated by planning policy. The emphasis placed by most planners upon the town centre as the focus of major commercial and social activity has led to a sympathetic attitude towards retail firms wishing to develop or expand town centre sites. Together with property developers, planners have carried out many schemes for expanding town centre shopping areas. This has greatly facilitated the expansion (in situ, or geographically) of multiple retail firms (4.3.2). The only major exceptions to this rule may have been in town centres of major historic interest, where conservation policies have created problems for retailers wishing to replace or alter their premises.

Hindrances to retail change have probably been most marked for the innovators in retailing (4.3.5). Those firms whose space requirements force them to seek cheap and large sites have generally received obstruction rather than cooperation from planners, who are generally reluctant to allow retail development outside established town or district centres (Schiller, 1974). There have also been many cases where small firms have not been allowed to rebuild, extend or alter premises, provide car parking facilities, or convert premises to retail uses.

The overall effect here has undoubtedly been a slowing down in the process of decentralisation of shopping facilities, which has been such a marked feature of post war retail change in other European and North American countries (Distributive Trades EDC, 1971; Davies, 1976a, Chapter 6). The rate of development of suburban shopping facilities has been much slower than one would have expected, given the general decentralisation of urban population and the increasing wishes of consumers to use cars for shopping trips, especially for convenience goods.

111

There remains however a considerable amount of change in retailing which has been affected relatively little by the town planning system. Such changes include the growth in comparison and specialist retailing; the decline in numbers of convenience goods shops, especially grocers and tobacconists; decline in certain types of shopping centre, especially those in inner parts of towns and conurbations. It is noteworthy that the decline in small shops and inner city areas has occurred despite the concern of many planners that such decline is undesirable on social grounds.

These themes have been outlined rather briefly, and without full empirical support, because they will be examined again in detail in Chapters 7-9. In these chapters the reasoning behind planning policies for town centres, hypermarkets, and local shops respectively will be discussed, and the impact of these policies upon consumer and retailer decision making examined.

6.4. CONCLUSIONS

This chapter has attempted to describe and explain typical attitudes of British town planners to retailing and retail location. The level of discussion has been general, so that some consistent themes can be established as a background to the more specific retail planning issues to be discussed in Chapters 7-9.

The planning system has been considered here mainly in terms of its influence upon the location of retail stores of various types, and upon the growth or decline of shopping centres of various types. It has been shown that the system has had considerable influence, which has stemmed not only from deliberate policies of intervention in retail decision making processes on behalf of wider societal goals, such as the welfare of consumers; but also as the largely unintended effects of policies which derive from the traditional concerns of British planners. These unintended effects have not been fully understood by planners, and they certainly have not been evaluated. It is clear that in some instances planning policies - for example containment ('green belt') policies which result in refusals for applications for out-of-town stores - have prevented the provision of substantial savings in costs for certain retailers and groups of consumers. Planners might argue that the goal of containment is worth this cost, but in fact they are rarely called upon to argue such a case. Planners can through their policies perpetuate inefficient patterns of retail location, and the costs imposed by these patterns have to be met ultimately by consumers.

Many planners have since the mid 1960s become aware of economic and social factors, and have gained some insight into possible economic and social effects of planning policies. It has also been suggested that planning policies themselves can create beneficial economic and social effects through selective intervention in market processes. This argument does not appear to be supported well by recent evidence, partly because planners tend to misunderstand the market (Stewart, 1974), and partly because their powers of intervention and implementation are themselves severely limited (Broadbent, 1977). This point is clearly exemplified in retail planning, where it appears that attempts by planners to 'forecast' floorspace 'requirements' in shopping centres may have adverse economic effects rather than beneficial (6.2.4). There are however some matters in which developers and retailers welcome intervention in the market by planners, and planning policies should recognise thus. One example here is the provision of large sites for

shopping centre development;   compulsory purchase by the public sector
can reduce the amount of time needed to create new centres.   This has
long been accepted within town centres (Chapter 7);   planners have in
some instances extended this principle to hasten the development of new
district centres and local centres (Chapters 8 and 9).

It is depressing though to find that few planning policies for the
retail sector are explicitly justified through arguments about costs and
benefits to demand and supply sides.   Methods of evaluating alternative
policies, or for that matter specific retail proposals, with reference
to retailers' requirements, consumers' requirements, and other planning
requirements (such as the avoidance of negative externalities), are
poorly developed and little used. (17)

Given this state of affairs, it is not entirely unfortunate that
development control planners tend to pay little attention to planning
policies in statistical or written form, and rather more to those
policies which provide specific proposals for specific parcels of land.
The extent to which structure plan policies for retailing can
successfully be implemented remains very much in question.   It seems
likely however that local plan policies will be much more specific.
It is here that the critical attention of retailers, their advisors,
and other observers of the scene should be directed in the years to come.

NOTES

(1)   Much of the detailed discussion in this Chapter relates to England
and Wales only.
(2)   Generally a district or metropolitan district council (in England
and Wales).
(3)   While 1968 marks the change in legislation which brought in the
two tier development plan system, approved structure and local plans
still do not exist in many areas at the time of writing (1979).
(4)   In England, the Department of the Environment;   in Wales, the
Welsh Office.
(5)   This requirement is likely to be abolished by the present
government.
(6)   Until 1974, and for development plan purposes, a county or county
borough council.
(7)   The second edition of this book is dealt with here, as it portrays
more clearly than the first edition (1952) the principles and methods
in use over much of the period under review.
(8)   The comprehensive redevelopment schemes common in the 1960s in
town centres were usually prepared as amendments to the original
development plans (see below).
(9)   Schaffer (1972, Chapter 10) describes the principles used in retail
planning in British new towns, with many examples.
(10) Some of the principles involved in town centre developments in new
towns are explained in more detail by Price (1972).
(11) Address given by Secretary of State for the Environment to the
Royal Town Planning Institute Summer School, September 1979.
(12) This method clearly stems from principles of normative decision
making (2.2).
(13) It is possible also to derive an 'optimal' system of allocating
floorspace increases to shopping centres from nonlinear programmes based
on spatial interaction theory (Openshaw, 1975, pp.28-30;   Coelho and
Wilson, 1976).   This approach has not yet, to the author's knowledge,
been used in planning practice.

(14) The present government is likely to pass legislation which will reduce the extent of county involvement in development control.

(15) This may arise because of the views of local politicians, as well as the planning traditions discussed above. Political influences are however not discussed specifically in this chapter, because of a complete lack of empirical evidence.

(16) At present, the Secretary of State for the Environment, or the Secretary of State for Wales.

(17) Further discussion of evaluation according to these principles is presented in 8.3.3.

7 Retailing and planning in town centres

7.1 RETAIL PROVISION IN TOWN CENTRES: SUPPLY AND DEMAND

7.1.1 Introduction

It has been suggested (6.3.3) that one major impact of post war town planning policies has been to accelerate processes of growth and redevelopment in town centres. This chapter examines these processes. First, a brief review is made of attitudes of supply and demand sides to retail provision in town centres: in particular some perceived advantages and disadvantages of 'traditional' town centres, compared with suburban or out of town centres, will be discussed. In section 7.2, the belief of many town planners in the importance of town centres will be discussed, along with some of the planning policies which have been influenced by this belief. Section 7.3 contains a brief historical review of processes of central area development since 1950. It emphasises firstly the changing roles of property development firms and local authorities over this period, and secondly the changing attitudes of the public to large scale comprehensive redevelopment in central areas. The events of the 'boom' and 'slump' years are briefly described and explained. In the final section, some conclusions and implications for future town planning policies in town centres are drawn.

7.1.2 Attitudes of retailers to town centres

It is useful first to examine typical decisions of retail firms with respect to town centres: one may draw attention to conclusions reached in earlier chapters. There can be little doubt that in most town centres in Britain a strong demand has existed since 1950 for retail floorspace. This demand has been manifested mainly by multiple retail firms. Even in the inter war period some major firms such as Woolworth were expanding their business through building new stores in town centres (Thorpe, 1966; Marriott, 1967, pp.28-29). This process accelerated after the war, one notable feature being attempts by multiple firms operating in one region of Britain to extend their market to other regions or the whole country (Scott, 1970, pp.49-53). This situation could result in a demand for retail floorspace even in towns where there appeared to be little or no demand from consumers for extra facilities (4.3.2). In the long term, however, these firms generally benefited from increases in consumer expenditure over the post war period. This happened in two ways. Firstly, expenditure has tended to rise most rapidly in durable and household goods, clothing and footwear, and least rapidly in foods. This trend favoured those firms selling comparison goods, which would normally, up to the late 1960s, have chosen central area locations. Secondly, expenditure has increased more rapidly in multiple owned stores than co-operatives or independent owned (Davies, 1976a, Chapter 3). This trend is linked with the first, but it also stems from the relatively greater efficiency of the multiple firm, which leads to more attractive and convenient display of goods, and more opportunity for cutting prices. These trends in consumer expenditure have reinforced the policy still favoured by many multiple firms of locating new retail space in town centres.

Since the late 1960s two important changes have occurred in the nature of the demand by retailers for central area space. Firstly, a number of multiple firms have lost interest in acquiring central area space. These include firms in which price cutting policies are important: for reasons discussed above (4.2.3), expensive central area sites are unnecessary as well as being inadvisable financially. These policies have applied particularly in food retailing and for certain household and electrical goods. Not only has any demand for additional central area space virtually ceased from these firms, but many of their central area shops have been closed. This has occurred partly through the collapse of a few firms, especially in electrical goods; also through policies of selective closure of shops by other firms; and probably, in part, through a wish to profit from the sale of valuable central area property.

It is not clear to what extent these changes have affected the overall demand for central area retail space. They have occurred at a time when, for other reasons, the supply of new central area space has greatly diminished (7.3.6). But it is very likely that the increasing demand for space outside town centres, and especially for large free standing stores, has led to a corresponding decline in demand for retail space within central areas.

The second important change has to some extent obscured the effects of the first change described above. This has been a change in the nature of demand for space in shopping centres. Economies of scale and a desire to increase the variety of goods sold have led to store expansion programmes among several firms, of which Marks and Spencer, British Home Stores, Boots and W.H. Smith are important examples. For the latter two firms, stores built or occupied before the 1960s have often proved inadequate and are being gradually replaced within town centres by much larger stores. The sites needed, of 60,000 - 80,000 square feet gross internal area in the case of Boots (Northen and Haskoll, 1977, p.45), are not easily found in prime locations within town centres. Because of delays in obtaining such sites, the expansion programmes of such firms are likely to continue for several years.

A demand for space in large shopping centres is not exactly equivalent to a demand for space in central areas of towns. The first type of demand has in fact been met almost entirely within central areas, since in Britain there are very few large shopping centres outside town centres. Before 1950 this observation would not have required further comment. Since then, the dominant position of town centres appears to have been maintained largely through planning policies of restriction of large scale suburban shopping development, for reasons discussed below (8.2). The few entirely new major centres built in suburban or rural locations have all, to the author's knowledge, proved successful in attracting multiple firms. (1) Thus it is not clear whether most multiple firms have any particular commitment to central area locations, despite their willingness to occupy postwar central area development.

One should ask then what particular advantages a town centre as opposed to suburban development, may have for the retailer. Three advantages appear to be important, although they may not apply equally to all retailers. The first is that town centres generally represent points of maximum accessibility, especially to users of public transport. The second is that town centres attract shoppers for reasons unconnected with their retail facilities (7.1.3): thus all town centre shops benefit to some extent from 'suscipient' business as well as 'shared' (4.2.1). The third advantage applies mainly to independent retailers: in almost

all British town centres there are relatively cheap shop premises
available in side streets or covered markets. These are promising
locations for the small shopkeeper selling specialty or certain
comparison goods. These opportunities are not available in purpose
built suburban centres, which, like town centre precinct schemes, tend
to be dominated by multiple branches (3.3.3).

7.1.3 Attitudes of consumers to town centre shopping

The distinction can again be made between reasons why consumers benefit
from large shopping centres offering a wide range of goods and services,
and reasons why they may benefit from urban central area locations for
such shopping opportunities.

In theory, two main types of benefit accrue to the consumer in a large
shopping centre: one is concerned with the purchase of comparison goods;
the other with the range of goods and services available. The first
aspect has tended to be emphasised by market researchers, the second by
geographers in studies based on Central Place Theory. In practice it
would be difficult to separate these two aspects. It is sufficient to
state that most consumers will, occasionally at least, wish to visit a
centre where for some goods (e.g. clothes) there is a wide range from
which to choose, and also where certain specialised goods (2) and
services are to be found. It is useful also for more commonly available
goods to be sold in such a centre, so that multi purpose shopping trips
may be made.

It is clear though that consumers' attitudes to shopping centres are
not concerned simply with the range, quality and price of the goods
available there. Firstly, many stores possess a distinctive image
(5.3.2), and the presence of a particular store may itself attract
consumers to the centre concerned. Secondly, there are qualities of a
shopping centre itself which appear to attract or repel consumers. For
example, Downs (1970) found from responses to home interviews that
housewives in Bristol identified four main attributes of large shopping
centres that characterised the shops there (quality of service, prices,
shopping hours, and range and quality of shops); and four attributes
characterising the centre as a whole (layout and design, internal
pedestrian circulation, visual appearance and traffic conditions).
Of these attributes 'service quality' was the most important.

If Downs' four 'centre' attributes are used to evaluate shopping
centres, the typical modern purpose built shopping centre might score
rather more highly than many established town centres. The latter would
probably rate more highly for 'visual appearance', but the modern centre,
if built as a pedestrian precinct, is likely to be more compact, thus
offering better internal layout and pedestrian circulation, and to be
significantly safer from traffic hazards. Many precincts have of course
been provided within established town centres, thus adding to their
attractiveness and safety, but one could argue that a policy of providing
complete new major shopping centres would have fulfilled consumer
requirements better than adapting old town centres. Three main counter
arguments, already mentioned in 7.1.2, can be made in defending the
value of existing town centres to the consumer.

Firstly, existing town centres are generally more accessible than
purpose built new centres, which are likely to have a suburban or semi
rural location. Town centres are almost always the focus of public
transport networks, and therefore offer special advantages of access for
shoppers who do not own cars.

Secondly, existing town centres, with their usual mixture of properties of varying size condition and age, are likely to offer a far greater variety of shopping opportunity than the modern centre with its rather standardised format and high shop rents. Many town centres contain areas of high quality specialised boutiques, etc., usually in architecturally attractive streets; and areas of low quality discount or second hand goods shops. Both these types of retailing have particular requirements in terms of property and location: these cannot be met in a purpose built centre.

Thirdly, existing town centres contain several other important functions: public offices, educational and cultural facilities, entertainment, etc. In addition, they offer employment to many of those who carry out most of the household's shopping. These facilities allow many people to carry out trips involving shopping and some other business, social or cultural activity. Even where the trip has no purpose but shopping, many will prefer to carry out their shopping in a centre where other types of activity take place. This is a view strongly held by many town planners (7.2.1). However, it is not clear from direct evidence of shopper attitudes (e.g. Downs, 1970; Daws and Bruce, 1971; Bradley and Fenwick, 1975) whether these feelings are strongly held amongst shoppers. (3)

It appears then that the traditional town centre, despite its traffic problems, has some advantages for the shopper in general, and strong advantages for certain types of shopper. Modern suburban shopping centres of comparable size will fulfil most, but not all, of the functions of a town centre.

7.2 PLANNING POLICIES FOR TOWN CENTRES: A CRITICAL REVIEW

7.2.1 Town centres: planners' opinions and values

One of the most widely held beliefs among British planners and others concerned with the built environment has been in the importance of town and city centres. This belief has been founded on a number of ideas. One such idea is that the town centre is the natural focus of urban social and cultural activity: a meeting place for citizens. This has been emphasised by historians such as Mumford (1961), who also draw attention to the supposedly calamitous decline of American city centres in this century, hastened by the flight of population, industry and business to the suburbs. If one supports these views it is natural to attempt to ensure that British town centres remain prosperous, in the belief that this will maximise their economic, social and cultural value to the town's residents.

Allied to this is a belief that the appearance and prosperity of a town centre is, or should be, a matter for pride amongst citizens. Marriott (1967, Chapter 9) has shown how the early post war development in town centres was hastened not only by war damage, but also by 'a simultaneous attack of folie de grandeur among a great many local councils' (p.147). This was particularly strong in towns who regarded themselves as being in competition with neighbouring towns: a bigger and better town centre would provide more business, and also more prestige.

A third principle, already discussed (6.2.1), is that of the value of a clearly articulated hierarchy of shopping centres. This principle, although based explicitly upon central place theory, fitted in well with the tradition in town planning of purpose and order in the spatial distribution of land uses. It is a short step from observing that the largest existing business centres contain the largest number of functions and attract the most custom, to claiming that this state of affairs is entirely proper and should be maintained through planning policy.

These beliefs, together with the more prosaic but important considerations of consumer welfare discussed above (7.1.3), have led to general support for stability or growth in town centre retailing, and opposition to the development of out of town or 'regional' centres in the American fashion. These themes are exemplified by Burns (1959, p.103):

> 'The regional centre, however well designed, must surely be regarded simply as an economic development ... (it) is not part of civic life: it does not exist for its own environment but for a population living miles away ... it can never be a satisfactory replacement for the town centre or 'downtown' shopping district. It can never be part of the wider city culture. From this point of view, therefore, the out of town shopping centre must be regarded as inhuman'.

7.2.2 'Obsolescence' and comprehensive redevelopment

Burns, as in the extract above, was concerned to paint a picture of the awful consequences of neglecting to adapt town centres to twentieth century conditions. Town centres would have to be altered substantially to avoid being 'swamped' by traffic (see also Buchanan, 1963). The growth in motor traffic during the 1950s had led to four problems in town centres: noise, pollution and danger for pedestrians; difficulty in delivery and servicing for shops; difficulty for car borne shoppers in obtaining parking space; and delay for traffic forced to travel through the town centre but not wishing to stop there. Conditions in many high streets had become extremely unpleasant, with through traffic, car borne shoppers, public transport, delivery vehicles and pedestrians all occupying the same confined space. It was felt that relief of such conditions was essential, not just for social reasons but also for economic; if shops could not benefit from improvements in access for their suppliers and car parking provision for customers, then their owners would take them elsewhere.

In hindsight it appears that several solutions to these problems were available to planners. Some of these would involve reducing the volume of traffic and pedestrians by facilitating the removal of some retail activity to other centres. This would to some extent replicate events in America. However, because of commitment to the principle of maintaining the importance of town centres, such measures were unacceptable to almost all local authority councillors and planners. Another broad type of solution was to maintain or increase the level of economic activity, and at the same time attempt to solve traffic problems by improving both road and pedestrian circulation systems. In many towns this clearly implied a substantial amount of demolition and redevelopment: this was however seen not as a problem, but as an opportunity to enhance the prestige of the town as a whole by providing new attractions for both shoppers and other town centre users.

It was emphasised frequently that 'bold' or 'radical' plans should be prepared for city centres, with the central shopping area devoted entirely to pedestrians, and vastly improved car parking facilities and approach roads provided, usually within a near motorway standard ring road for through traffic. The early postwar redevelopment of Coventry city centre (Davies, 1972) had demonstrated that such plans could be successfully carried out, where sites had already been made available through war damage. However, the implementation of such schemes in other town centres could require much demolition, in order to allow some redistribution of land uses, and perhaps the provision of new social, civic or cultural facilities, as well as the traffic improvements. These ideas received official support in the Ministry of Housing and Local Government/Ministry of Transport joint publication 'Town Centres: Approach to Renewal' (1962) (for a summary see Davies, 1976a, pp.177-181). The financial cost of such plans could be enormous, but, as Burns (1959, p.102) stated:

> 'The folly of parsimony in dealing with town centre improvements cannot be stressed too much. Just because the dividends from the capital invested in large scale reconstruction are diffuse and cannot be pinpointed on a balance sheet, it does not follow that the operation is uneconomical'.

Of vital importance was the fact that local planning authorities possessed the means to implement even the most radical town centre scheme, at least so far as acquiring the land was concerned. The Town and Country Planning Acts gave authorities the power to designate Comprehensive Development Areas: if the designation was approved by central government, then the authority gained special rights to compulsory purchase of land and buildings within the area. (4) This legislation, originally intended to deal with the reconstruction of areas affected by war damage, was used extensively by local planning authorities in the redevelopment of central areas in the late 1950s and 1960s.

In the following section the connections between this principle of comprehensive development in town centres and its consequences for retail and other property development will be examined.

7.3 TOWN CENTRE DEVELOPMENT PROCESSES, 1945-1975

7.3.1 Introduction

In this section a brief review is given of the processes by which over 300 town centre retail development schemes came into being in the thirty years or so after 1945. These schemes generally resulted from some combination of potential for profitable development (3.1 - 3.2), and central area planning policy (7.2). Processes of development have varied according to the relative importance of these two factors. The following discussion draws distinctions between schemes developed primarily by the private sector, and those developed by the public sector or by a formal partnership between the two sectors. Finally, there is provided a brief examination of the recent reduction in town centre development activity.

Generally, a development scheme will be considered if it promises a reasonable rate of return on the capital invested (3.1). The capital itself usually emanates from financial institutions, mainly banks, insurance companies and pension funds. It has been shown by Ambrose and Colenutt (1975) that the rate of development activity as a whole in Britain is directly related to the willingness and ability of the financial institutions to lend money for property development. This itself is influenced by estimates of the likely profitability of investment in property compared with other types of investment: in industrial firms, overseas opportunities, or gilt edge securities, for example. Detailed evidence is given in Ambrose and Colenutt (1975, Chapter 2), and in Massey and Catalano (1978, Chapter 6).

There are two important implications of this situation. The first is that the extent of opportunities for profitable redevelopment in town centres reflects not only the policies of local authorities, or the demand for new retail premises, but also the general financial and economic situation. The second is that local authorities, where cooperating with financial institutions or property developers, can be regarded as a type of agent whose effect, if not purpose, is to facilitate the private accumulation of capital. This is exemplified in cases where local authorities have given direct or indirect financial assistance to developers and/or retailers in order that a scheme can be completed (McDougall et al, 1974; Dumbleton, 1977).

7.3.2 Developer-led schemes

In the interests of simplicity one may distinguish three modes of town centre redevelopment: these and their implications are discussed in this and the following two sub sections. The first mode is development which is almost entirely planned and organised by a property development firm, which is then responsible for letting space to tenants. This mode has probably occurred most often in the first half of the period under review, and for relatively small schemes. Developers' criteria for decisions on such schemes have already been discussed (3.2).

This mode was practicable in the early part of the review period for a number of reasons. There was ample opportunity for small town centre schemes because of war damage. There was relatively little competition between development firms, allowing one firm (often based in local estate agents) to acquire suitable land piece by piece. Local authorities were prepared to allow small new precincts rather than insisting on large scale 'comprehensive' schemes. Thus, the early success of property development firms outside London was founded largely upon these opportunities (Marriott, 1967, Chapter 5).

The results of this developer led process were often minor in terms of their impact upon retailing, although in later years some major schemes such as the Whitgift Centre in Croydon were built largely on the initiative of private landowners and developers, with relatively little intervention by local authorities.

7.3.3 Partnership schemes

During the 1950s and early 1960s, local authorities became more and more involved in the planning and financing of town centre redevelopment. There were two broad reasons for this. The first was that authorities gradually became convinced of the need for substantial improvements in road access and car parking in town centres, and hence foresaw a need for comprehensive redevelopment, rather than 'piecemeal' development on small sites (7.2.2). As well as proposals involving road improvements etc., it would usually be held desirable to improve the economic and social well being of the town by providing additional shopping and office space. At this point it would be logical to hire a property developer to plan, build and let the additional space. From the authority's viewpoint, the 'commercial' aspects involving the developer would seem relatively unimportant compared with the supposed benefits of the scheme as a whole.

A second reason for local authority involvement was a growing feeling that in some cases developers (or their financial backers) had made unreasonably high profits, with little benefit accruing to the town as a whole. Thus the principle arose that in being allowed to profit from the development of property, the developer should provide certain benefits for the public in general. This would save public money, and 'justify' the main part of the development in the eyes of the local authority and the public. Probably the most common form of this 'planning gain' associated with retail developments in central areas was the multi storey car park. This was in any case a desirable addition from the developer's viewpoint; but it also met an important objective of the local authority. Other forms of planning gain have included meeting halls, libraries, churches, and council housing.

If both local authority and developer accepted the principle of planning gain, the logical step was for the two sides to cooperate in order to produce schemes which would produce private financial return and public benefits. This suggested a 'partnership' between the two sides as a means of implementing plans for central areas.

'Partnership' implied a formal agreement between authority and developer, in which financial arrangements would be clearly set out. The most common arrangement was probably 'sale and lease back', wherein the local authority would buy the land, by compulsory purchase if necessary, and subsequently let it, usually for 99 years, to the developer. The local authority would thus receive merely a ground rent from the developer, who would receive rent payments from the occupiers. In this way the local authority would avoid incurring financial risk, but would also gain relatively little of the financial rewards from a successful scheme. Further details of typical financial arrangements are given by Stocks and Gleave (1971); Jennings (1974); Department of the Environment (1975, pp.30-31).

It was commonly the case that the approximate area and location of the new retail space were decided by the local authority, and property development firms would then be invited to tender for the development. Certain details would remain negotiable. This procedure involved two disadvantages for the developer. Firstly, there would be less opportunity to profit from increases in land value created by the development itself. However, as far as at least one major developer in this field was concerned (Chippindale, 1974), the question of who owned the land was unimportant. A second disadvantage was that the area of land to be devoted to retail and office uses, and its location, was decided by the local authority, and not the developer. Many local authority schemes of this kind were, according to Chippindale, too small and in the wrong location.

On the other hand there were two major advantages for developers in this arrangement. First, there was no need to go into the time consuming and expensive business of purchasing the land needed for redevelopment. Second, because of the local authority involvement from the beginning, there was likely to be no problem over obtaining planning permission.

Partnership schemes could also arise through a different sequence of events. Here the developer would take the initiative, deciding where and how large the development should be. He would then contact the local authority (often by-passing officials and dealing directly with councillors) and 'sell' his scheme. The local authority would probably be involved to the extent of helping with the purchase of land, and would try to extract some 'planning gain' from the developer. This process was initiated by Chippindale himself, working in the north of England in the 1950s (Marriott, 1967, Chapter 9). He and other developers were very persuasive in describing the advantages of pedestrian precincts, free of traffic hazards and offering some protection from bad weather.

It is important to note that, whether the scheme was initiated by the local authority or by the developer, the local authority would normally bear none of the actual profit or loss to be derived from running the development itself. The developer would almost always deal directly with retailers, assigning units in the scheme and fixing rent levels. The local authority would (it was hoped) gain in three other ways: first, there were normally some planning gains, as already described; second, there was a new source of income from rates charged on the new shops and offices; third, a less tangible benefit of increased trade in the town centre and increased importance and prestige for the town as a whole. Some experts have claimed that this arrangement has been of dubious benefit to local authorities: the planning gains could have been made more simply by increased general expenditure, which could have been partly financed by a share in the profits from the developments themselves.

In this partnership process, it was unlikely that either local authority or developer would base their proposals for retail floorspace on any rational assessment of shopping needs. Instead, the situation would often arise that a group of towns or suburban centres were independently proposing and even building new developments whose combined floorspace would greatly exceed the amount actually needed in the foreseeable future to cater for increases in demand for retail goods in the sub region. This was emphasised in a Ministry of Housing and Local Government (1966) circular.

The results of partnership schemes were often large additions to town centre shopping areas: in many cases these additions were provided through a combination of civic pride and financial imperative, rather than to meet any demand from retailers and shoppers. In some cases that demand was in fact lacking to such an extent that the new shops remained mostly unlet (Marcus, 1978). In other cities the new developments were successful, but temporarily at the expense of older parts of the city centre. (5) One should of course acknowledge that consumers in many towns have benefited from the addition of a modern weatherproof pedestrian precinct which has also allowed the entry of new retail firms to the town centre. While these gains are important, one remains unconvinced that they have been made in the most efficient or socially desirable manner.

7.3.4 Local authority-led schemes

Two lessons were learned by some local authorities from the experience of partnership schemes: first, that developers were not infallible; second, that the financial benefits from a successful scheme generally accrued entirely to the developer and any other agencies responsible for funding the scheme. Some authorities decided that, given good professional advice, they could perform the role of developer themselves. This led to the formation of a new kind of partnership, between a local authority and a financial institution. The role of the latter was simply to supply the capital and reclaim an agreed return, augmented possibly by a share of any extra profit derived from the scheme when fully operational. Thus the financial institution would demand a reasonable rate of return and would not incur the risk involved in a major development. On the other hand, the local authority stood to gain substantially from a successful scheme. Further details are given by Stocks and Gleave (1971).

No independent assessment of the degree of success of this type of
scheme appears to have been made. Casual observation of completed
schemes planned and run by local authorities and new town development
corporations suggests that they have largely been successful (in terms
of letting retail space and attracting consumers). Physically they are
indistinguishable from schemes planned and built by developers or
partnerships. It is not clear whether any authorities have made
substantial profits from these schemes, and, if so, how this gain has
been used.

7.3.5 Popular reactions against town centre development

It has been shown that planners' and developers' solutions for city
centre problems often involved substantial demolition and redevelopment.
This appeared necessary in order to provide large scale access and car
parking facilities, and also to accumulate sites worthwhile for shop and
office development. Planners and councillors generally believed that
the sacrifice of older parts of the town centre, perhaps containing many
buildings of historic and architectural interest, was worth making.
However, substantial opposition to this process became apparent during
the late 1960s. Protest movements against demolition and redevelopment
arose separately in many towns, and eventually these gained a wider
audience through the publication of books such as Amery and Cruickshank
(1975), and many critical articles in architectural magazines and
popular press. In some cases the local opposition was strong enough to
change councillors' minds about the virtues of redevelopment; in other
cases, opposition led to the intervention of the Secretary of State for
the Environment, who would hold a public inquiry so that the cases for
and against could be aired thoroughly. The result of a public inquiry
was occasionally the refusal of permission to go ahead.
 At the same time another rationale for opposition to large scale city
centre development was becoming established. This concerned the
political and economic aspects of development: it was argued that local
authorities, often assisted by central government, were acting as agents
of capital, in facilitating or even subsidising the activities of
financiers and developers. This argument, with detailed examples, is
provided in several sources such as Ambrose and Colenutt (1975) and
Dumbleton (1977); a theoretical discussion is provided by Cooke
(forthcoming). At a simplistic level, the argument that local
authorities should spend money on housing or social services, rather
than subsidising developers, has some appeal to Labour Party councillors,
who tend nowadays to oppose local authority involvement in development
schemes much more than in the 1960s.
 As a result of these ideas, any scheme for town centre development can
now expect to receive close and critical attention, on grounds both of
physical impact and financial arrangements. In addition, large scale
improvements in access and car parking have become much harder to
justify in a new climate of opinion on urban transport planning. The
perceived need for substantial town centre development is thus less than
in the 1960s.

7.3.6 Town centre development in the 1970s and 1980s

The early 1970s featured an increased number of large town centre
schemes, compared with the 1960s (Table 7.1). This was mainly because
schemes prepared in the late 1960s often took several years to be
completed, and in fact a few of these are still awaiting completion at

the time of writing.

Table 7.1   Numbers of central area shopping precinct developments
            by size and date of opening

	Retail floor space	
	50,000 - 250,000 ft^2	Over 250,000 ft^2
Opened before January 1970	43	13
Opened after January 1970	42	30
Proposed (with outline planning permission) but not opened prior to January 1977	19	20
Total	104	63

Source: Marcus (1978), Table 1.1

New proposals for town centre development have, according to several
commentators (e.g. Moor, 1976; Department of the Environment, 1975,
p.19) become uncommon in the 1970s. This may be due partly to the
changing climate of opinion noted above. However, problems associated
with the property slump (3.1.2) have probably been more important.
These have included a combination of sharp rises in building costs, high
interest rates, and uncertainty about future financial situations, which
have made the financing of a large scheme expensive and risky. In
addition, the provisions of the Community Land Act, and the Development
Land Tax, have partially removed a major incentive for development - the
capability to increase land values substantially through intensification
or change of land use (3.1.1).

It is possible that in the near future some of these constraints will
be eased. The new Conservative government has promised to repeal the
Community Land Act, and has reduced the rate of Development Land Tax.
The general climate for property development is likely to continue its
recent 'improvement', but there seems little likelihood of a major
revival in town centre shopping schemes. This statement can be supported
by three arguments. First, as discussed above (7.1.2), multiple retail
firms show less interest than formerly in town centre premises: some
firms have become developers of their own stores in suburban locations.
Secondly, in many town centres there is no apparent opportunity for
major development, either because of a low level of demand for retail
floorspace, or because suitable sites are not available. The latter
statement is of course one that can be made redundant by changes in the
property market or public opinion. Thirdly, as discussed above, local
authorities are unlikely today to wish to undertake substantial town
centre schemes. The situation may even return whereby most schemes are
initiated by developers (6) rather than local authorities.

7.4 CONCLUSIONS AND POLICY IMPLICATIONS

7.4.1 The bases for decision making

This chapter has shown that the post war boom in town centre development

resulted from a number of preconditions which are unlikely to recur in
the foreseeable future (Thorncroft, 1976). Its 'success' was enhanced
by cooperation from the state, in the form mainly of local authority
planning and compulsory purchase powers amounting often to an indirect
subsidisation of the developer, or financial institution; and also by
central government in the form of support for 'comprehensive' and
'radical' solutions to town centre traffic and environmental problems.

In chapter 3 a sequence of typical decisions for the developer was
outlined, and the type and quality of information used in making those
decisions was assessed. It was concluded that developers did not
generally appear to make well informed decisions, but that their eventual
success was always likely, given their monopoly position in supplying
new retail floorspace in many areas, and their partial subsidisation by
occupants of small size premises in the finished development. It appears
now that in general the developer's chance of success in a town centre
scheme has often been improved by the willingness of the local authority
to accept some of the costs of land acquisition, and of providing
vehicle and pedestrian access to the site.

Local authorities have also been shown to be somewhat less than fully
rational in their decision making. Large scale schemes costing many
millions of pounds were based not upon judgments of social need for new
shopping facilities, or upon economic forecasts of profitability
(although these could always be acquired from compliant consultant
firms): they were based more upon vague beliefs of the superiority of
central areas over all other types of retail location; and fortified
on the one hand by notions of civic prestige, and on the other by
alarmist statements of impending disaster, quite possibly the end of
civilisation itself, if motor traffic was not to be fully 'accommodated'
in town centres.

The financial success of most town centre schemes, taken in isolation,
cannot be disputed: it appears to have resulted partly from the
expansionist plans of multiple retail and service firms, but also from
the considerable popularity of covered shopping centres with the public.
Heavy financial costs have been incurred in the form of new roads, car
parks, service access, etc., and social costs in the form of losses of
historic buildings and attractive townscapes, and of existing town centre
shops and other property through competition or through the redevelopment
itself. It can also be argued that the high cost of central area
development leads to excessive rent demands on retailers, which in turn
forces them into policies of concentration on high margin luxury goods
(Jameson, 1976). Most of these costs have been ignored by the
principal decision makers - local authority councillors. There has been
no serious consideration of costs and benefits of alternative proposals,
such as the development of suburban covered shopping centres to the
scale found in American cities, or even the Paris region (Moor, 1974).

7.4.2 Rationales for planning intervention

Any assessment of present and future planning policy for intervention in
the market should stem from an examination of the necessity for
intervention. In 6.1.4 it was concluded that intervention was
justifiable for three basic reasons: to improve the performance of the
market; to provide facilities which the market could not adequately
provide to the public; and to restrain certain types of negative
externality which may result from development. Planners would probably
argue that town centre retail policies have been designed largely for
the first of these objectives. Processes of zoning and purchasing land

for the expansion of town centre shopping have assisted developers and
retailers by providing opportunities and reducing uncertainty about
rates of growth in floorspace. The seeking of 'planning gain' has to
some extent fulfilled the second objective, particularly in providing
otherwise uneconomic multi storey car parks. Pursuit of the third
objective has been partially achieved through normal processes of
development control.

This analysis is however incomplete, because these methods could
equally have been applied in the development of shopping centres in out
of town locations. Intervention such that development is steered into
town centres and away from other locations does not clearly follow any
of the rules given above. To some extent it reflects the application
of these rules to proposals for non central large scale development
(8.3.1), where planners have quite legitimately been concerned about
negative externalities. But it may be argued that important negative
externalities have stemmed from town centre developments (7.4.1).
These externalities have not been assessed properly by planners: the
main reason for this appears to be their habitual bias in favour of town
centre development and against suburban or out of town.

7.4.3 Future planning policies for retailing in town centres

The environment for planning policies in town centres has changed
considerably since the 1960s. 'Radical' solutions to traffic problems
are generally regarded as financially and politically infeasible. There
is much greater concern for the role of planning policies in remedying
economic and social problems in inner areas, and much less concern with
civic achievement and prestige. For these reasons, as well as the
relative lack of interest in town centre development as a commercial
proposition, the events of the 1960s are unlikely to be repeated in the
foreseeable future.

At the same time many planners and councillors see a continuing need
to maintain or improve town centre shopping facilities. This is partly
out of concern for the shopper, particularly where he or she is unable
to reach alternative facilities. This concern manifests itself in
policies for the improvement of the environment, such as pedestrianisation of main shopping streets. Another area of concern results
partly from the prior involvement of councils in town centre development.
This is a desire to protect the economic viability of such development
by restricting retail development elsewhere in the town or surrounding
area.

The first area of concern is justifiable in terms of general arguments
for planning intervention, particularly in improving the operation of
the market. Experience has shown that pedestrianisation and other
traffic management schemes in town centres bring considerable benefits
to consumers and retailers, at relatively low cost.

The second area of concern - protection of existing development in
town centres - cannot generally be regarded as justifiable. This reason
for intervention mitigates against improvement of the operations of the
market, and clearly stems from misuse of the system of control over
market operations. In principle there should be no justification for
limiting consumer choice of shopping opportunity, except where the
welfare of a significant number of consumers is threatened by the effects
of enlargement of that choice. This argument does not deny the validity
of refusing planning permission for specific suburban or out of town
schemes for specific reasons.

It seems that planning policies for town centres will in most cases have to acknowledge that future growth in retail sales is likely to be much less than would have been estimated ten or twenty years ago. There appear to be three elements of policy which are appropriate in this new situation. The first is to initiate or encourage gradual improvements in environmental conditions, as discussed above. The second is to continue to cooperate with developers in the provision of new retail space: it appears likely however that future schemes will generally be small scale, possibly in the manner of the early postwar schemes. The third element of policy is to continue to carry out development control, largely to maintain standards of visual attractiveness rather than to implement economic policies such as the achievement of floorspace targets. These rather modest suggestions for policy indicate that the greatest pressure for development has moved away from town centres: without this pressure, planners can perhaps paradoxically achieve more than hitherto in enhancing the specialised nature and attractiveness of town centre shopping.

NOTES

(1) Such centres include Brent Cross in north west London, and the centres of some new towns, such as Washington, Runcorn and Telford.
(2) Not necessarily confined to specialty goods as defined in 5.5.2.
(3) In one survey, housewives were asked their reasons for buying food and groceries in Watford town centre (Daws and Bruce, 1971, Table 23). The majority gave reasons connected with characteristics of food shops: only 19% agreed that 'I go there anyway, because of work etc.'
(4) After 1959, compensation for compulsory purchase had to be at full market value of the land. This may have created financial difficulties for some councils in their attempts to assemble central area sites.
(5) This type of impact has been studied in Nottingham (Bower, 1974) and Newcastle (Davies and Bennison, 1978).
(6) The 'developer' is increasingly likely to be in whole or part a financial institution rather than a property development firm per se; see Massey and Catalano (1978, Chapter 6).

8 Hypermarkets and superstores

This chapter deals with the important phenomena of hypermarkets and
superstores, and the nature of the British planning response to them.
In this initial section, definitions are attempted, and then the
reasons for the development of hypermarkets and superstores, and a brief
summary of their present importance, are presented. In subsequent
sections, the planning responses at local and central government level
are described and explained, and also critically assessed with reference
to empirical findings on the impact of existing hypermarkets and
superstores.

8.1.1 Definitions

A definition of hypermarkets and superstores has been made by the Unit
for Retail Planning Information (1976):

> 'Superstores are defined as single level, self service
> stores offering a wide range of food and non food
> merchandise, with at least 25,000 square feet sales area
> (2,500 square metres) and supported by car parking. Stores
> with 50,000 square feet or more are commonly referred to as
> hypermarkets'

Using this definition, it was estimated that by the end of 1977, 140
such stores had opened in Britain and a further 70 were under
construction or had received planning permission (Jones, 1978). Of
these, 31 (open in 1977) would qualify as hypermarkets under this
definition.

8.1.2 Superstore development in Britain (1)

The developments in methods of retailing which have led to the growth
of superstores have already been outlined (4.3). Superstores represent
a logical development of the supermarket, with the same self service
principle, but add significant economies of scale. They are generally
sufficiently large to be able to order goods direct from manufacturers,
and so cut out the costs of wholesale distribution: they may also
negotiate special terms with manufacturers, thus reducing prices further.

A high volume of sales is necessary to make this method of bulk
purchasing worth while. This is ensured, firstly by passing on to the
consumer many of the cost savings, such that food prices may on average
be up to 12 per cent cheaper than the national average (URPI, 1976,
p.10); secondly, by stocking a very wide variety of goods, so as to
encourage the 'one stop' shopping trip (ibid, p.6); thirdly, by
providing extensive free car parking facilities, at a rate of approximately one space per five square metres of sales area (ibid, p.5);
and finally, by choosing locations such that at least 50,000 people
live within about ten minutes car driving time of the store (ibid, p.5).

Superstores have been developed much more widely in certain continental
European countries than in Britain, and mainly by specialist retail
firms of which the French firm Carrefour is a particularly successful

case. Carrefour has extended its operation to Britain, with five
hypermarkets now open. The most important British specialist firm,
with 39 superstores open or planned in 1977 is Asda, a subsidiary of
Associated Dairies Ltd. (4.3.5). However, superstores have also been
developed by firms already established in food retailing, such as Tesco
(20 superstores open or planned in 1977); and also by the variety
store firm Woolworth's, with 14 'Woolco' superstores open or planned in
1977 (URPI, 1977b). The latter are somewhat different from the normal
superstore, with greater emphasis on durable goods.

Two further features of superstore development in Britain should be
mentioned. The first is the fairly consistent upward trend in rates of
store openings per annum since 1965 (Figure 8.1). This suggests that
superstores are rapidly becoming established features of retailing in
many areas. Secondly, their geographical distribution: Table 8.1 shows
considerable variation between the regions of Britain in terms of
superstore 'penetration'. This variation is due partly to the
geographical origin in the north of England of the firms Asda and
Morrison, but also apparently, to variations in planning policy with
respect to superstores.

The question of planning policy and its impact upon the development of
superstores in Britain has been controversial for several years, and
indeed is the main topic for discussion in this chapter. It is
sufficient to note here that planning policy in many areas has either
been totally opposed to superstore development, or has at least led to
development in locations which retail firms might not otherwise have
chosen. Therefore the existing pattern of superstores, in both number
and location, is substantially different from that which would have
arisen from the uncontrolled operations of the firms involved.

8.1.3 Consumer response to superstores

In general terms there is no doubt that superstores have proved
successful with the public. Several reports exist of sales well beyond
expected levels, but none of closures due to unprofitable operation.

Several surveys of shoppers at superstores have been carried out.
Particular attention has been given to the Carrefour stores at Caerphilly
and Eastleigh, due to the pioneering role of that firm in developing
out of town hypermarkets (Donaldsons, 1973, 1975, 1979; Department of
the Environment, 1976a, 1978; Cole, 1975).   These surveys have shown
that shoppers at these particular hypermarkets form a wide cross section
of the general public, but nevertheless tend not to be a fully
representative sample (Table 8.2). There is an overrepresentation of
car owning families (about 90 per cent of families, compared with about
55 per cent in the population as a whole). Married couples in the
26-45 age group are overrepresented and single person households and
elderly persons under represented. There is also a tendency for
shoppers to visit the hypermarkets in much larger family groups than is
normal in shopping behaviour.

The Carrefour stores draw shoppers from a much wider area than is
normal with convenience shopping stores. About a quarter of the
hypermarkets' customers live at distances of over 20 minutes' driving
time from the store (Table 8.2). Virtually all customers travelling
other than short distances to the stores come by car: a small minority
of those living close to the store travel there on foot or by bus.

It is not clear to what extent these findings apply generally to
British superstores and hypermarkets. A comparison of travel modes for
shoppers at 14 different stores (Maltby and Johnson, 1979) suggests

130

Figure 8.1   Hypermarkets and superstores opened each year in UK, 1967-1977

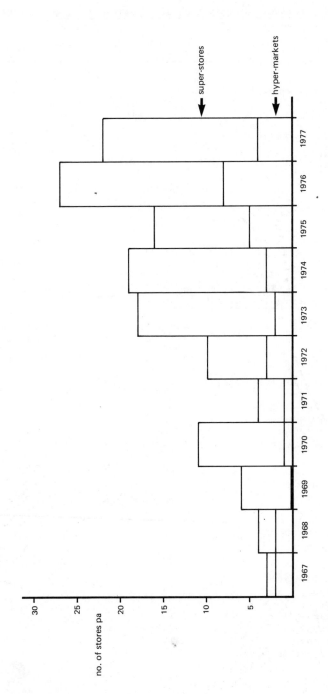

no. of stores pa

super-stores

hyper-markets

Source: Jones, 1978, Table A

131

Table 8.1   Regional distribution of superstores, compared with
             population, 1976

Region/country	% of British Superstores	% of population
North	8	6
Yorkshire & Humberside	15	9
North West	23	12
East Midlands	12	7
West Midlands	7	10
East Anglia	4	3
South East	7	31
South West	2	8
Wales	10	5
Scotland	12	10
Total	100	100

Sources: Jones (1978), Table C;
           Central Statistical Office (1978), Table 1.6.

Table 8.2   Consumer behaviour and attitudes towards hypermarkets
             at Caerphilly and Eastleigh

	Carrefour Caerphilly (1978) [1]	Carrefour Eastleigh (1977) [2]
	%	%
1. Time taken to reach the store:		
Under 10 minutes	49	45
10 - 20 minutes	33	35
20 - 30 minutes	7	11
Over 30 minutes	11	9
	100	100
2. Travel Mode:		
Car	86	91
Bus	5	2
Foot	8	5
Other	1	2
	100	100
3. Household size:		
1 person	3	4
2 persons	25	26
3 persons	23	20
4 persons	26	31
5 persons	14	12
Over 5 persons	5	6
Other	4	-
	100	100

Table 8.2 (continued)

	Caerphilly	Eastleigh
	%	%
4. Age of shoppers:		
18 – 25	14	
25 – 45	48	not
45 – 65	30	available
Over 65	8	
	100	
5. Reasons for using hypermarket[3]		
'Economy'		49 (30)
'Pleasant/convenient shopping'	not	43 (27)
'Convenience of site'	available	23 (14)
'Traffic'	in this form	18 (11)
'Other reasons'		29 (18)
		162 (100)

Notes:

1　Source:　Donaldsons (1979) Based upon interviews held on Fridays and Saturdays.　Figures given are means of Friday and Saturday results.

2　Source:　Department of the Environment(1978).　Based upon interviews held on all days that store was open.

3　More than one response to this question was allowed.　Figures in brackets are percentages of total responses.

---

that the overwhelming predominance of car trips noted above is typical only of edge of town superstores.　Superstores located in inner urban areas or town centres generate a much lower proportion of car trips (50 per cent in one case – Asda, Coatbridge), and much higher proportions of bus and walking trips.　Superstores located in new district centres in outer suburbs follow an intermediate pattern with around 70 – 80 per cent of trips being made by car.

　The 'in town' superstore thus possesses a partial role as a normal local centre generating a substantial number of walking trips.　For this reason the profile of shoppers, in terms of age, household size and social class, is much closer to the national average than is the case for edge of town superstores (e.g. Thorpe and McGoldrick, 1977).

8.1.4　Consumer attitudes to superstores

Shoppers interviewed at these stores have given reasons for their decisions to shop there:　these are listed in Table 8.2 for Eastleigh only.　Reasons of 'convenience' were mentioned most frequently, and the more detailed classification in the Eastleigh results (Department of the Environment, 1978, p.47) suggests that this means primarily convenience in being able to obtain many different goods in one place, rather than convenience of access, although the latter is also important.

　In this case, and also at Caerphilly (Donaldsons, 1979, Table 1.7), the number of respondents stressing reasons of 'economy' (i.e. price savings) has decreased, compared with surveys carried out shortly after the opening of the store.　This may be because initially many customers

are attracted to the store by price advantages, but those who become
regular customers find the store pleasant and convenient for their main
shopping trips.

In a tentative way it is possible to link these findings with the more
general considerations of consumer behaviour discussed in Chapter 5.
In terms of Stone's (1954) classification the typical hypermarket
shopper is 'economic', in wishing to save both money and time by buying
goods cheaply and in bulk. This attitude must result partly from family
circumstances: for married couples with children, the weekly food budget
is much larger than for smaller households. Access to a car is normally
essential in order to shop at these stores, when they are poorly located
with respect to public transport routes. However, the pattern of bulk
buying, which is encouraged by the characteristics of the store itself,
means that a car is in any case essential in order that the purchases
can easily be brought home.

It is possible, by implication, to identify sections of the public who
derive relatively little advantage from the opportunities offered by the
hypermarket. These include single people or small households, whose
weekly food budget is relatively small; people who cannot use cars to
take their purchases home; people who are unlikely to have sufficient
money available to be able to buy food in bulk; and people who simply
find hypermarkets to be unpleasant environments for shopping. The
latter will include those whose attitude to shopping can be
characterised as 'personalising' or 'ethical' (Stone, 1954).

These considerations may help explain a finding from an interview
survey of shoppers in four areas in Britain, two of which included a
hypermarket or large superstore (Bruce and Delworth, 1976). Respondents
were asked to 'rate' various types of shopping centre in terms of their
utility for convenience shopping, by giving them scores out of ten.
To anchor the scale at one point, one supermarket on its own was given
a predetermined value of 5.0. It was found that 'one hypermarket on
its own' received a relatively high mean rating (6.58), somewhat below
'two supermarkets with some smaller shops' (7.01). A significant
minority gave the hypermarket very high scores (8, 9, or 10), but many
respondents gave much lower ratings. This distribution was in sharp
contrast to those for other centres, which were approximately normal
(in the statistical sense). Thus, opinions about hypermarkets appeared
to vary substantially. This phenomenon was noted in all four areas
surveyed.

Again, it is not clear to what extent these findings apply generally.
Much depends upon the identity of the firm involved; for example,
customers of Woolco and Co-operative superstores place less emphasis
upon price advantages (e.g. Thorpe et al, 1972, Section 7; Thorpe and
McGoldrick, 1977, Chapter 7), probably because grocery prices here are
typically higher than for certain other firms (Which, 1979). However,
there is considerable strength of agreement amongst the various surveys
on the perceived 'convenience' of superstore shopping.

8.2 PLANNERS' ATTITUDES TO SUPERSTORES

In this section some typical attitudes of local authority planners to
proposals for superstores are reviewed. First, these attitudes are
summarised from structure plan and other policy statements: attention
is paid particularly to locational policies. An attempt is then made to
explain typical policies, in relation to traditional planning concerns
of physical containment and the minimisation of negative externalities

arising from new development. Policies which emphasise the impact of superstores upon existing retail systems are then reviewed in the light of evidence about such impact. Finally, the role of central government, and in particular the Department of the Environment, is discussed.

8.2.1 Planning policies for superstores

As with any form of commercial development, the superstore can operate only after receipt of planning permission. In most cases superstore proposals have been regarded as a matter on which the advice of the county council should be sought. This means that development plan policies, particularly structure plan, normally deal specifically with superstores in their sections concerning shopping.
  At the time of writing, the only reasonably full review of planning policies for shopping is that of Thorpe (1975b): he devotes some attention to policies for 'new types of trading', which include superstores. This review however predates the majority of structure plans, and the almost universal antipathy noted by Thorpe is no longer the case.
  Observation of a number of structure plan statements suggests that current attitudes of county planners to superstore proposals fall into three broad categories. In almost all cases the planners recognise that superstores form an important recent development in retail methods, and also bring certain advantages to the consumer. However, some authorities still consider that any development of superstores in their area is unsuitable and should be rejected. This may be stated explicitly, or implicitly: in the latter case, a statement may be made that any application will be considered 'on its merits', but then several conditions to be fulfilled are specified, which taken together are so onerous as to rule out almost any conceivable scheme.
  A second attitude, which is probably the most common at present, is to favour the development of superstores in certain types of location only, and also subject to several conditions. Such policies are concerned generally to incorporate superstores into the existing 'hierarchy' of shopping centres in urban areas, by locating them in town or district centres.
  A third type of policy is more positive than the first two, in proposing superstore development in certain locations, which may be specified either in general terms or fairly precisely.
  Of crucial importance also is the attitude of district level planners, particularly as recent government pronouncements indicate that districts are likely to be given full responsibility for almost all development control decisions. It is not clear whether district planning policies tend to be more strongly opposed to superstore development than county policies. There is evidence to support this proposition, in Chester and York for example (Lucas, 1979). It has however been pointed out that the majority of superstores in existence have been approved by local authorities in the first instance, rather than being allowed by central government after an appeal against refusal of planning permission (URPI, 1976, p.19). In many of these cases, permission was granted with relatively little local opposition or delay. More recently, some districts have taken a lead in agreeing district centre development schemes with certain superstore firms (URPI, 1977a). Overall it may be supposed that district policies fall into the three categories outlined above, but more often into the first or third than in the case of county authorities.

Published policies concerning superstores, especially in structure plans, tend to include arguments about both the benefits and costs of superstore development to the community at large. The nature of the benefits to consumers follows the arguments discussed above (8.1.3). The costs which are identified in most policy statements, and which also have been discussed in numerous planning inquiries (Department of the Environment, 1976b; Donaldsons, 1976, 1978), can be classified into three types. These are:

i) the unquantifiable costs that arise from the violation of established planning principles of order and containment;

ii) economic costs that arise from the impact of the new store upon existing retail facilities, and from other external effects;

iii) social costs that arise from (ii), and from the income redistribution effect upon consumers.

Each of these types of cost will be considered in detail in the following three subsections: the arguments put forward by planners will be critically examined in the light of empirical evidence.

8.2.2 Order and containment

It has been shown above (6.1) that British town planners, although claiming always to be governed by the needs of the community as a whole, have been influenced strongly by concepts arising from the concerns of their professional forbears - engineers and architects. Two major principles - 'order' and 'containment' - implicit in much policymaking and decision making have been discussed.

It has been shown (4.3.5) that firms normally prefer to build superstores in edge of town locations, because such land tends to be cheaper than true urban premises or sites, and also because large undeveloped sites are more readily available. The free standing edge of town store however violates established planning principles regarding the location of commercial activity in at least one of three possible ways.

Firstly, the proposed store is likely to be on a site previously unused for commercial activity - often agricultural land, or land zoned for industrial purposes but not used as such. Thus the proposal will be contrary to the zoning in the development plan, if this was formulated at a time when no need for edge of town commercial facilities was foreseen. This itself may be seen by planners as sufficient justification for refusal of planning permission. A more recent argument of this kind has been that a proposal should be refused permission on the grounds that its approval would prejudice the formulation of structure plan policies for shopping or for the use of the land concerned. This argument seems particularly illogical and unfair, and has been generally given little credit by government inspectors at planning inquiries (Donaldsons, 1976, pp.14-17).

Secondly, it follows that the proposed store will lie outside the established hierarchy of shopping centres in the area. Planners have tended to identify 'hierarchies' almost at will, since the concept suggests a degree of orderliness in the urban or regional system (6.2.1). It is held that the 'hierarchy' represents an optimal method of serving consumers in a town or region, and that new retail facilities outside established centres are therefore disorderly and unnecessary. This facile and erroneous argument appears to be important in the reasoning behind planning policies which favour continuing development in existing centres. An argument allied to this, which Thorpe has discussed (1975b, p.11, is that retail and other business or service facilities with perhaps some social and community facilities, ought to be grouped together into all purpose local centres. This is intended not only to facilitate multi purpose trips, but also to engender a 'sense of community' among local residents. The validity of these arguments seems doubtful, but in any case it is wrong to state that any shopping proposal which does not fulfil this criterion is bad and should not be allowed.

A third argument that has been applied in certain cases is that the site lies in 'green belt' (2) land and is thus unsuitable for development of any kind. It occurs thus that superstore proposals, even on sites which are themselves unattractive or derelict, are turned down because they would result in loss of green belt (Lucas, 1979). Two arguments are used in defending such decisions. First, the development could result in 'visual intrusion' of urban uses in the green belt. Second, the development would create a 'precedent' for urban use in the green belt which would mean that future applications by other commercial firms could not logically be refused. Of these arguments, the first may clearly have merit in certain situations, although retailers are normally prepared to carry out substantial landscaping in order to minimise the visual impact of a large store and its car park. The second argument is illogical if one believes the frequent claims of central government departments that appeal decisions, in the green belt and elsewhere, are always decided 'on their own merits'. These arguments related to order and containment appear to form a basis for the opposition of many planners and councillors to out of town superstore proposals, although their detailed statements of opposition also include reference to economic and social costs of the proposal. These can now be discussed.

8.2.3 The economic impact of superstores

In examining any proposal for a superstore, an essential consideration for the planner is the economic impact of the store. This includes the impact of the store upon existing retail facilities, and its impact upon traffic patterns.

Planners' concern for impact upon existing facilities tends to form part of a somewhat schizophrenic attitude. They will declare that it is not the planners' task to prevent competition between retailers or to protect existing interests. They will then show concern that a superstore will adversely affect existing shopping centres. This duality also occurs in statements by retailer organisations such as Local Chambers of Trade, which may have considerable influence over councillor opinion and thus over planning policy.

The case for concern can be summarised as follows. The superstore's turnover is mainly in convenience goods, for which the demand is relatively inelastic. This means that sales at the superstore will be made, it is claimed, at the expense of other shops in the area. Some shops will thus become unprofitable and will eventually be closed by their owners. This is detrimental in four ways. Firstly, there may be hardship to independent shopkeepers who lose their livelihood. Secondly, empty shops are unattractive and lower the image to consumers and retailers of a shopping centre, thus causing further deterioration in trade. Thirdly, consumers depending on local shops which have closed down are disadvantaged. Fourthly, if the superstore because of its successful competitive impact has established a near monopoly position, it can then dictate its terms to the consumer, for example by raising prices (Pickering, 1972).

The evidence of superstore impact in Britain can now be reviewed in these terms. It should first be noted that the initial stage of the argument - that a superstore draws convenience goods trade away from other shops - has not been fully proven. It seems possible that the price reductions and displays in superstores render goods more attractive to consumers, and hence some expenditure takes place which would not have occurred in other shops. This suggests that the use of spatial interaction models to assess the impact of a superstore on expenditure patterns (e.g. Guy, 1977b) may be inappropriate, since these models assume that expenditure by people living in an area is fixed in sum, no matter what shopping opportunities are available.

However it is clear that much of the expenditure in superstores is on basic food which would have been bought elsewhere. It is of interest then to know what type of shop or centre tends to be rejected in favour of the superstore, by typical superstore shoppers. The latter, as explained above (8.1.3), tend to be from relatively large households with a substantial weekly budget for food. The commonly observed pattern of once weekly or less frequent 'bulk buying' is both a response to the characteristics of the superstore itself, and a response to personal conditions such as limited car availability. It is likely that households choosing to buy most of their groceries in once weekly trips to a superstore would previously have shopped in much the same manner, at any supermarket which offered price reductions and contained a sufficiently wide range of goods.

This tends to be confirmed in surveys of superstore shoppers. It is generally found (e.g. Rogers, 1974; Thorpe and McGoldrick, 1977) that the majority of shoppers regularly using superstores previously carried out most of their grocery shopping at other superstores or at super- markets owned by multiples or co-operatives. Under ten per cent of such shoppers previously relied on small local shops. It follows that, given typical patterns of supermarket location, the centres most affected by superstore competition are generally town or district centres. It should be emphasised that this competition is mainly for convenience shopping, which in any case forms a small and declining sector of town centre trade.

It has also been found that, because superstores attract shoppers from much greater distances than is normal for convenience opportunities, their impact is spread over several centres. For individual centres the impact is usually slight, especially where the superstore is located at the edge of an urban area. This is however not the case where the superstore is well within an urban area, and close to a district centre. In these circumstances it may divert a substantial number of consumers from the district centre or other local shops. It appears though that this type of consumer, who is likely to walk to the superstore, will continue to spend more of her food budget outside the superstore, than the car borne consumer who has previously shopped at other superstores or multiple owned supermarkets (Thorpe and McGoldrick, 1977, pp.96-97).

The impact of superstores upon other shopping facilities has also been assessed by surveys of retailers. The existence of superstores is regarded generally as a minor problem by independent grocery retailers (Bates, 1976, p.79), and in towns where superstores have opened, trade losses have been small for independents; but for multiples and co-operatives, substantially greater (Thorpe et al, 1976). It is not clear whether superstore competition has in fact caused smaller supermarkets to close down. It has to be remembered that several multiple chains and co-operative societies have in any case undergone policies in the 1970s of closing smaller stores, as these are the least profitable element in their operation (9.3.3). A firm which opens superstores will probably close some of its smaller stores, but not necessarily in the same area (Hallsworth, 1978).

Information about actual shop closures in areas adjacent to superstores is also unclear. Donaldsons (1975) reported that in the two years following the opening of the Carrefour hypermarket at Caerphilly, the number of food shops had declined by 45 in the study area, from a total of 321 in 1972. This area included the centre and northern suburbs of Cardiff, and several other towns within ten miles of the hypermarket. The decline was three times as great as the national average decline in numbers of food shops over that period. Donaldsons (1975, p.8) point out that those 45 shops would only have had trade equivalent to about one quarter of the hypermarket's. Therefore it is possible that many other shops were affected by the hypermarket, but were continuing to trade.

In locational terms the impact upon shops appeared to be much as one would expect from considerations of changes in consumer behaviour (above). The only substantial centre which can compete with the hypermarket for walk in customers is Caerphilly town centre: this had suffered a net loss of eight food shops (40 per cent of the 1972 total). Most of these premises were subsequently taken up by non food trades or services (Donaldsons, 1979). Further afield, the loss of premises was more pronounced in town and district centres than in neighbourhood centres or isolated shops. It should be noted however that many of these losses were in areas north and west of Caerphilly, which have in any case suffered losses of employment and population in recent years.

In assessing the impact of superstores on existing shops, it follows that one should attempt to control for other changes in the environment for retailers. This is also shown by events close to the Eastleigh Carrefour: the only local centre to experience a substantial net loss in food shops (five over three years) was Eastleigh town centre, about two miles away. This may however have been due mainly to the opening of a large Tesco supermarket in Eastleigh town centre itself (Department of the Environment, 1978, p.57).

One other type of impact of superstores upon nearby shops has been demonstrated in the Caerphilly area: this is tendency towards reduction in food prices, and is clearly a competitive response by shopkeepers (Cole, 1975). This evidence clearly refutes Pickering's (1972) claim that a superstore could establish monopoly advantages, to the detriment of shoppers.

Finally in this subsection, the impact of superstores upon road traffic patterns can be mentioned. The superstore is designed basically to serve the car borne shopper, and one must therefore expect substantial traffic generation. However, one should distinguish three types of effect, according to size and location of the superstore (Maltby and Johnson, 1979).

Firstly, the edge of town hypermarket. Around 90 per cent of trips to hypermarkets are made by car, and thus the traffic generation effect is considerable. The following estimates have been given for Carrefour Caerphilly:

'i)   over 1,000 trips per day to the hypermarket from outside the immediate urban area (i.e. over ten minutes off peak journey time); and

ii) at least 2,800 trips to the hypermarket from within the immediate urban area (i.e. under ten minutes off peak journey time); and

139

iii)   over 800 trips by 'through movement' visitors.'

(Kelly, 1979, p.260)

The effect of a petrol station at the site is also substantial: 12 per cent of the trips to Caerphilly Carrefour were made simply to buy petrol. Kelly's figures are based upon monitoring of trips on Fridays, and the impact on other days of the week is probably less.

The impact of hypermarket traffic on the road system has been studied for the Minworth hypermarket near Birmingham (Harris and Andrew, 1979). This store, with a sales area of 70,000 square feet, attracted some 1,000 vehicles per hour at peak periods. This the authors regard as 'a significant volume of traffic which may in some circumstances require grade separation at the access point' (ibid, p.8).

On the surrounding highway network the increase in traffic was also substantial, but the survey established that there was no significant increase in congestion. This was because the peak flows to and from the hypermarket occurred at times other than the normal peak flows on the main road system.

Secondly, edge of town superstores. These tend also to draw a very high percentage of car borne shoppers, with relatively few walking or bus trips. The rate of generation of trips, expressed for example as trips per 1,000 square feet sales area, tends to be similar to hypermarkets (Kelly, 1979), although substantial variation exists (Maltby and Johnson, 1979). Because of the smaller size, the actual impact upon the local road system is less than for the hypermarket. It is also generally found that a smaller proportion of trips emanate from outside the local urban area.

Thirdly, in town superstores. These show lower percentages of car borne shoppers, possibly as low as 50 per cent. This means that impact upon the local road system is rather less. It is not clear whether peak flows to in town superstores are complementary with peak flows on the road network, as is the case at Minworth. But it seems likely that problems will occur where a superstore is located near a district or town centre. This is because the capacity of roads in the centre itself would be reduced during shopping hours by the presence of delivery vehicles and of shoppers attempting to park.

One must conclude that the economic impact of superstores has generally been much less serious than many councillors and planners feared. Any diversion of trade to superstores seems to have led to the closure of very few convenience shops, except where superstores have been built close to district centres. This may have been mitigated to some extent by increased rates of price reduction in existing stores. The impact upon traffic patterns has been substantial in some cases, such that problems of congestion may occur unless special provision is made for superstore traffic.

It appears then that if planners wish to minimise the economic impact of superstores, they should prefer them to be located at the edge of urban areas and adjacent to major roads. This is so that the impact upon district centres will be least, and so that problems of congestion and disturbance to residents by heavy traffic are minimised. An in town location, especially within or close to a district centre, may have much greater economic impact locally.

8.2.4 The social impact of superstores

The social impact of superstores has also been a subject of concern to British planners. There are four basic causes for concern: firstly, that shop closures instigated by the success of the superstore impose social costs on their users; secondly, that superstores create other negative externalities; thirdly, that superstore development pre-empts other, more socially useful, development; and fourthly, that through reducing prices to the more mobile and affluent consumer, the superstore increases disparities between rich and poor. These arguments will be assessed against the evidence already mentioned.

The first of these arguments was given considerable weight by writers such as Hillman (1973). He painted a picture of rapid rates of closure of small local shops, to the detriment of the poorer shopper who could not travel to the superstore. This argument however seems inconsistent. It is more reasonable to assume that shoppers who cannot get to the edge of town superstore will continue to use their local shops, which therefore remain in business (T. Sainsbury, 1973). This conclusion has been borne out by events, and some writers would claim that small shops have become more popular after the opening of superstores in an area. This is because they tend to be used by superstore shoppers for 'topping up' trips during the week (Cole, 1975).

It would be foolish to claim that there are no social costs as a result of the economic impact of superstores. However, since this impact tends to be diffused over a large area, and has little effect upon small food shops, it cannot be said generally to be serious. The author (Guy, 1977b) has shown by means of a simulation model of shop closures, and by use of access measures, that the impact of a hypermarket upon shoppers' access to local shops would generally be very small, even given very pessimistic assumptions about rates of shop closure.

The second argument, about other possible negative externalities, needs to be examined through case studies and cannot easily be discussed in general terms. Of concern here is the effects upon local residents of traffic generated by a superstore. Some of this traffic would in any case have occurred in trips to other shopping opportunities in the same area, but the studies mentioned above (8.2.3) show a substantial volume of traffic which would otherwise not have visited the area concerned.

The third argument, concerning alternative uses of superstore sites, can again only be assessed through case studies. Some planning authorities have objected to superstore proposals on the grounds that land zoned for industry has been lost. However, it has generally been agreed at planning inquiries that such land at the time of the proposal was not in fact in demand for industrial purposes, and that other industrial land was still available if needed (Donaldsons, 1976, pp.24-25). In conventional terms it might be argued that in town sites, with their greater general accessibility, are more valuable to the community than edge of town sites. However, as Tesco (1977) have pointed out, much land in the inner parts of large cities is currently vacant or underused, and therefore the opportunity costs of building a superstore in the inner city may be low.

The fourth argument, that superstore use increases income disparities, is the most difficult to resolve. Evidence of shopper characteristics shows broadly that the argument is correct, although more so for edge of town superstores than in town. The difficulty arises in deciding whether this constitutes a matter for planning intervention.

The profile of typical superstore shoppers (8.1.3) is one that virtually excludes non car owning and elderly single person or married couple households. In social class terms middle class and skilled working class households predominate. Thus, the people who use the store least are those who would appear to need its price savings the most.

Two broad reasons for this are connected with the characteristics of

141

the superstore itself. Firstly, poor families generally have little money available at any one time and hence cannot buy food in bulk. They also lack facilities for transporting goods in bulk. Secondly, some shoppers prefer the small shop anyway: the little evidence available suggests that elderly people accustomed to the 'corner shop' will not always take kindly to the superstore with its impersonal atmosphere. This is not entirely irrational behaviour, since shopping in large stores for a small volume of goods is also wasteful of effort.

The third reason for underuse of most superstores by poor families is connected with their location and accessibility. Superstores in edge of town locations are usually accessible by car and perhaps one or two bus routes. (3) This precludes their use by more than a few non car owning households. In town superstores, with much higher percentages of users travelling by bus or on foot, may have slightly different consumer profiles. For example, the Co-operative superstore at Failsworth, an in town site near Manchester, attracts a substantially higher proportion of shoppers aged over 60 than do other superstores in the area (Thorpe and McGoldrick, 1977, p.54). Even then, this store still attracted well below the national average of both elderly people and households headed by a semi skilled or unskilled worker. The question whether an in town superstore can prove fully adequate for the food shopping needs of the poor and elderly is thus not yet answered.

The evidence suggests then that the superstore offers its price and other advantages mainly to the better off customer. This is mitigated to some extent by locating the store so as to be accessible to non car owners. The question now is whether the inequitable effects of the superstore matter. On the one hand it can be argued that the introduction of a superstore into an area is desirable because it makes some people better off and no one worse off (unless a significant number of other stores close as a result of competition). On the other hand, if disparities between rich and poor are increased, then deprivation (which is usually assumed to be relative in nature) is increased. This would be especially true if the poor were aware that lower prices were obtainable in stores that they could not reach.

The argument about relative deprivation is becoming more apparent in planning policies. The solution usually put forward is for superstores to be provided at in town locations accessible by bus and foot. Some non car owners can then visit the store without difficulty if they wish to. An alternative policy is to ban superstores altogether, but a logical extension of this policy - where applied on social grounds - would be to ban any store which promised to offer price reductions. It is of course impossible for any physical planning policy to eliminate all sources of inequality in an area. Inequity (4) can however be minimised by ensuring that all sections of the community have access to a variety of opportunities, in shopping as in other respects.

These arguments appear to support the in town superstore at the expense of the edge of town. It should be remembered that impact upon local shopping facilities, and generation of external effects, appear to be more severe in the case of the in town superstore. This raises problems in policy making, which will be discussed further (8.3.3).

8.2.5 Central government planning intervention

Two important general points arise from the discussion above. First, the evaluation of the economic and social benefits and costs of superstores is a complex operation; second, local authority planners are unlikely to be able to make entirely fair decisions, being constrained by the biased objectives of councillors and also by their own professional traditions.

For these reasons there is a good case for central government intervention in local decision making. This was particularly true at the beginning of the 1970s, when relatively little was known about super-stores and their effects. It seemed likely that misinformed and unfair decisions, against or in favour of superstore proposals, would be made. Hence the Department of the Environment took two steps in 1972. Firstly, it provided 'advice' in the form of a Development Control Policy Note on 'Out of town shops and shopping centres' (Department of the Environment, 1972). In this note the benefits of edge of town shopping were explained, and it was stated that

'It is not the function of land use planning to prevent
competition between retailers or between methods of
retailing nor to preserve existing commercial interests
as such' (para 6).

However the note then proceeded to warn planners of the dangers of 'over provision' of shops, thus reverting to the stance of encouraging the forecasting of floorspace 'requirements' as set out in the Development Plans Manual (Ministry of Housing and Local Government, 1970) (see 6.2.4). The note also warned against locally adverse effects of out of town development.

The second step taken by the Department was a request to local authorities to be informed of all applications for stores of over 50,000 square feet gross floor area outside existing town or district centres. The Department would then decide whether to 'call in' the application for its own decision; this was subsequently done in several cases, for which public inquiries were held.

In 1976 local authorities were sent a summary of the main issues which had been relevant in the Secretary of State's decisions at 21 inquiries over the period 1972-75 (Department of the Environment, 1976b). This summary indicated a variety of attitudes of inquiry inspectors to the main issues of economic impact, siting considerations and traffic generation, such that it was extremely difficult to discern any consistent attitude to these issues or to edge of town superstore proposals in general. Donaldsons (1976) in a much more thorough summary of these and other such inquiries, attempt however to draw some common conclusions. This report detects among inspectors a concern primarily for 'urban form and containment and the proper physical development of a site' (p.61); and rather less concern for 'functional and locational needs in development' (ibid). Also, the possible effects of the development upon existing retail facilities was overall the most important single reason for refusal, although in other cases this factor was stated by the inspector to be insignificant.

At the 24 inquiries into hypermarkets or superstores included in the Donaldsons review, 16 resulted in refusal while eight were approved.

At the same time the Department raised the limit for notification of superstore proposals to 100,000 square feet. This suggested that, partly as a result of the evidence on superstore impact, the Department now considered that a superstore (as opposed to hypermarket) application would be unlikely to raise major strategic planning issues. The Department has of course continued to be involved in planning inquiries held when the firm has appealed against refusal of planning permission.

In 1977 local authorities were asked to comment on a draft revision of the Development Control Policy Note, which indicated a more liberal attitude: a summary of the results of impact studies was also sent (Department of the Environment, 1977a). Subsequently a definitive new version of the Policy Note, now entitled 'Large new stores', was issued (Department of the Environment, 1977b).

Although containing much material from the 1972 Note, the new version, as implied in its title, brought a changed emphasis. The statements of factors to be taken into account by planning authorities remained much the same, but the emphasis was now upon superstores rather than out of town developments per se. The most important new recommendation was that large new stores should be located 'where they can serve not only those able to travel by car but also customers travelling on foot and by public transport' (para 10). Furthermore,

'Edge of town sites are only likely to be considered for developments where size, land requirements or some other factor precludes their location within the built up area and where such siting will not be detrimental to the interests of the inner areas of our towns and cities'. (ibid)

This policy appears to result more from the concern of a Labour government with inner city problems and the revival of public transport than from assimilation of the evidence of superstore impact. In particular, it is hard to see how an edge of town store could have much impact upon inner areas, except possibly in adding to the sense of deprivation felt by inner area residents. The note is also unhelpful in emphasising the importance of estimating the effect of a proposed development upon existing centres, and then in rejecting the use of mathematical models for this purpose.

Since this Note there have, at the time of writing, been no further major pronouncements. It remains to be seen whether the Conservative administration will adopt a new stance.

It must be concluded that this history of intervention and 'advice' does not do the government very much credit. At first attention was devoted, reasonably so, to the possible impact of large new stores on existing centres. Impact studies at Caerphilly and Eastleigh were supported by government funds, but their results were virtually ignored subsequently. The continued emphasis on economic impact involves planners in an area where there is no clear rationale for intervention, and where forecasting and evaluation are extremely difficult (Henderson, 1978). Finally, at no time has government advice concentrated on positive aspects of planning: that planning authorities might recognise the benefits of superstores and seek actively to incorporate proposals for them in structure or local plans. It is clear that this approach would be welcomed by the retail firms involved, who are naturally unhappy not only at being refused planning permission, but also at the length of time taken for a decision to be reached (Lee, 1976). Because of generally negative attitudes to superstore provision, firms have often presented proposals for almost any sites that can be made available to them: these sites, naturally, may be unacceptable on local land use planning grounds.

An example may make clearer the negativity of government policy taken as a whole. The 1972 Note (Department of the Environment, 1972, para 9) mentioned with approval the possibility of planning new district centres on the edge of urban areas, but did not make clear whether these might include superstores or not. This was not followed by any detailed advice on the planning of such centres. Perhaps partly as a result, development of such centres has been slow, and the proceedings of a seminar held to discuss such centres reveal much confusion over size, location, characteristics and mode of development (URPI, 1977a). The 1977 Note lacks any reference to edge of town district centres, presumbly because this would be inconsistent with its emphasis on inner area location.

The overall conclusion here must be that central government guidance to local authority planners is necessary, but that it should be much more positive. The rationale for planning intervention should be more clearly stated: the issues that planners should or should not take into account, and their relative importance, should be stated: the results of research should be related in a straightforward manner to these issues. Advice should be related to the incorporation of superstore proposals into planning policies, rather than focussing simply on reactions to planning applications.

8.2.6 Conclusions

This review of planning policies regarding superstores has shown that planners have been faced with very difficult decisions, in which they have had to take several factors into account. These relate to the welfare of consumers, both prosperous and poor: the economic health of existing retail facilities; and the general welfare of residents, which may be affected by negative externalities from development. These considerations could of course influence any planning decision on retailing matters. However the 'debate' over superstores has been a prominent feature of the planning press for several years: this seems to be partly because the superstore, especially where proposed for out of town locations, is far removed from the typical planner's vision of ideal retail facilities. In this he is usually supported by the local authority councillor, although perhaps for reasons connected more with the support of existing business interests. This means that the arguments against superstore proposals, although all valid in certain circumstances, have been used indiscriminately and often wrongly. Central government intervention has helped to clarify some of the issues involved, but has probably helped little towards making local authority decisions fairer and more consistent.

8.3 TOWARDS PLANNING POLICY GUIDELINES FOR SUPERSTORES

This final section suggests some guidelines for fair and positive planning policies with regard to superstores. The emphasis is not on finding a universal compromise which will meet the requirements of all parties, but more on providing a clear framework for policies. It is up to planners and politicians to decide which are the most important factors to take into account, but it is also necessary for the implications of any system of weighting of objectives to be fully understood.

8.3.1 A rationale for planning intervention

The existence of any planning policy to control superstore location must mean that it is considered necessary to intervene in the 'market' - here, in the locational decisions of superstore operators. Justification for such intervention can be examined with reference to the arguments developed in 6.1.4. It was concluded there that under present political conditions, intervention was required when market action would bring unacceptable negative externalities; or where it would have the effect of improving the operation of the market. This improvement could be measured against social as well as economic criteria; but extensive intervention on the grounds of social improvement would be limited by the need to retain profitability in the market's operations.

It follows that there are two reasons for planning intervention in the operation of retail firms that wish to build superstores. The first is that a superstore could bring unacceptable negative externalities: these could include visual effects, traffic generation, or severe economic impact resulting in closures of other shops. The second reason for intervention is that the planner wishes to maximise the benefits that superstores bring to the public. Intervention here is most likely to be in respect of location, and possibly also of timing and mode of development.

Intervention should be based upon decisions at local level. Central government involvement is necessary only to provide information upon which local decisions can be made, and also to rectify local decisions which appear to breach the limits of intervention as already discussed, or which are wrongly informed and unfair.

A further proposition should be made. If intervention is desired for the second reason discussed above - improvement of market operation on social and/or economic grounds - then it is necessary for planners to provide the market with guidelines, such that the market can adjust its plans in order to meet the social or economic objectives considered important. In the case of market operation involving development at specific locations, it will be helpful for planners to suggest actual locations, possibly after discussion with the private sector. The point here is that it is not sufficient for planners to oppose development of certain kinds in certain places on the grounds that such development is not of maximal benefit to society. It is essential to take positive steps in guiding development to the most appropriate locations, but such guidance must also take into account the costs of development at various locations.

8.3.2 Policies for development control

The stance explained above allows the planning refusal of superstore proposals on the grounds that the store would create significant negative externalities. Opposition simply on the grounds that the store is less than ideally located is as discussed above, invalid unless the planners can demonstrate that 'better' specific locations are available.

The nature of negative externalities from superstore development has already been discussed. Circumstances will vary between locations, and with size of store. However, some general guidelines have emerged from the research discussed in 8.2.3. The economic and traffic effects of a superstore are likely to be most severe where it is sited close to or within existing shopping centres, and least severe in an edge of town or rural location close to a major road. A large superstore will probably necessitate improvements to the immediately local road system to facilitate access by motorists, but it is within the spirit of the 'rules' of planning intervention, as discussed above, to ensure that any such costs are met by the firm.

Control over superstore development in the interests of visual impact and/or urban containment is also legitimate, but here it must be realised that such criteria are subjective. It is difficult thus to suggest any general rules for superstore location. However it would seem legitimate to oppose development on the grounds of 'loss of amenity' or other local land use reasons, only where appropriate policies have already been formulated. These policies should derive from a political will for containment and preservation of amenity, and they should apply to all forms of development.

8.3.3 Planning policies for superstore location

The case has been made above for positive policies for superstores:
this involves the planning authority in decisions concerning the number
of superstores in an area, and their approximate location and size. If
precise locations are proposed, then the planners should be able to
indicate that the land involved is actually available for development.

Definition of 'suitable' and 'unsuitable' locations requires knowledge
of particular circumstances, and it would be wrong to make dogmatic
general statements. The following discussion may however serve to
clarify the issues involved.

In an urban area six types of location for superstores may be
discerned, as follows:

    I)   In or at the edge of a town centre
   II)   In or at the edge of a district centre (existing)
  III)   In a proposed district centre in the inner urban area
   IV)   In a proposed district centre in the outer urban area
    V)   In some other location within the urban area
   VI)   In an edge of town or rural location, not associated with
       other shops.

In a broad statement of planning policy one would expect some choice
of one or more such general locations for superstores. Choice should be
made according to the principles established above: firstly, that
negative externalities, including economic impact upon other shops,
should be minimised. Secondly, the social benefits of the store should
be maximised. Thirdly, the store(s) must be economically viable and on
sites which are suitable physically.

It is necessary now to examine how well each of the types of location
is likely to perform in respect of these criteria. Figure 8.2 represents
an attempt to express this process of comparison. The six types of
location are as described above. The external, social and economic
criteria are derived from arguments from earlier parts of this chapter:
each is given in terms of minimising costs or maximising benefits.

In the limited space available it is not possible to discuss every
entry in the matrix. Generally speaking the ticks represent locations
which appear in principle to be advantageous in terms of specific
'benefit' criteria: the crosses similarly show disadvantages in cost
terms. In order that this treatment can be understood in terms of its
limitations, three assumptions should be stated. The first is that, no
matter what location, the same facility is proposed - a single storey
superstore with adequate car parking provision. The second is that
economic impact upon other shopping facilities (criteria A1-3) tends to
vary inversely with distance from the superstore: it is therefore
greatest in the centre within which it is located. The third is that
inaccessibility to a superstore (by any transport mode) is not a social
cost, but simply lack of benefit. This assumption is somewhat arguable
(see 8.2.4).

This matrix could be used in two broad ways. The first would be to
assign monetary values to all costs and benefits, or just to those
indicated as being of particular importance, and compute the total net
benefit for any locational type. It would be preferable to allow special
weighting for certain criteria which were considered to be particularly
important or unimportant. The exercise could also be extended to examine
costs and benefits to various social classes, or geographical areas.
All this would be very complex and would almost certainly involve a
number of dubious assumptions. The exercise would be more valuable if
actual locations were compared according to these criteria.

Figure 8.2   A simple evaluation process for superstore location policies

Criteria	I	II	III	IV	V	VI
			Locations			
A1	x					
A2		x	x	x	x	
A3			x	x		
A4	x	x				
A5		x	x	x		
A6	x	x				
A7						x
B1			✓	✓		
B2	✓	✓	✓			
B3		✓	✓	✓		
B4	✓	✓	✓	✓		
C1	✓					✓
C2				✓		✓
C3	x	x				
C4	x	x	x			

Key Locations
I   City Centre
II   Existing District Centre
III Proposed District Centre (inner)
IV   Proposed District Centre (outer)
V   Other urban
VI   Edge-of-town

Criteria   A External Costs

A1 Minimise economic impact upon town centre shops
A2 ----------------------------- suburban shops
A3 ----------------------------- proposed new centres
A4 Minimise traffic congestion
A5 Minimise disturbance to local residents by traffic
A6 Minimise intrusion into urban fabric
A7 ----------------------- countryside

B Social Benefits

B1 Maximise accessibility by car
B2 --------------------- by public transport
B3 --------------------- by foot
B4 Maximise potential for multi purpose trips

C Economic Benefits and Costs

C1 Maximise catchment population
C2 Maximise ease of car access and car parking
C3 Minimise land costs
C4 Minimise costs of site preparation

Symbols
✓   advantageous location in principle
x   disadvantageous location in principle
(blank) advantages and disadvantages slight

The second type of use is in identifying which costs (or absences of benefits) need correction through other planning action. For example, if in general terms a policy of inner urban new district centre location was favoured, then the costs of competition with existing facilities (A2), with other new shopping investment (A3), disturbance to local residents (A5), and cost of site preparation (C4), would have to be examined. It might be possible to choose a location for the district centre which rendered these costs insignificant, while retaining the four types of benefit identified.

One general point is clear from this matrix. Most superstore applications have been for locations V and VI, which appear from this analysis to offer relatively few substantial benefits or costs. Planners and councillors will favour locations I-IV, which offer substantial benefits and costs. Choice of any of these locational types means that planners must take a lead in identifying actual sites which are acceptable both to the retailer and to local residents. Locations V and VI appear in general to involve fewer problems, and therefore might be a wiser choice for the planning authority which is not prepared to intervene positively in the market.

A final word of caution is due in respect of the true hypermarket. It is unlikely that such a store with its considerable car parking requirements can be satisfactorily fitted into any town centre or district centre, except in special circumstances such as a new town. It appears by default that V and VI have to remain the most suitable hypermarket locations: if these are considered undesirable, then there is no place for the true hypermarket in many urban areas.

8.3.4 Conclusions

This chapter has examined the British evidence about hypermarkets and superstores, their characteristics and impact. The reaction of planning authorities has been shown to be often ill informed. More and more authorities now appear however to be considering more positive policies in which superstores are treated in much the same way as other modern forms of development: welcomed in principle and steered to locations where they can prove to be of greatest net benefit. It is hoped that the main value of this chapter is in setting out systematic principles for fair and productive planning policies of this kind.

NOTES

(1) The term 'superstore' in this chapter includes superstores and hypermarkets, except where indicated.
(2) Green belts, which may be 'official' (approved in Ministerial statements) or, more often, 'unofficial' or 'interim', are designed so as to limit the expansion of urban areas within them. A secondary purpose is to provide outdoor recreational opportunities for residents of these urban areas. Once designated, green belts are usually protected consistently against any urban development.
(3) Some superstore firms provide free bus services from more accessible locations. Their impact is not clear.
(4) Inequality and inequity are not identical concepts: the term equity 'implies fairness or justice in the distribution of society's benefits and penalties' (Smith, 1977, p.138).

9   Local shopping problems

This chapter deals with an issue very different in character from that
discussed in Chapter 8. The central theme is pressures created by
decline instead of growth: the decline is in standards of local
shopping. In this chapter an attempt is made firstly to provide a
structured description and explanation of local shopping problems in
Britain, and then, to examine the present and possible future role of
town planning policies in alleviating such problems.

'Local shops' is a term incapable of exact definition. It suggests
proximity of shops to consumers, but almost any shop will be local for
some people. As used in this chapter, it indicates those shops which
are useful to consumers mainly because they are local. Almost all
consumers have routine shopping needs that have to be fulfilled
frequently, and it is convenient that these needs should be met close to
the home.

The differences between 'local shops', 'small shops', and 'small
shopkeepers', should be clarified. 'Local shops' as used in this chapter
is a term relating shops spatially to their consumers: there is no
direct implication of size or type of shop. 'Small shops' are usually
defined as being below a certain size, although there is no clear
agreement on actual size limits. The 'small shopkeeper' may either be
the owner of a small shop, or the owner of an 'independent' retail firm
(4.4.1). It is usually implied that the small shopkeeper both owns and
manages one or a small number of shops. Now clearly many small shopkeepers will own shops which serve almost entirely a local function;
and many shops which are used mainly by local people will be small and
independent owned. But there is by no means an exact congruence.

It follows that in discussing local shopping problems it is not
sufficient simply to discuss problems of small shops or small shopkeepers, as has been done elsewhere (A.D. Smith, 1971; Kirby, 1975;
Davies, 1976b; Berry, 1977; 1978).

Since the term 'local' relates to retailers and consumers, it is
necessary in defining local shopping problems to involve consumers.
The view is taken in this chapter that local shops should fulfil certain
requirements of consumers. When consumers find that their requirements
are not being met satisfactorily, or less so than before, then 'local
shopping problems' can be said to exist.

The next section discusses the nature of consumers' general
requirements for local shops, using evidence of shopping behaviour and
attitudes from several British surveys. The following section describes
and explains the important current types of local shopping problem,
using evidence of difficulties met by the supply side in providing and
maintaining local shops in various types of geographical environment.
Finally, an attempt is made to suggest realistic public sector policies
for tackling local shopping problems, consistent with the views on
rationales for intervention developed in previous chapters.

9.2 CONSUMERS' REQUIREMENTS FOR LOCAL SHOPS

Consumers' requirements for local shops have to be inferred from two
kinds of evidence. The first is of actual usage of local shops: some
general points can be made from the results of recent shopping surveys
in Britain. The second type of evidence is that supplied by shoppers in
answer to questions about their attitudes to local shops. In both cases
it is necessary to generalise from evidence of diverse behaviour and
attitudes, and one important conclusion must be that local shops are of
far greater importance for certain groups in the population than for
others.

9.2.1 Walking to the shops

A relevant specification for local shops, in urban areas at least, is
that they should be within walking distance of the home. This statement
needs to be justified first, and then an attempt can be made to define
the limits to 'walking distance'.

It can be established that in the recent past, walking has been the
most common mode for shopping trips in Britain; it seems very likely
that this is still the case. Its precise degree of importance is
unclear. The survey carried out for the IPC Women's Weekly Group (1970,
Table 2) shows that in 1970, 59 per cent of the housewives interviewed
carried out their main grocery shopping trip on foot. In response to
another survey held in 1970, only 41 per cent of female respondents
stated that they made their main 'household' shopping trip on foot
(Bradley and Fenwick, 1975, Table 13). The percentage of all food
shopping trips may be higher, since both reports show that nearly all
housewives made more than one trip per week, and that most of them would
not call every trip a 'main' trip. It is reasonable to suppose that
many of the non-main or 'subsidiary' trips are usually made on foot since
they involve a lower volume of purchases than the main trip.

An important reason for this state of affairs is that only a small
minority of housewives have access to a car for shopping trips at any
time of the week. Only about 20 per cent of the adult women in the UK
held driving licenses in 1972 (Hillman, 1973), and not all of these
would have a car available at all times. Variations in licence holding
and car availability among housewives have been investigated by Hillman
et al (1973; 1976). The latter survey found that even within the
prosperous London Outer Metropolitan Area, only 29 per cent of women
with young children had full optional use of a car for shopping (Hillman
et al, 1976, p.64). As only a small percentage use bicycles for food
shopping (IPC, 1970, Table 2), the choice for most housewives is between
public transport (usually bus) and walking. The latter is normally
quicker than public transport for journeys of up to one mile or more
(Hillman et al, 1973, p.23); it is also cheaper, except where free bus
travel is made available to pensioners and disabled people. Walking
provides more opportunity for chance meeting with acquaintances; is
healthier; and more convenient for the housewife taking small children
or pets on the shopping trip.

The topic of 'walking distance' is one which has concerned planners
for many years, and distances of a quarter mile (0.4 km) or a half mile
(0.8 km) are variously given as acceptable maxima. Evidence of behaviour
suggests that many shoppers are prepared to walk much greater distances,
as Table 9.1 shows. It has also been inferred from a survey of housewives' shopping behaviour carried out in 1969, that:
    'Watford housewives who opted to walk to their nearest

shops rather than use an available car lived within 600m
or so, and those who opted to walk rather than bus lived
within a radius of about 1 km.' (Daws, 1974, p.13)

Table 9.1   Transport mode analysed by length of journey

Transport Mode	Under ½ ml. %	Length of Journey ½-1 ml. %	1-2 ml. %	2-3 ml. %	Over 3 ml. %
Walk	86	55	27	6	3
Car	11	29	36	54	68
Public Transport	4	17	34	44	33
Other	1	3	5	1	-
Base (informants mainly responsible for household shopping)	485	161	209	108	192
Base as % of sample	42.0	13.9	18.1	9.4	16.6

Notes: 1. The data refer to main 'household' (i.e. convenience goods)
          shopping trips.
       2. Questions asked were: 'When you go shopping on your main day,
          ... how far is that from your home (workplace, etc.) ... how
          do you usually get there ?'
       3. Figures in this table consistently add up to slightly over
          100 per cent. The reason for this is not given in the source
          table.
       4. Source: Bradley and Fenwick, 1975, Table 14(ii).

9.2.2 Usage of local shops

Relationships between household shopping and local shops can now be
examined. Bruce (1976), drawing upon experience of several surveys
carried out by the Building Research Establishment, makes two important
points:
    'Over a long period there is some evidence that average
    shopping frequency has been declining gradually. However,
    one would hesitate to say that the national average for food
    shopping is now less than three and a half trips a week.
    There is probably one extra trip or visit to shops to buy
    other goods or to use services. But the data ... suggest
    quite strongly that the trend to one major food shopping
    expedition a week is continuing.'
Bruce shows that in deciding upon the destination for the main food
shopping trip, distance of the centre from the home is merely one of
several important considerations, which include the selection of shops,
parking facilities and typical price levels. Travel time may appear more
important than physical distance, and many housewives use a car for main
food shopping trips. In these circumstances it appears that the major
role of local shopping centres (especially when these are small) is to
supply food and household goods in non main trips. Surveys have shown
local shops to be used often, but for relatively small sums to be spent
there. For example, Day (1973) found that in Crawley New Town 82 per
cent of his sample used local food shops, but only 37 per cent of total

expenditure on food took place in them. Small local shops and centres will also continue to act as main sources for a minority of housewives, particularly those who buy food almost every day of the week. Housewives without access to a car may be prepared to carry out their main food shopping trip in a town centre, using public transport; otherwise they will probably have to rely on their local shops.

These conclusions have to be offered tentatively, and without proper quantification, because comparative studies of behaviour such as Bruce (1976) show a great deal of variation between one area and another. Surveys in Britain (e.g. Daws and Bruce, 1971; Davies, 1973b; Bradley and Fenwick, 1975) have demonstrated some consistent variations with age, social class, income and car ownership (5.4). In particular, it appears that young (18-24) or old (over 65) shoppers are more likely to use small local shops for main household shopping trips. This appears to reflect preferences as well as mobility, since non car owners in other age groups appear more prepared to use public transport for main trips. However, car owners in general are likely to use cars for main shopping trips, and often travel to centres outside the immediately local area. It appears also that differences in the size and quality of local shopping centres influence behaviour (Hillman et al, 1976, pp.80-83). But all types of shopper, even including those with cars available all week, tend to walk to local shops for secondary or 'topping up' trips.

9.2.3 Attitudes to local shops: general findings

Attitudes to local shops have been expressed by consumers in response to several surveys. These include opinions of the value of local shops in principle; and opinions of the most useful combination of shops comprising local centres.

It seems that most consumers value 'convenience' very highly with regard to their food and household shopping. For example, while 90 per cent of the IPC sample said that they usually used the same shops for food purchases, half of this number said that this was because they were the nearest and most convenient shops (IPC, 1970, p.12). The OPCS survey relates preferences more clearly to actual behaviour. Those shoppers who found their household shopping in general to be 'very convenient' (47 per cent of the total) were more likely to walk to the shops, and undergo shorter trips than other shoppers (Bradley and Fenwick, 1975, p.13). The authors thus suggest that 'no matter how useful a car may be, living within easy walking distance of the shops cannot be beaten for shopping convenience' (ibid).

The percentage of housewives wanting to have shops locally appears to be higher than the percentage actually using them. The survey of Watford housewives carried out in 1969 by the Building Research Station found that 95 per cent of those interviewed felt that 'it really mattered' to have shops near where they lived (Bruce, 1974). In subsequent surveys, between 81 per cent and 92 per cent of respondents agreed with the more searching proposition that 'small local shops are essential, even if their prices are higher' (Bruce, 1976). In the Bowlby (1979) survey, 58 per cent agreed and 32 per cent of the sample disagreed that 'the convenience of local shops is worth the extra it can cost' (Table 14.7).

9.2.4 'Essential' and 'desirable' local shops

Further questions in the Watford survey asked which types of shop were most desired locally (Daws and Bruce, 1971, Table 39). Those which were mentioned by a majority of respondents are listed in Table 9.2. The list

Table 9.2   Shops required near the home

'Essential' Shops	%	'Desirable' Shops	%
Chemist	98	Fishmonger	66
Post Office	97	Bank	65
Grocer	96	Hardware	63
Baker	95	Draper	62
Butcher	94	Shoe Repairer	57
Greengrocer	94	Hairdresser	52
Newsagent	94	Dry cleaner	51

Notes: 1. This table is based upon interviews held with 1,003 housewives
in the Watford area in 1969. The percentages represent those
respondents who said they definitely would require these
types of shop locally, on moving to a new house.

2. The terms 'essential' and 'desirable' are the present
author's.

3. Source: Daws and Bruce (1971), Table 39.

Table 9.3   Housewives' ratings of shopping centres

Type of Centre	Average Scale Score
One grocer's shop	3.01
Five or six small shops	4.81
(One supermarket on its own)	5.00)
A lot of small shops	5.39
Two supermarkets together	6.12
One supermarket together with some small shops	6.14
One hypermarket on its own	6.58
Two supermarkets with some smaller shops	7.01

Notes: 1. This table is based upon interviews held with about 800
housewives in four different areas in 1974-75. Respondents
were asked to rate the different types of centre as places
for getting their food shopping, by giving them scores out
of ten. 'One supermarket on its own' was allocated a score
of 5.0, to anchor the scale at one point.

2. Source: Bruce and Delworth (1976), p.33.

---

falls conveniently into two groups, which may be termed 'essential' and
'desirable' shops. The seven essential types of shop were each mentioned
by over 90 per cent of respondents, and the seven desirable types by
between 50 per cent and 66 per cent. Inclusion of chemists and post
offices in the first group indicates that these facilities are desired
by all segments of the population and not just by the elderly, who may
apparently need them the most.

The nature of the shops themselves seems to be at least as important
as the range of goods that they supply. Table 9.3 based upon the
surveys described by Bruce (1976), shows that one supermarket may be
regarded as slightly preferable to 'five or six small shops'. This is
because the supermarket often carries out the functions of the baker,
butcher and greengrocer, as well as that of the grocer, selling many
kinds of packaged and fresh foods under one roof. There is clearly no

longer any significant consumer resistance in principle to supermarkets, but there is still evidence that they are not generally regarded as ideal sources for all types of food. The IPC survey shows (IPC, 1970, Section V) that supermarkets are more popular than counter service grocers for packaged groceries; this seems to be partly because of the advantages of self service, and partly because supermarkets usually have a much wider selection of goods, and at somewhat lower prices. However, the same survey shows (Section VII) that supermarkets are much less popular for perishable foods. For example, of housewives who went to a super- market on their main food shopping trip (69 per cent of the total), only 26 per cent bought fresh meat there, and 51 per cent bought fresh meat elsewhere (presumably at a specialist butcher). Freshness of food bought in specialist shops was the most important single reason for buying food there. (1)   All this suggests that one supermarket is not adequate for food shopping, but one supermarket plus some specialist food shops may be so. A centre comprising two supermarkets plus smaller shops is rated very highly (Table 9.3).

This should be expected from a consideration of 'attitudes' to shopping as an activity (5.3.3). The 'economic' shopper will want to compare prices between a number of stores, and may be suspicious of the potential 'monopoly' position of one isolated store.   Other types of shopper will discriminate between shops on grounds of atmosphere, cleanliness, friendliness of staff, etc.   So most shoppers are likely to prefer to choose between a number of stores, even for the most basic food requirements, rather than be restricted to just one shop.

9.2.5 A 'basic' local shopping centre

From the evidence presented in this section, it is possible to derive the composition of a 'basic' local shopping centre which would meet the immediate requirements of local shoppers. The question of economic viability of the shops themselves is being ignored for the moment.   The centre could then be as follows:

    1 Supermarket selling a wide range of packaged groceries, plus
      meat, bread, fruit and vegetables;
    1 Butcher's shop;
    1 Baker's shop*;
    1 Greengrocer's shop*;
    1 Newsagent/Confectioner/Tobacconist;
    1 Dispensing Chemist;
    1 Sub Post Office+.

    * Either or both of these shops could store some packaged groceries.
    + To share premises with one of the other types, probably the
      Newsagent.

The centre might also include one or more of the 'desirable' types, depending on circumstances.

The list given above would meet the basic criteria for local shopping centres. Fresh meat, vegetables and bread would be available, and the additional presence of these items in the supermarket would introduce an element of competition over price and quality. Those who disliked the supermarket would be able to buy many of their food goods in the other shops. On the other hand, there seems little point in having more than one newsagent or chemist, as the goods and services here do not vary much from one small shop to the next.

9.2.6 Conclusions

This section has attempted to show that it is possible to derive outline standards of local shopping provision and location from the requirements of shoppers. The basic requirement is that routine purchases of food and household goods can be made within walking distance of the home. This need seems to be felt whether or not the shopper is likely to use local shops at all regularly. It appears also that the larger a local centre is, the more popular it will be - this relationship is probably more important than the classic 'distance decay' relationship, which holds that (ceteris paribus) the closer a centre is to the home, the more popular it will be. Since most shoppers seem to be prepared to walk at least half a mile to the shops, the distance decay factor is probably unimportant at this very local level. On the other hand, shoppers value highly the presence of a supermarket (or better, two supermarkets), fresh food shops, a post office and a chemist in their local shops. Even with these facilities provided, a substantial number of shoppers will choose to travel further on their main trip, and possibly on subsidiary trips, to take advantage of lower prices, better selection of goods, and other advantages at more distant centres. Thus the main value of local shops is often in meeting immediate needs during the early part of the week, when main trips are uncommon.

The nature of these requirements raises some problems, which are discussed further in the rest of this chapter. It is unlikely that substantial shopping centres can be provided within walking distance of all the population in all urban areas, especially if many of the shoppers in these areas are not going to use those centres to the full. Compromises have to be made, and the nature of these compromises will reflect the requirements of developers, retailers, and planners as discussed below.

9.3 LOCAL SHOPPING PROBLEMS: A DESCRIPTION AND EXPLANATION

9.3.1 Introduction

As suggested in 9.1, local shopping problems arise when consumers find their local shopping requirements are not being met by the local shopping system. This implies either that changes have occurred in the system, or that consumers have moved to an area in which the system appears inadequate. In order to investigate local shopping problems it is necessary to examine the supply side - retailers, developers and local authority planners.

This section starts with a summary of recent trends in local shop provision in general. This is followed by a discussion of the impact upon local shopping systems of supermarkets and superstores. Finally a brief review of local shopping problems is given for three types of geographical area. Firstly, inner urban areas, where two types of change in the supply side have occurred. The first is a tendency for small shops which serve local shoppers to close down; the second, much more localised, is the change of shops from the types identified in 9.2.5 to other types of little specific local value. The second geographical area is the outer suburb, where it is shown that local shopping facilities provided in recent years have tended to be inadequate. The third area discussed is the rural settlement, where trends similar to those observed in inner urban areas have led to serious deprivation for those shoppers lacking adequate transport arrangements.

9.3.2 National trends in local shop numbers

There is an immediate problem in examining trends in the provision of
local shops in Britain: the 'local shop' as defined in this chapter
does not strictly resemble any category of shop for which statistics are
available. The most appropriate statistics available in Census of
Distribution tables are those for the classes of shop usually termed
'convenience' in this country – food retailers, and confectioner/tobacc-
onist/newsagents. This is by no means an exact fit with the whole set
of local shops as defined above. The definition of shop types in Census
data, particularly for 1961 and 1966, is not sufficiently detailed for
one to be able to discriminate between shops selling true convenience
goods, and those of the shopping and specialist categories. No shop
will sell goods entirely of one of these categories, but most will deal
mainly in one, with 'local' shops dealing mainly in convenience goods.
In addition, some 'convenience' stores are of more than local importance.
The 1971 tables, with a more detailed classification of types of shop,
and with tabulations of goods sold against types of shop, are much more
helpful than earlier versions, but the presence of useful data for just
one point in time does not allow the discernment of trends.

With these provisos in mind, one can use time series derived from
Census data to give some indication of trends in the provision of local
shops. Table 9.4 shows total numbers in those shop types most likely to
include a substantial proportion of local shops, for the years 1961,
1966 and 1971. The table shows an overall decline in the number of
retail shops, slightly more rapid in the first five years than the
second. The rate of decline in most types of 'convenience' shops was
well above the overall average: if defined as food retailers plus
confectioner/tobacconist/newsagent, their total fell by 81,670 (24.6 per
cent of the 1961 total) over the ten years. The number of other shops
rose slightly in the same period, by 12,360 (5.9 per cent).

The form of organisation within which a shop belongs may also have
some bearing on whether it serves 'local' functions or not. Other
commentators in describing recent trends in numbers of 'small' shops
(e.g. Davies, 1976b) have concentrated on data of 'independent'
retailers (i.e. those retail firms with 1-10 branches). While many local
shops will be owned by large multiple firms or co-operatives, the
independently owned convenience shop is most likely to have a purely
local function. Table 9.5 shows that over 1961-1971 the rate of decline
of independently owned shops was slightly below the overall rate. Here
the rate of decline eased considerably in the second five year period,
for independently owned shops in general, and for independently owned
food shops, but not confectioner/tobacconist/newsagents.

The evidence suggests a steady decline in numbers of local shops, due
more to the nature of the goods sold in them than to factors concerned
with their organisational structure. This seems likely from the wide
variation in rates of decline between the type of trade included in
Table 9.4 and the much smaller degree of variation between rates of
decline between independently owned and other shops.

The variations between trades are of some interest, although in the
absence of more detailed knowledge of changes in organisational structure
or location of shops, it is difficult to suggest consistent arguments of
cause and effect. In a general manner the changes reflect changes in
retail organisation and in consumer behaviour, discussed elsewhere (e.g.
Distributive Trades EDC, 1971; Davies, 1976a). The declines in numbers
of food shops and tobacconists must, as discussed below, stem partly
from the rapidly increasing competition by supermarkets over this period,

157

Table 9.4   Changes in selected shop types, 1961-1971

Type	Number of Retail Shops 1961	1966	1971	Change 1961-71 as % of 1961
All retail establishments	542,301	504,412	472,991	-12.8
Grocers and provision dealers	146,777	123,385	105,283	-28.3
Other food retailers	114,655	104,359	92,524	-19.3
Butchers	42,419	38,351	33,939	-20.0
Fishmongers & poulterers	6,330	5,466	4,678	-26.1
Greengrocers & fruiterers	33,073	27,172	23,318	-29.5
Bread and flour confectioners	17,260	18,099	17,299	+ 0.2
Off-Licences	9,000	10,815	9,437	+ 4.9
Confectioners, tobacconists, newsagents	70,108	63,333	52,064	-25.7
Hardware, china, paints and wallpaper	25,103	25,809	26,461	+ 5.4
Chemists and photographic dealers	18,097	17,959	16,670	- 7.9
Shoe repairers	11,154	8,769	5,494	-50.7
Hairdressers	40,152	47,632	47,191	+17.5

Notes: 1. Figures are for Great Britain
        2. This table is not comprehensive, but covers those shop
           types in which local shops are most likely to occur.
        3. Source: Department of Industry (1975), Table 3, Table A.

Table 9.5   Changes in independently owned shops, 1961-1971

Type	Number of Retail Shops 1961	1966	1971	Change 1961-71 as % of 1961	Indep. as % of total 1971
All Retail establishments	446,204	403,876	390,793	-12.4	82.6
Grocers and p.d.'s	116,336	96,451	86,565	-25.6	82.2
Other food retailers	89,811	77,563	72,198	-19.6	78.0
Con/tob/news	64,054	56,899	46,260	-27.8	88.9
Hardware etc.	22,438	22,949	23,728	+ 5.7	89.7
Chemists and photo.	14,375	14,290	13,447	- 6.5	80.7

Notes: 1. 2. and 3. as in Table 9.4.
        4. 'Independent' ownership means that the firm owning
           the shop possesses 1-10 shops.

although surprisingly there was no decline in bread shops or off-licences, which might also have suffered this competition. The increases in numbers of off-licences hardware stores and hairdressers probably reflect real increases in consumer expenditure for goods or services available in these shops.

It is clear that most of the shop types required near the home (Table 9.2) were in decline over this period. Of the 'essential' types, all except baker, post office (2) and chemist (3) declined in numbers at a rapid rate, but the performance of the 'desirable' types was more variable. Generally, the figures indicate a rate of decline in local shops more rapid than the overall rate, and within the population of local shops, a more rapid decline in food shops and confectioner/tobacc-onists. This means that standards of provision are both declining and changing in nature.

9.3.3 The impact of supermarkets

Many writers have ascribed the decline in the numbers of small food shops to the effects of increased competition from larger supermarkets and other convenience outlets. The widespread introduction of super-markets in the 1960s was associated with an increase in the rate of decline in food shops generally, although the links between cause and effect are not straightforward. Two separate processes occurred during this period, and continue in the 1970s. The first is that large retail firms and co-operative societies make decisions to close some of their smaller branches which are regarded as unprofitable. The closure of many small stores is thus associated with the opening of a few very large stores, but it cannot be said that one event leads to the other. The second process is that the small shop loses part of its custom, which is said to be lured to the larger stores by factors such as lower prices, greater variety of goods, and other advantages of self service operation. After this loss of trade the shop may become unprofitable, and is forced to close.

There is clear evidence of the first of these processes. In the 1960s rates of closure were somewhat faster in food trades for both multiple and co-operative owned shops than for independent owned, although the latter with their high share of the total accounted for most of the loss in numbers (Table 9.5). In the 1970s, multiple branches are continuing to close at a high rate as a result of the policies described above (Tisdall, 1976a; Benwell Community Project, 1979).

Documented instances of substantial loss of trade caused by retail growth nearby are rare. One can, however, postulate a number of ways by which this process could take place. The first would be that the shopper deserts the small shop and visits the new, larger competitor instead, simply because of price advantages etc. This is plausible, but there are several advantages held by the small local shop, such as familiarity and accessibility (4.4; 9.2) which mean that it will retain much of its trade in the face of competition. The second possibility is that the shopper switches her attentions to a larger store after her favourite small store closes down. In these circumstances the store, when reopened by a new owner, may not recapture this trade and may thus be unprofitable. The third possibility is that the shopper moves house and, having no loyalties to any of the new set of local shops, decides to patronise a supermarket. This can mean a net loss for small shop-keepers. The fourth is longer term: in any area the older shoppers suffer loss in income, illness, and death, and are in effect replaced by young shoppers who are less likely to establish loyalties to

159

particular shops. This represents a net loss of trade for the small shop sector without any conscious change of habit by consumers.

It would be impossible to determine the importance of each of these sub processes, or even to distinguish their operation in any empirical study. But if we allow that the indirect sub processes are as important as the direct, then it follows that changes in the use made of local shops – and thus in their general viability – reflect demographic changes among both shopkeepers and consumers as much as any direct impact of new shops themselves.

9.3.4 The impact of hypermarkets and superstores

Concern has been expressed in recent years that hypermarkets and super-stores will drain custom from local shops and force them to close (e.g. Hillman, 1973). This view seems somewhat alarmist in the light of recent reports on the impact of superstores and hypermarkets in this country (8.2.3). These have shown little evidence of small food shops closing as a direct result of competition from the new store. Also, the reports agree that the new stores attract shoppers from existing medium sized supermarkets to a much greater extent than from small local shops. This is not surprising, because (as established above) the shopper using local food shops is unlikely to be tempted entirely away from them.

This argument is perhaps simplistic. In many cases the 'local shop' will in fact be a medium sized supermarket owned by a large firm or co-operative. In this instance the local shop will probably lose some of its trade. For this reason it seems likely that the impact of large new developments may be greatest in newly developed residential areas, served only by a small number of supermarkets.

It appears though that the more traditional small local shop is little affected, at least in the short term, by retail developments elsewhere. (4) It seems possible that the impact of supermarkets in the 1960s has been gradual and indirect rather than sudden and direct. Many traders have in any case attempted to establish a competitive position with the supermarket by introducing self service, or by subscribing to 'voluntary' groups to take advantage of bulk purchasing facilities (Kirby, 1974; 1975). It follows that much of the decline in the numbers of local shops should be ascribed to causes other than the impact of retail developments elsewhere. These will be discussed in the following three sub sections.

9.3.5 Local shop closures in inner urban areas

A very large part of the decline in numbers of local shops noted above (9.3.2) has been caused by the closure of small shops in inner urban areas – those areas built substantially before 1914. It is this phenomenon that has attracted most of the recent attention to local shopping problems.

The concept of 'stress' as a precondition of locational decisions has become familiar in industrial location studies (e.g. Hamilton, 1974; Cooper, 1975). Stress may be caused by internal forces, such as the need to increase production or sales beyond the limits possible within the confines of the site; or external forces. These external forces may either derive from within the industry concerned, for example increased competition from other firms; or they may be imposed by agencies unconnected with the operations of the firm. Examples of the latter are population movements, termination of lease, takeovers, and compulsory purchase for redevelopment.

Retailers may respond to stress in a variety of ways. The well organised multiple firm will react by closing 'unprofitable' branches. The independent retailer may however attempt to continue for as long as possible under increasingly difficult conditions. Moving to another location is likely to present problems of reorganisation and finance to shopkeepers already under pressure. In any case, rents and rates for new premises are far higher than for most existing shop premises, thus constraining the shopkeeper's choice of location. Since the small shopkeeper is often unwilling to consider expanding his business, (4.4.3) he is unlikely to want to move his location, and under pressure to do so may decide to close instead.

At this point it is necessary to consider the events that create this pressure, and to attempt to assess their effects upon local shops in Britain. Here one should distinguish between external events that affect the viability of a shop, and those that actually force the retailer to close down.

Events affecting viability of a shop include changes in catchment population, and changes in the shopping centre of which the shop itself forms a part. Changes in catchment population – both in numbers and socio economic characteristics – have been widespread in inner city areas in Britain. The most common trend has been a fall in population due partly to local authority slum clearance programmes, and partly to a general fall in average household size. (5) Slum clearance programmes can have dramatic effects on catchment populations even where the shop itself is not demolished: case studies show that redevelopment programmes can lead to very high rates of vacancy of shop premises in inner city areas (Butler, 1976, p.53; Maroney, 1976, Table II; Benwell Community Project, 1979, Chapter 2).

At a more general level, Shepherd and Thorpe (1977) have identified housing clearance as a major contributory factor to the decline in numbers of food shops during the 1960s. They demonstrate a strong statistical relationship between percentage loss in number of shops of all types and percentage of housing stock demolished, for a sample of towns. The relationship was strongest for grocers, clothing shops and household goods shops: independent and multiple/co-operative stores were all strongly affected. It is not clear whether this relationship is due mainly to physical loss of premises through clearance, or to loss of population catchment. The former appears to be important, since the relationship between retail change and population change itself over the same period was generally much weaker.

9.3.6 Other local shop changes in inner urban areas

As well as absolute decline, other important changes have taken place in inner urban areas. These may be categorised into three types, although they all represent a slowing down of the process of absolute decline.

Firstly, ethnic changes in ownership. Inner urban districts with substantial non white populations tend to develop local shops owned by the same ethnic group. Research by Cater and Jones (1978; 1979) shows that these shops often have extremely long opening hours, but appear to present very low financial rewards for the owners. Almost certainly, many shops are thus being kept alive which in other circumstances would have closed for lack of trade.

The second and third types of change are both from traditional convenience goods stores to other trades. In areas of declining population and static or declining demand for retail space, the convenience goods stores that close may be partially replaced by 'marginal' traders.

These sell cheap and poor quality new or second hand goods, or offer
repair services (Benwell Community Project, 1979, pp.23-24): they tend
to close after a short period and appear similar to the 'unstable' small
shops discussed in 4.4.5. In similar vein, Davies (1976b, 1977b) has
described 'twilight' activities typically found in inner city shopping
ribbons.

A final type of change occurs in circumstances of economic revival
caused by an influx of higher income groups into an area. The most
striking examples of this have occurred in inner London, where commercial
premises of almost any kind in certain areas are in demand for uses such
as boutique, restaurant or antique shop. These types of trader can pay
much higher rent than ordinary shopkeepers, and many local shops have
thus disappeared, especially after landlords' rent reviews. The
situation has become serious in some cases and local consumers have
formed pressure groups, the most notable of which is the 'Save Our Local
Shops' campaign (Brown, 1977; Lock, 1976). Here the problem is not
likely to be a total loss of useful local shops, but the loss of some
shops such as greengrocers and their replacement by shops or services
used only rarely by local people.

It seems that this type of problem occurs mainly in inner London at
present: the likelihood of it becoming serious in other cities seems
fairly remote. Recent years have seen the growth of the types of shop
mentioned above in many provincial cities and tourist centres, but in
most cities there is a selection of readily available and cheap property
on the fringe of the town centre, or in inner suburbs. This will often
satisfy the locational requirements of traders such as antique dealers.

The Save Our Local Shops Campaign has gained a lot of attention in the
press, partly one suspects because of its espousal by articulate middle
class residents of the areas which have suffered from this invasion of
non local shops and services. This problem has tended to become
confused with the much more pervasive and serious problem of the general
decline of local shops in inner city areas. This confusion enters not
only the descriptions of local shopping problems but also proposals for
remedies (e.g. AMA, 1976; Brown, 1977; see below).

9.3.7 Local shopping in outer urban areas

Problems of adequacy of local shops in outer urban areas have received
much less attention in the planning press. This may seem surprising,
since local shops are generally far less numerous in residential areas
built largely since 1918, and especially so in recent suburban estates.
Residents of such areas appear to have far poorer standards of access to
essential or desirable goods and services than do those in inner areas,
as the author's studies of the Reading area demonstrate (Guy, 1976a;
1977a, Chapter 8; see also Bowlby, 1979).

There are two basic reasons for this situation. Firstly, post-1918
residential areas are generally of much lower population density than
pre-1914. This means that even if shops are provided at the same rate
per 1,000 population (say) as in inner areas, there will be far fewer
shops per unit area. Secondly, the supply of shop premises in outer
areas has been controlled by policies of land use zoning, whereas in
inner areas shops have arisen largely through the conversion of houses.
Zoning policies existed before 1939 and led to purpose built 'shopping
parades', usually located at major road intersections. Shops were
typically small with living accommodation provided for the shopkeeper
behind and above the shop.

Since the war there has been an intensification in the process of

providing new shops in purpose built units located in planned shopping
centres. These centres have been developed by property development
companies, or local authorities and new town development corporations,
or partnerships, or in recent years by retail firms. The most significant trend however has been a reduction in the number and variety of
local shops typically provided in new residential developments. This is
clearly demonstrated in a historical review of shopping provision in new
town neighbourhoods since the start of the new towns programme in the
early 1950s. Up to the mid 1960s it was normal to provide centres of
about 8-12 small shops for residential 'neighbourhoods' of 5,000 or so:
in addition, larger 'district centres' were often provided for groups
of three or four neighbourhoods. But more recently the local or
neighbourhood centres have often been no more than one shop unit
comprising a supermarket and newsagent-tobacconist. The district centres,
increasingly likely to be based around a superstore, continue to be
built, but now have to provide many of the functions formerly fulfilled
by neighbourhood centres, without offering their accessibility. A more
detailed review is available in Guy (1976b; 1977a, Chapter 6).
    There appear to be two broad reasons for this state of affairs. The
first is that loyalty to local shops in new residential areas is likely
to be low: young married couples are usually strongly represented in
such areas, and these households are likely to use 'economic' criteria
in choosing where to shop, and to own cars to enable them to reach
larger stores and centres. The second reason is that new premises cost
far more to buy or rent than pre-war, and therefore the turnover in a
new shop has to be much higher than normal for a local shop. Retailers
are therefore unwilling to take what they regard as substantial risks.
The price is high and the rewards uncertain.
    These factors have led to an inadequacy in local shops in many new
residential areas. For most households the inadequacy is in terms of
emergency or topping up trips, but for a minority without cars a
necessity arises for tedious and possibly expensive trips to town or
district centre in order to buy everyday convenience goods.

9.3.8 Local shopping problems in rural areas

Local shopping problems clearly exist in rural areas, but there is little
conclusive information on their extent, or on recent trends.
Commentators (e.g. Dawson, 1976a) suggest that there has been a
substantial decline in numbers of food and other convenience shops in
villages in Britain during this century. In recent years the decline
appears to have continued, except in scenically attractive areas where
village stores have been popular acquisitions for exurbanites. The
decline in numbers of local shops has also been obscured in Census data
by growth in rural souvenir, craft and antique shops which deal mainly
with tourists and have little if any local function.
    Surveys of Norfolk villages (Norfolk C.C., 1976; Harman, 1978) have
shown that villages of similar population may vary widely in numbers of
food shops: it is clearly incorrect to assume some general 'threshhold'
population for a village local shop. The former report does however
show that about 90 per cent of villages with over 250 population
possessed at least one food shop.
    Such shops share a number of characteristics with the urban 'corner
shop'. They tend to have limited stocks, especially of fresh food, and
charge high prices compared with supermarkets. They are thus unlikely
to appeal to the 'economic' consumer. Their importance lies in three
aspects. Firstly, they represent an accessible source of goods in

emergency or for 'topping up' between major shopping trips. Secondly, for shoppers without the use of a car, they represent a main source of goods; in addition, small rural shops are often prepared to sell goods to pensioners in very small quantities. Thirdly, village shops tend to be important social centres for exchange of information and advice. The closure of the village shop may have a social significance unknown in the present day city, symbolising the decline of the village itself.

The rural shopkeeper clearly has to accept a moderate level of turnover and standard of living, but his environment is rather less susceptible to the shocks of rent reviews or slum clearance encountered in inner urban areas. His position appears to have worsened gradually under the impact of increasing consumer mobility, declining population, and increasing difficulties involved in obtaining goods from wholesalers (Dawson, 1976a; Joseph, 1977).

Studies of rural accessibility suggest that generally only a small minority of rural dwellers – those in small settlements and without cars – are seriously inconvenienced for their everyday shopping. For example, in two rural parts of Norfolk, only eight per cent of households questioned stated that there was no 'local shop' available, and a further seven per cent did not use local shops because they were inaccessible (Harman, 1978, Tables 7, 8). However many suffer in relation to the standards of variety and price enjoyed by most urban dwellers.

9.3.9 The nature of local shopping problems

The decline in numbers of local shops, and any associated changes in their nature, may not be problems in themselves. In this context, the 'problem' should be definable as something experienced and perceived as such by the people involved, and preferably it should in some way be measurable. In order to define problems, it is necessary to consider each of the actors involved in retailing, and examine their attitudes to and expectations for local shops. Where events act to frustrate these expectations, then problems may exist.

Retailers experience local shopping problems in that they are affected directly as the owners of local shops. Spokesmen for the retail trade such as Seeney (1976) paint a picture of the small shopkeeper constantly harassed by actions of developers and planners who buy up shop premises, remove support populations, create blight and uncertainty over large areas, and can offer new premises only at prohibitive cost or in unsuitable and remote suburban locations. While there is some truth in this, the whole picture is reminiscent of the small entrepreneur's attitude generally to government intervention of any kind (Golby and Johns, 1971; see 4.4.3).

At a more local level the reaction of retail trade organisations is also directed against those agencies deemed responsible for changes in the small shopkeeper's environment. Developers and landlords are criticised for charging excessive rents; multiple retailers for unfair competition; 'planners' for blight, redevelopment, population change, car parking restrictions, and anything that appears to threaten the viability of a shop or centre. It is not often admitted that small local shops may seem old fashioned, inefficient and expensive to many consumers, and that the retailer himself can do much to attract (or deter) trade.

Consumers also experience local shopping problems; indeed, these should be given special emphasis because the word 'local' implies the fulfilment of consumer requirements. Consumer problems here are essentially of two kinds: those problems of adjustment caused by change in the supply side, and the more lasting problems of inadequacy of the

available system of local shops. In considering either of these types
of problem, there is little of value that one can obtain from published
sources. Research on local shopping behaviour has tended to take a
descriptive stance without probing into possible problems, and there are
few published statements about local shopping problems from consumer
interests. Those that exist tend to provide an unrepresentative view
(for example, the Save Our Local Shops Campaign, see above).

The problems of adjustment to changing supply of local shops are
essentially short term. The consumer who finds that her favourite local
shop for certain types of good has closed or changed in some unacceptable
way, must seek an alternative. Many consumers are consistently loyal to
certain shops, and their closure or change will bring a certain amount
of discomfiture. However, in finding an alternative source the consumer
can use informal local sources of information and will probably quickly
adjust her shopping trip pattern. In the absence of any published work
on this topic it is difficult to be more precise.

The problems of inadequacy are easier to discuss, since it is possible
to examine existing local shops and assess the extent to which they meet
consumers' requirements (9.2). In general the requirements of consumers
for local shops appear to be that the shops should be readily accessible
(i.e. within walking distance); should offer those goods required most
frequently and at short notice; and should do so with adequate standards
of selection, price, and quality of goods, and of cleanliness, efficiency
and friendliness of shop and staff. This is an idealised account because
many consumers would consider some of these items unimportant, or would
accept that the small shopkeeper cannot provide an adequate service in
all respects. Nevertheless, standards of this kind can be used in an
objective assessment of local shopping provision.

Thus, two major types of inadequacy may be apparent in a pattern of
local shops. The first, more serious, is that local shops are so few
or so limited in their scope that certain essential convenience goods
are simply not available locally. At present, this situation is most
probable for chemist's goods and post office services, since their sale
is restricted to particular outlets whose total number in any area is
far less than for the most common types of convenience store. (6)

The second types of inadequacy is in the other requirements listed
above: goods may be available, but not in the form or at the price
required. Furthermore, the shops may be perceived as inadequate,
unsuitable or unpleasant. It follows that most consumers will appreciate
a choice between local shops for food and some other items.

In discussions of the evidence of declining numbers of local shops,
little attention is generally paid to the needs of consumers, except in
that the decline is usually portrayed as an undesirable trend because it
reduces the number of local shopping opportunities available, or removes
the much loved 'corner shop' from the urban scene. It has, however,
been argued (e.g. Davies, 1977b, p.47) that there is still a 'surfeit'
of corner shops and other small businesses in inner cities. These shops
tend to command very small catchment populations, and so are scarcely
profitable: this means that improvements which would benefit the
consumer as well as the retailer cannot be carried out. Thus a decline
in the number of such shops would be beneficial in that the remaining
shops could establish a better competitive position. They would then be
able to carry out improvements to make their shops more attractive to
consumers. In this way, a decline in numbers can make local shops more
capable of meeting consumers' requirements.

This argument seems to beg a number of questions, including that of
the average small retailer's willingness or ability to improve his shop.

But it does warn against uncritical acceptance of the view that any decline in numbers of shops is bad for the consumer.

It follows that local shopping problems are not synonymous with reductions in the numbers of small shops, although planners have tended recently to equate the two areas of concern (e.g. AMA, 1976). In the final part of this chapter, an attempt is made to suggest ways in which planners can assess local shopping problems, and put forward partial remedies.

9.4 TOWARDS PLANNING POLICIES FOR LOCAL SHOPS

In this section the ways in which central and local government can respond to local shopping problems are discussed. As in previous chapters, it is necessary first to establish a rationale for planning intervention. Methods of valid intervention by government at various levels are then discussed, either by evaluating current methods, or by examining the potential of new methods which have been suggested by commentators.

9.4.1 A rationale for planning intervention

Under the view of planning intervention established in Chapter 6, there are three types of rationale for intervention in a situation character- ised by stagnation and decline rather than growth. The first is to help create a suitable economic environment for the operation of the market: in this case, the profitable operation of local shops. The second is to help adjust market forces to optimise the benefit that people derive from local shops, without making their operation unprofitable. The third is to compensate if the market is unable to provide an adequate service to consumers, and if this level of inadequacy is socially unacceptable.

These arguments suggest a number of stances that central and local government should adopt in response to local shopping problems. The first is to investigate the extent to which their present policies, particularly those designed for purposes unconnected with local shops, have exacerbated the problems. Secondly, it is necessary to develop methods of examining consumers' requirements for local shops, and identifying or predicting local shopping problems in specific places. One may then consider the need for intervention, and the forms that it can legitimately take at national or at local level. These stances form the subjects of the following four sub sections.

9.4.2 The effects of present government policies

Small retailers' hostility to central government financial and adminis- trative controls has been mentioned above, although the extent to which these controls have actually driven retailers out of business is hard to detect. Of much greater importance have been local government policies, particularly of slum clearance, which has removed both population and shops from inner cities. Furthermore, levels of compensation paid to small shopkeepers whose properties have been cleared have been inadequate (Berry, 1978, p.18). In general terms it may also be argued that planning policies have restricted the entry of new retailers by preventing the partial conversion of houses to shops.

Whether these factors have exacerbated local shopping problems is not clear. If one regards quality of local shops as being more important than quantity, it may then be reasonable to erect certain barriers against entry to shopkeeping. This of course has not been the intention of government at central or local level and the policies discussed above have been directed towards other ends.

One should conclude that central and local government policies have not strongly contributed to local shopping problems, except in two types of instance. The first is where slum clearance has led to a severe reduction in the stock of local shops. The second is where restrictions on the conversion of property have led to inadequacies in shopping provision in newly developed areas, especially where there is no economic basis for purpose built shops.

It follows that local government should on occasion be more observant of the local shopping needs of the community, and should avoid taking action which intensifies inadequacies and is not sufficiently necessary for other reasons. For example, development control policies which restrict conversion of premises to retail use often seem to derive from dogma rather than rational economically or socially based argument, and could frequently be relaxed without serious harm to the environment.

9.4.3 The identification of local shopping problems

Identification of problems is a prerequisite to the consideration of methods of intervention. In this case problems are local in nature and so the investigation should take place at local government level.

One hesitates to recommend complex methods of survey and analysis to local planners who would no doubt claim already to be overworked. However, a few relatively simple methods of appraisal may be sufficient in many areas to reveal the presence (or absence) or potential local shopping problems. These methods of desk analysis should be backed up with exercises in communication with retailers and consumers, as discussed below.

In order simply to identify problems, expensive surveys of shopping behaviour or retailer performance should not be necessary: a full knowledge of the existing stock of retail premises is, however, advisable since it is this stock rather than aspects of behaviour which is amenable to direct control by planners. Data of premises can be analysed so as to examine variations in access to food shops, chemists and post offices in urban areas (Guy, 1977a, Chapter 8). Recent changes in stock should also be examined, through the comparison of commercial directory data if necessary, although this may incur some loss in accuracy. Typical conclusions from these types of desk study might be that certain districts were poorly provided with local shops in general; or that the location of chemists or post offices appeared to present problems for the elderly; or that changes in the stock were proceeding at such a rate as to suggest that consumers were finding problems of adjustment, and retailers were in a general state of uncertainty about the future.

At this point it would be necessary to enquire whether these conclusions were justified or not, through discussions with the retailers and consumers involved. Representative organisations of retailers (Chambers of Trade) and consumers (Consumer Groups) exist in many towns, and are often consulted over planning matters, for example as part of the process of public participation for structure plans. Discussions specifically on local shopping problems could be held with these bodies. Representative local bodies exist in many areas, such as parish, 'town', community and neighbourhood councils; and also associations representing small residential areas. These could similarly be involved.

What is being suggested here is simply a formalised version of the informal contact that already takes place at a number of levels. This process is as important as the analytical desk study, since it involves the actors concerned in a definition and discussion of problems, rather than regarding this simply as a technical 'planning' exercise.

9.4.4   Intervention by central government

A number of suggestions have recently been made concerning government support for the independent retail sector: these include subsidies, direct and indirect, or removal of certain forms of control (Berry, 1978). It is however by no means certain that such measures would help alleviate local shopping problems. General subsidies for small shop-keepers favour the efficient and inefficient alike, and do not necessarily lead to improvement in standards. In any case, local shopping facilities are often provided by multiple firms, and it would be difficult to subsidise just their local shopping functions and not other aspects of their business.

A possible exception to this argument lies in the isolated rural store: these are subsidised by central government in some European countries (Dawson, 1976a, 1976b). This would seem justifiable under the first rationale for intervention discussed in 9.4.1, and precedents exist, for example in the current subsidisation of rural public transport services run by private firms.

Another suggestion for government intervention, or rather, a slight modification to existing powers, has been made in response to the problem noted in 9.3.6 of shops changing from local to other functions. This is to modify the Use Classes Order (6.3.1) such that changes from 'local' to other types of shop were defined as 'development' and would require planning permission (AMA, 1976). This proposal was rejected by the Department of the Environment in 1977, arguably correctly, since it would involve planners in considerable extra work over the whole country to deal with a problem which occurs in a very small number of areas.

It should be noted finally that some suggestions for local government initiative, to be discussed below, would require central government assistance in formulating legislation and/or supplying finance. Thus these changes require some basic changes in central government attitudes to the retail sector from its present stance of non interference and non support.

9.4.5   Intervention by local government

Local government intervention in respect of local shops can take three forms. Firstly, an attempt can be made to preserve or improve local shopping provision through land use planning policies. Secondly, local shops can be given selective financial support. Thirdly, local government can itself build and run local shops.

Land use planning itself would seem to have little potential in this respect. Planners have only very limited scope in dealing with existing premises: they cannot make existing shops more efficient, or prevent them from closing down. One can suggest that development control decisions should reflect the needs of the retailer as well as other priorities. For example, an application for expansion of premises into adjoining floors or adjacent properties probably stems from a successful small business, and ought normally to be allowed, even in locations such as shopping ribbons, where planners have in the past attempted to restrain retail expansion. Any policy which aims to extinguish retail activity in certain locations seems wrong, since the entry of new firms is eased when the stock of retail premises is at a high level. At the

same time, it is reasonable to allow premises to change to non retail
uses, especially residential, unless there appears to be considerable
pressure of demand upon the existing stock.

The argument here then is that planners might usefully intervene
rather less than they have done in the past: but knowledge of recent
trends in the use of retail premises is valuable when detailed development control policies are under examination.

Certain more conventional planning policies, such as the improvement
of car parking facilities and rear access at small shopping centres, can
be considered as indirect subsidies to the retailers involved. These
policies, while probably of benefit to these retailers, have to be
applied selectively because of problems of resource and land
availability. They also discriminate in effect against the smallest
centres or isolated shops, which are unlikely to merit such improvements.

Financial support has been discussed in general terms above (9.4.4).
Local authorities themselves could act in two ways to improve the
viability of local shops: in reducing their outgoings, or in encouraging
improvements in their attractiveness to consumers. One method of
reducing outgoings would be to allow some relief on rate payments: these
can amount to several hundred pounds a year even for small corner shops.
However, rateable values are determined by a central government agency
(Inland Revenue), and local authorities have no power to allow rate
relief for commercial premises. There are probably other, legally
permissible ways of subsidising existing small shops but it is difficult
to believe that these would be of more than very marginal benefit to the
small shopkeeper in financial difficulties. Such a policy would also be
politically unacceptable to both right and left wing opinion.

Measures to improve the attractiveness of small shops - especially the
counter service grocer - may be cheaper to implement, and more beneficial
in the long term. Such measures could include special grants or loans
for modernisation of shops: one proposal is for the extension of the
improvement grants scheme to apply to small shop units as well as
residential accommodation (Maroney, 1976, p.43). This again would
require new central government legislation.

A local authority can most directly affect local shopping by providing
new shops itself, or buying existing shops. The latter policy appears
uncommon, except as an incidental and temporary effect of compulsory
purchase for eventual redevelopment. However, local authorities have
built shopping centres for many years, either in partnership or as sole
developer. Standards of provision have declined severely in the past 30
years (9.3.7), and it appears that new policies of shop design and
location in new residential areas are needed (Guy, 1976b). These
conclusions apply equally to the shops provided in redeveloped inner
city areas, except that here there is an additional problem. The new
premises are usually offered to traders displaced by the redevelopment
but there is evidence that they are often unwilling to pay the high
rents involved. The premises may instead be occupied by local multiple
firms or new entrants to retailing, who tend to stock a more standardised range of items than were found in the old shops (Davies, 1977b,
p.47). It is clear that small premises should be made available to
local displaced traders as cheaply as possible - covered markets or lock
up garages have been suggested by Davies. These solutions will unfortunately be unacceptable to many planners who have been accustomed to
thinking of environmental quality as an element of paramount importance
in the design of new residential areas. Alternatively, planners can
encourage the development of small shops and businesses in new
residential units: some experiments, apparently successful, have been

made, but again many planners are loath to see any mixture of residential and commercial use, believing that the latter should be provided only in purpose built centres (Low, 1975, provides a detailed documentation and critique of this attitude).

So far as conventional shop units are concerned, local authorities build to much the same standard as private developers, and tend to charge 'commercial rents' which will guarantee a profit on the development. Despite this, there is still some advantage in having new local shops provided by the public rather than the private sector: first, because the public sector may adopt a more flexible attitude toward rent levels in individual shops, realising that certain retailers can only afford low rents, but that others in the same centre can in effect subsidise them. Second, the local authority can restrict the tenant in many ways through the terms of his lease, in a more flexible and enforceable manner than through any conditions on planning permission. Many local authorities control the nature of goods sold, and prohibit sub letting. Also, if the tenant leaves, a replacement suitable for a local shop can be installed. No such procedure is enforceable for a privately owned shop.

All this indicates that in certain circumstances it would be desirable for local authorities to purchase existing shops and let them to suitable tenants. Here the emphasis should be on buying premises as they become available and at normal market prices, rather than on compulsory purchase, which seems unjustifiable for this purpose. Political pressures however are against any extension of local authority commercial operations, and a policy of buying existing shops in order to safeguard local shopping standards would probably not receive support from central government.

9.4.6 Conclusions

This section has demonstrated that, despite fairly strong justifications for planning intervention in certain circumstances, planning policies are likely to be ineffective in resolving local shopping problems. This is in strong contrast to the previous chapter, in which it is shown that planning intervention has been of major importance in controlling the impact of superstores.

Given that direct intervention appears at present to be impractical, one should ask whether local authorities, and particularly their planners, have any role to fulfil in tackling local shopping problems. One answer is that the planner should become more and more a 'reticulist' (Friend, Power and Yewlett, 1974), establishing channels of communication between interested parties, such that problems can be dealt with by direct negotiation between, for example, residents' associations and local Health Authorities, in respect of provision of pharmacies. This process would follow the identification of problems as discussed above (9.4.3), which seems to be a task for the local planner, if only by default.

If local shopping problems continue to become more severe, such that a large minority of the population are severely disadvantaged (a condition which does not appear to hold at present), local shops will have to be regarded as a social rather than commercial service. Then the political arguments against intervention will thus need to be reassessed. In the meantime it seems likely that, as with many social services, initiatives for change will arise from voluntary effort. Thus we may find increasingly that local shopping problems are being partially resolved by the introduction of co-operatives and other 'self help' schemes

(Lock, 1976). The public sector, in the form partly of local planning initiative, can aid this process to some extent, but must at the same time avoid stifling it in mistaken interests of intervention.

NOTES

(1)   At the same time, many housewives consider specialist food shops, especially greengrocers, to be more 'dirty', 'old fashioned', and 'dishonest', than supermarkets (Bruce, 1970).
(2)   Comparable details for post offices are not available, but the number of sub post offices in the UK decreased by about 4.1 per cent over the period 1964-74 (POUNC, 1976, p.25).
(3)   The moderate rate of decline in the 'chemist and photographic' category conceals, however, a 17 per cent loss in registered pharmacies (Bates, 1977).
(4)   Surveys of small retailers have shown that V.A.T. and local authority rates are widely regarded as 'problems' by retailers; far more so than the impact of multiple firms or hypermarkets, or of local authority redevelopment (Bates, 1976, pp.78-82; Berry, 1977, pp.133-135).
(5)   For example, inner city areas of Newcastle-upon-Tyne (i.e. those areas developed before 1900) lost 33 per cent of their population and 42 per cent of their shops over the period 1960-1975 (Butler, 1976, p.51).
(6)   In 1971 there were 22,799 sub post offices (UK figure) and 12,250 dispensing chemists in Britain, compared with 105,283 grocers.

N.B.

171

10   Conclusions

This final chapter has two purposes. Firstly, it summarises previous
chapters and presents some general conclusions. Secondly, it suggests
some possible future trends in retailing and retail location in Britain,
and appropriate ways in which planning policies may be modified in order
to deal with future problems.

10.1   TOWARDS AN UNDERSTANDING OF RETAIL LOCATION AND PLANNING
          INTERVENTION

Throughout this book there has been a movement from a descriptive to a
prescriptive stance. This has been necessary, because in order to
formulate conclusions about effective methods of planning intervention
in the market, one must first understand the workings of the market.
The term 'market' is a construct involving actors in retailing and their
decisions, and the spatial manifestation of these decisions. Thus, the
first five chapters have established an overall picture of these
decisions and their ultimate effects upon patterns of retail location.
Chapter Six combines an analysis of this type, considering town planners
in terms of their decisions affecting retail location, with a discussion
of the purposes of planning intervention in this respect.
  These chapters discussing 'attitudes to retail location' have drawn
upon a great deal of empirical evidence in their attempt to build up
consistent pictures of decisions and their spatial effects. Much of
this evidence has however been indirect or anecdotal. In several areas
there is a lack of factual information on decisions either of general
policy, or concerning retail location in particular. The material
reviewed on supply side decisions (Chapters Three and Four) is generally
atheoretic; this creates problems in generalising empirical results.
While the basic framework of decision theory adopted in this book has
proved valid in terms of classifying and organising discussion of the
empirical material, it is difficult to know to what extent the empirical
material itself can be held to be generally applicable.
  In the discussion of the demand side (Chapter Five), a different
situation has emerged: an abundance of theories and empirical survey
results. On closer attention, it has been shown that much of the theory
is of rather limited value since it is either untested or has been
relatively poorly supported by empirical results. The decision theory
framework enables identification of a number of gaps in knowledge of
consumer behaviour. Other more general problems remain unsolved, one
being the nature and extent of effects of characteristics of the local
shopping environment upon characteristics of shopping behaviour.
  A further class of problem arises. It is concluded in later chapters
that planners' understanding of retailing and retail location is not
adequate for the proper formulation of policies for intervention in the
market. It seems however that in some important areas an understanding
may be reached only through consideration of relatively complex theory
and empirical research methods, for example in applications of
psychological choice theory or revealed preference theory to tackle the

environment-behaviour problem noted above. Analytical and forecasting techniques used by planners tend to derive from simpler but inadequate theoretical statements of supply and demand factors and their relationships. One pressing task for researchers then is to explain new methods to practitioners, in the interests of improving understanding of the market.

The discussion of planners' 'attitudes' in Chapter Six has led to prescriptive conclusions in Chapters Seven, Eight and Nine on planning responses in three types of situation. Here, it is proposed that intervention should take place according to consistent rules appropriate within a mixed economy, but that the particular mode and extent of intervention must reflect circumstances. The planners' position is also established as being unsatisfactory, in that available methods of intervention are not always adequate to ensure that intervention has the appropriate effect. This is particularly the case with local shopping problems, where logically valid forms of intervention such as subsidies to certain types of shopkeeper are ruled out at present because of constraints on public sector expenditures.

The most important general conclusion from these chapters is that it is possible to frame consistent 'rules' for planning intervention from which policies can be derived to meet particular problems or opportunities. These policies include much currently normal town planning activity, although certain planning policies and attitudes are shown to be of dubious merit. Also, it appears that some relatively novel types of planning policy are valid and feasible, for example the formulation of policies for guiding superstore development to preselected locations which maximise net benefits from the development.

10.2 RECENT EVENTS AND THE FUTURE OF RETAILING

Retailing in Britain is becoming dominated more and more by a small number of large firms. The desire of these firms to establish secure and expanding positions in a virtually stagnant total market has intensified competitive processes and led to important changes. The search to cut operating costs has led to expansions in sizes of store, and major changes in methods of store management. The search for increasing shares of the market has led to price wars, advertising campaigns, and in-store gimmicks to attract shoppers. The striving for profitability has led to the closure of small multiple owned stores, especially in grocery chains. The growth of the multiples has also created substantial problems for the independent shopkeeper, who has tended to react in three ways: firstly, to copy the multiple; secondly, to remain small and emphasise personal relationships with the shopper; thirdly, to introduce new products and services to the market, taking risks where the multiples are unwilling.

Consumers have often been given little choice but to adapt their shopping behaviour to these changes. However, in certain respects the new phenomena in retailing clearly suit the requirements of many of today's consumers. In particular, the married couple household, with both adults working and/or young children, appear to be adopting increasingly a pattern of stereotyped shopping behaviour, involving one main weekly food shopping trip, usually made by car to a store chosen on grounds of price advantage and selection of goods; subsidiary walking trips to local centres; and approximately once weekly trips to major centres for comparison shopping. This pattern characterises at present a minority of shoppers, but may be expected to extend gradually to a variety of age groups and family types.

These trends on the supply and demand sides appear likely to intensify the trends in growth and change in retail location patterns discussed in Chapter One. Town centres appear likely to maintain or increase their importance for comparison goods and some specialty goods, but their role for convenience shopping is likely to decline to that largely of a local centre for people working in the centre itself. It seems inevitable that food shopping will continue to show a net movement to outer suburban locations, as superstores open at an increasing rate and small shops close. The efficiently run small food shop will continue to serve an essential role, but its viability will depend partly upon the influence of factors over which the shopkeeper has no control. Suburban locations of almost any type will continue their attraction for price cutting retailers of bulky goods such as furniture, and also for specialty goods retailers who can advertise their location and attract special trips.

A conclusion in Chapter One was that the rate of development in many of these areas was a function of the attitudes of planners. This is still true in principle, but it appears likely that in the future planners will be less willing to intervene negatively by imposing bans on development regarded as unsuitable. This may arise partly from the adoption of more rational planning policies, as discussed in Chapters Six and Eight. It is likely to arise also from the increasing bargaining power of retail firms in a situation of economic decline. In order to induce development at all, planners will often have to allow development according to the wishes of retailers.

This does not mean however that there is no important role remaining for the town planning profession in respect of retail planning. Firstly, it is clear that collaboration between private and public sectors can produce results of mutual benefit. Here it is necessary for planners to consider much wider definitions of 'benefit' than, for example, in the 1960s developments in town centres. Secondly, as the decline in variety and total number of shops continues, it will become more necessary for planners to investigate the extent to which consumers become disadvantaged. This involves the development of methods of survey and analysis, and in some instances the operation of political pressure to initiate new modes of public intervention, for example in ensuring adequate local shops in rural areas.

What is needed is a change in the whole manner with which the planning profession views the retail sector. Planners have tended to regard new developments in retailing, particularly where of locational impact, as 'problems' which should be dealt with through traditional planning processes of control. This attitude has led to a decade of conflict between private and public sector. It is valid for planners to intervene in the market, but they have not presented a convincing case for intervention solely on the grounds of containment or preservation of amenity.

A more valid rationale for intervention can proceed from the arguments adopted in this book. Arguably, the main criterion for planners to adopt in considering retail development should be the welfare of consumers. This may enable planners to indicate positive modification to private sector locational policies, or to propose direct action to meet the needs of disadvantaged consumers. This is a flexible stance which will remain valid in the face of unforeseen changes in retailing. Thus, the most important task of planner and researcher alike is not simply to predict future change, but to identify the conditions in which intervention on behalf of consumers is necessary; and to develop methods of retail planning which ensure that new developments are of maximum benefit to all those involved in the retail sector.

Bibliography

Ambrose, P.J., 1968, An analysis of intra-urban shopping patterns,
  Town Planning Review, vol.38, pp.327-334.
Ambrose, P.J. and Colenutt, R.J., 1975, The property machine, Penguin,
  Harmondsworth.
American Marketing Association, 1948, Report of the Definitions
  Committee, Journal of Marketing, vol.13, pp.202-217.
Amery, C. and Cruickshank, D., 1975, The rape of Britain, Paul Elek,
  London.
Anon, 1972, Get shopped, London Property Letter, February 1972, pp.9-12.
Anon, 1973, The big one said turnover, London Property Letter,
  September 1973, pp.7-9.
Applebaum, W., 1961, Teaching marketing geography by the case method,
  Economic Geography, vol.37, pp.48-60.
Association of Metropolitan Authorities, 1976, The preservation of
  essential shopping facilities, in Jones, P. and Oliphant, R., (eds),
  Local shops: Problems and prospects, Unit for Retail Planning
  Information, Reading.
Bacon, R.W., 1971, An approach to the theory of consumer shopping
  behaviour, Urban Studies, vol.8, pp.55-64.
Bates, P., 1976, The independent grocery retailer: characteristics and
  problems - a report of a survey, Retail Outlets Research Unit,
  Manchester Business School Research Report 23.
Bates, P., 1977, Retail pharmacies: their changing distribution,
  Retail Outlets Research Unit, Manchester Business School Research
  Report 21.
Batey, P.W.J. and Breheny, M.J., Methods in strategic planning:
  Part I: A descriptive review, Town Planning Review, vol.49, pp.261-273.
Batty, M., 1976, Urban modelling: algorithms, calibrations, predictions,
  Cambridge University Press.
Bauer, R.A., 1960, Consumer behaviour as risk taking, in Hancock, R.S.,
  (ed), Dynamic marketing for a changing world, American Marketing
  Association, Chicago.
Baumol, W.J., 1967, Calculation of optimal product and retailer
  characteristics: the abstract product approach, Journal of Political
  Economy, vol.75, pp.674-685. Reprinted in Tucker and Yamey, op.cit.,
  Chapter 17.
Baumol, W.J. and Ide, E.A., 1956, Variety in retailing, Management
  Science, vol.3, pp.93-101. Reprinted in Tucker and Yamey, op.cit.,
  Chapter 19.
Beavon, K.S.O., 1977, Central place theory: a reinterpretation,
  Longman, London.
Bechhofer, F. and Elliott, B., 1975, A progress report on small
  shopkeepers and the class structure, Social Science Research Council,
  Project HR 216, research report.
Bechhofer, F., Elliott, B. and Rushforth, M., 1971, The market situation
  of small shopkeepers, Scottish Journal of Political Economy, vol.18,
  pp.161-180.
Bechhofer, F., Elliott, B., Rushforth, M. and Bland, R., 1974a,
  The petits bourgeois in the class structure: the case of the small

shopkeepers, in Parkin, F., (ed), The social analysis of class structure, Tavistock Publications, London.

Bechhofer, F., Elliott, B., Rushforth, M. and Bland, R., 1974b, Small shopkeepers: matters of money and meaning, Sociological Review, n.s., vol.22, pp.465-482.

Benwell Community Project, 1979, From blacksmiths to white elephants: Benwell's changing shops, Benwell Community Project: Final Report Series No.7, Newcastle.

Berkshire County Council, 1976, Central Berkshire Structure Plan: Report of Survey, Royal County of Berkshire, Reading.

Berry, B.J.L., 1963, Commercial structure and commercial blight, University of Chicago, Department of Geography Research Paper 85.

Berry, B.J.L., 1967, Geography of market centres and retail distribution, Prentice Hall, Englewood Cliffs, NJ.

Berry, B.J.L. and Garrison, W.L., 1958, Recent developments of central place theory, Papers and Proceedings of the Regional Science Association, vol.4, pp.107-120.

Berry, L.L., 1969, The components of department store image: A theoretical and empirical analysis, Journal of Retailing, vol.45, pp.3-20.

Berry, R.K., 1977, Small unit retailing in urban Britain: a review of present trends and the policies affecting the small shop, Lampeter, St Davids University College.

Berry, R.K., 1978, Public and private policies towards small shops, Retailing and Planning Associates, Corbridge, Northumberland.

Blake, J., 1976, Brent Cross shopping centre, Town and Country Planning, vol.44, pp.231-236.

Booth, D. and Jaffe, M., 1978, Generation and evaluation in structure planning, Town Planning Review, vol.49, pp.445-458.

Bower, M.D., 1974, Victoria Centre, Nottingham, Proceedings of the Seminar on Retailing, PTRC Summer Annual Meeting.

Bowlby, S.R., 1972, Spatial variation in consumer's information levels, Unpublished PhD dissertation, Department of Geography, Northwestern University, Evanston, Ill.

Bowlby, S.R., 1979, Accessibility, mobility and shopping provision, in Goodall, B. and Kirby, A., (eds), Resources and Planning, Pergamon Press, Oxford.

Bradley, M. and Fenwick, D., 1975, Shopping habits and attitudes to shop hours in Great Britain, Office of Population Censuses and Surveys: Social Survey Division, HMSO, London.

Britt, S.H., (ed), 1970, Consumer behavior in theory and in action, Wiley, New York.

Broadbent, T.A., 1977, Planning and profit in the urban economy, Methuen, London.

Brown, A., 1977, Small shops in jeopardy, Planning, no.208, pp.8-9.

Brown, A. and Deaton, A., 1972, Surveys in applied economics; models of consumer behaviour, Economic Journal, vol.82, pp.1145-1236.

Bruce, A.J., 1970, Housewife attitudes towards shops and shopping, Proceedings of the Architectural Psychology Conference, Kingston Polytechnic, Surrey.

Bruce, A.J., 1974, Facilities required near home, Built Environment, vol.3, pp.290-291.

Bruce, A., 1976, shopper preferences and attitudes, Proceedings of the Seminar on Retailing, PTRC Summer Annual Meeting.

Bruce, A. and Delworth, K. Shopping behaviour in four areas, Building Research Establishment Note N3/76, Garston, Herts.

Buchanan, C.D. et al, 1963, Traffic in Towns, HMSO, London.

Bucklin, L.P., 1967, The concept of mass in intra-urban shopping, Journal of Marketing, vol.31, no.4, pp.37-42.

Bucklin, L.P., 1969, Consumer search, role enactment, and market efficiency, Journal of Business, vol.42, pp.416-438.

Burnett, K.P., 1973, The dimensions of alternatives in spatial choice processes, Geographical Analysis, vol.5, pp.181-204.

Burnett, K.P., 1977, Tests of a linear learning model of destination choice: Applications to shopping travel by heterogenous population groups, Geografiska Annaler, vol.59B, pp.95-108.

Burnett, K.P., 1978, Markovian models of movement within urban spatial structures, Geographical Analysis, vol.10, pp.142-153.

Burns, W., 1959, British shopping centres, Leonard Hill, London.

Butler, P., 1976, A study of local shopping in Newcastle upon Tyne, in Jones, P. and Oliphant, R., (eds), Local shops: Problems and prospects, Unit for Retail Planning Information, Reading.

Byron, C.H., 1967, Shopping; work for women; leisure, Basildon Development Corporation, Basildon, Essex.

Cadman, D. and Austin Crowe, L., 1978, Property development, Spon, London.

Campbell, B.M., 1969, The existence of evoked set and determinants of its magnitude in brand choice behavior, Columbia University Press, New York.

Capital and Counties Property Co Ltd., 1970, Design for Shopping, London.

Carruthers, W.I., 1967, Major shopping centres in England and Wales, Regional Studies, vol.1, pp.65-81.

Carter, H., 1975, The study of urban geography, (Second edition), Edward Arnold, London.

Castles, F.G., Murray, D.J. and Potter, D.C., (eds), 1971, Decisions, organizations and society, Penguin, Harmondsworth.

Cater, J., 1979, Asian and non-Asian retailing in inner city areas: A preliminary report on a survey of Bradford, Leicester and the London Borough of Ealing, Paper presented to the Urban Study Group of the Institute of British Geographers.

Cater, J. and Jones, T., 1978, Asians in Bradford, New Society, vol.44, pp.81-82.

Central Statistical Office, 1978, Social Trends No.9, HMSO, London.

Centre for Advanced Land Use Studies, 1975, Rent assessment and tenant mix in planned shopping centres, College of Estate Management, Reading.

Chadwick, G., 1971, A systems view of planning, Pergamon Press, Oxford.

Cherry, G., 1974, The development of planning thought, in Bruton, M.J., (ed) The spirit and purpose of planning, Hutchinson, London.

Chippindale, S., 1974, Property is money, Lecture given to Faculty of Urban and Regional Studies, University of Reading.

Christaller, W., 1966, Central places in Southern Germany (trans. C.W. Baskin), Prentice Hall, Englewood Cliffs, New Jersey.

Clark, W.A.V., 1968, Consumer travel patterns and the concept of range, Annals of the Association of American Geographers, vol.58, pp.386-396.

Clark, W.A.V. and Rushton, G., 1970, Models of intra-urban consumer behaviour and their implications for central place theory, Economic Geography, vol.46, pp.486-497.

Coelho, J.D. and Wilson, A.G., 1976, The optimum location and size of shopping centres, Regional Studies, vol.10, pp.413-421.

Cohen, S.B. and Lewis, G.K., 1967, Form and function in the geography of retailing, Economic Geography, vol.43, pp.1-42.

Cole, H.R., 1966, Shopping assessments at Haydock and elsewhere: A review, Urban Studies, vol.3, pp.147-156.

Cole, H.R., 1975, Up the hypermarket, New Society, vol.34, pp.542-543.

Cooke, P.N., forthcoming, Capital relation and state dependency: An analysis of urban development policy in Cardiff, in Rees, G. and Rees, T., (eds), Poverty at the periphery, Croom Helm, London.

Cooper, M.J.M., 1975, The industrial location decision making process, University of Birmingham, Centre for Urban and Regional Studies, Occasional Paper 34.

Copeland, M.T., 1924, Principles of merchandising, Shaw, Chicago.

Cox, D.F., 1963, The audience as communicators, American Marketing Association, Chicago.

Cox, R.K., 1968, Retail site assessment, Business Books, London.

Cullingworth, J.B., 1976, Town and Country Planning in Britain, (Revised 6th Edition), Allen and Unwin, London.

Cyert, R.M. and March, J.G., 1963, A behavioral theory of the firm, Prentice Hall, Englewood Cliffs, New Jersey.

Darlow, C. (ed), 1972, Enclosed shopping centres, Architectural Press, London.

Dash, J.F., Schiffman, L.G. and Berenson, C., 1976, Risk- and personality- related dimensions of store choice, Journal of Marketing, vol.40, no.1, pp.32-39.

Davies, R.L., 1972, The retail pattern of the central area in Coventry, in I.B.G. Urban Study Group (eds), The retail structure of cities, Institute of British Geographers, London.

Davies, R.L., 1973a, Evaluation of retail store attributes and sales performance, European Journal of Marketing, vol.7, pp.89-102.

Davies, R.L., 1973b, Patterns and profiles of consumer behaviour, University of Newcastle, Department of Geography Research Series 10.

Davies, R.L., 1976a, Marketing geography, Retailing and Planning Associates, Corbridge, Northumberland.

Davies, R.L., 1976b, The recent history and problems of small shops and related small businesses, in Jones, P. and Oliphant, R., (eds), Local shops: Problems and prospects, Unit for Retail Planning Information, Reading.

Davies, R.L., 1977a, Store location and store assessment research: the integration of some new and traditional techniques, Transactions of the Institute of British Geographers, n.s. vol.2, pp.141-157.

Davies, R.L., 1977b, A framework for commercial planning policies, Town Planning Review, vol.48, pp.42-58.

Davies, R.L. and Bennison, D.J., 1978, The Eldon Square Regional Shopping Centre - the first eighteen months, Retailing and Planning Associates, Corbridge, Northumberland.

Daws, L.F., 1974, On shoppers' requirements for the location of shops in towns, Building Research Establishment Current Paper 23/74, Garston, Herts.

Daws, L.F. and Bruce, A.J., 1971, Shopping in Watford, Building Research Station, Garston, Herts.

Dawson, J.A., 1976a, The country shop in Britain: objectives and background to a research project, in Jones, P. and Oliphant, R., (eds), Local shops: Problems and prospects, Unit for Retail Planning Information, Reading.

Dawson, J.A., 1976b, Public policy and distribution in the EEC, in Lee, R. and Ogden, P.E., (eds), Economy and society in the EEC, Saxon House, Farnborough.

Day, R.A., 1973, Consumer shopping behaviour in a planned urban
environment, Tijdschrift voor economische en sociale geografie, vol.64,
pp.77-85.
Department of Employment, 1972, Family expenditure survey: report for
1971, HMSO, London.
Department of Industry, 1975, Report on the census of distribution and
other services 1971, part 1, HMSO, London.
Department of the Environment, 1972, Development Control Policy Note 13:
Out of town shops and shopping centres, HMSO, London.
Department of the Environment, 1974, Land, Command No.5730, HMSO, London.
Department of the Environment, 1975, Commercial property development,
First report of the Advisory Group on Commercial Property Development,
HMSO, London.
Department of the Environment, 1976a, The Eastleigh Carrefour: a
hypermarket and its effects, DoE Research Report 16, HMSO, London.
Department of the Environment, 1976b, Large new stores, DoE Circular
71/76, HMSO, London.
Department of the Environment, 1977a, Large new stores, DoE Circular
96/77, HMSO, London.
Department of the Environment, 1977b, Development Control Policy Note 13:
Large new stores, HMSO, London.
Department of the Environment, 1979, Memorandum on Structure and Local
Plans, DoE Circular 4/79, HMSO, London.
Departments of the Environment and Transport, 1978, The Eastleigh
Carrefour hypermarket after three years, DoE and T. Research Report
27, HMSO, London.
Department of Transport, 1978, Transport statistics Great Britain
1966-1976, HMSO, London.
Devletoglou, N., 1965, A dissenting view of duopoly and spatial
competition, Economica, vol.32, pp.140-160.
Diamond, D.R. and Gibb, E.B., 1962, Development of new shopping centres:
Area estimation, Scottish Journal of Political Economy, vol.9,
pp.130-146.
Dichter, E., 1964, Handbook of consumer motivations: The psychology of
the world of objects, McGraw-Hill, New York.
Distributive Trades Economic Development Council, 1970, Urban models in
shopping studies, HMSO, London.
Distributive Trades Economic Development Council, 1971, The future
pattern of shopping, HMSO, London.
Dommermuth, W.P. and Cundiff, E.W., 1967, Shopping goods, shopping
centers and selling strategies, Journal of Marketing, vol.31, no.4,
pp.32-36.
Donaldsons, 1973, Caerphilly hypermarket study, Donaldsons Research
Report, London.
Donaldsons, 1975, Caerphilly hypermarket study; year two, Donaldsons
Research Report 2, London.
Donaldsons, 1976, Planning inquiry study, Donaldsons Research Report 3,
London.
Donaldsons, 1978, Planning inquiry study two, Donaldsons Research
Report 5, London.
Donaldsons, 1979, Caerphilly hypermarket study year five, Donaldsons
Research Report 6, London.
Douglas, E., 1962, Size of firm and the structure of costs in retailing,
Journal of Business, vol.35, pp.158-190, reprinted in Tucker and
Yamey, op.cit., Chapter 13.
Downs, R.M., 1970, The cognitive structure of an urban shopping centre,

Environment and Behavior, vol.2, pp.13-39.

Doyle, P., 1973, The use of automatic interaction detector and similar search procedures, Operational Research Quarterly, vol.24, pp.465-467.

Doyle, P. and Fenwick, I., 1974, Store image and store choice, Paper prepared for the Third Annual Workshop on Research in Marketing, Brussels, April 1974.

Drake, M., McLoughlin, J.B., Thompson, J.R. and Thornley, J., 1975, Aspects of structure planning in Britain, Centre for Environmental Studies Research Paper 20.

Dumbleton, R., 1977, The second blitz: the demolition and rebuilding of town centres in South Wales, Cardiff.

Dunlop, J., 1976, The scope and effect of structure planning, The Planner, vol.62, pp.48-51.

Economist Intelligence Unit, 1973, The future of pedestrianised shopping precincts, Retail Business, no.190, pp.20-27.

Economist Intelligence Unit, 1976, Retail distribution in Britain, London.

Ehrenberg, A.S.C., 1969, Towards an integrated theory of consumer behaviour, Journal of the Market Research Society, vol.11, pp.305-337; reprinted in A.S.C. Ehrenberg and G.F. Pyatt (eds), Consumer behaviour, Penguin, Harmondsworth, 1971.

Ehrenberg, A.S.C., 1972, Repeat buying: theory and applications, North Holland, Amsterdam.

Epstein, B.J., 1971, Geography and the business of retail site evaluation and selection, Economic Geography, vol.47, pp.192-199.

Evans, A.W., 1972, A linear programming solution to the shopping problem posed by R.W. Bacon, Urban Studies, vol.9, pp.221-222.

Festinger, L., 1957, A theory of cognitive dissonance, Row, Peterson, Evanston, Ill.

Fiber, A., 1972, The complete guide to retail management, Penguin, Harmondsworth.

Finney, J.E. and Robinson, J., 1976, District shopping centres: some case studies, Proceedings of the Seminar on Retailing, PTRC Summer Annual Meeting.

Foxall, G.R., 1977, Consumer behaviour: a practical guide, Retailing and Planning Associates, Corbridge, Northumberland.

Frank, R.E., 1967, Correlates of buying behavior for grocery products, Journal of Marketing, vol.31, no.4, pp.48-53; reprinted in A.S.C. Ehrenberg and F.G. Pyatt (eds), Consumer behaviour, Penguin, Harmondsworth, 1971.

Friend, J.K., Power, J.M. and Yewlett, C.J.L., 1974, Public planning: the inter-corporate dimension, Tavistock, London.

Fudge, C., 1976, Local plans, structure plans and policy planning, The Planner, vol.62, pp.174-176.

Gabor, A., 1974, Customer oriented pricing, in Thorpe, D. (ed), Research into retailing and distribution, Saxon House, Farnborough.

Goffman, E., 1959, The presentation of self in everyday life, Doubleday Anchor Books, Garden City.

Golby, C.W. and Johns, G., 1971, Attitude and motivation, Committee of Inquiry on Small Firms Research Report 7, HMSO, London.

Golledge, R.G., 1970, Some equilibrium models of consumer behaviour, Economic Geography, vol.46, Supplement, pp.417-424.

Golldge, R.G.and Brown, L.A., 1967, Search, learning and the market decision process, Geografiska Annaler, vol.49B, pp.116-124.

Golledge, R.G., Rushton, G. and Clark, W.A.V., 1966, Some spatial characteristics of Iowa's dispersed farm population and their implications for the grouping of central place functions, <u>Economic Geography</u>, vol.42, pp.261-272.

Goodall, B., 1972, <u>The economics of urban areas</u>, Pergamon Press, Oxford.

Gornall, E., 1954, Some aspects of the retail greengrocery trade in an industrial working class district, <u>Journal of Industrial Economics</u>, vol.2, pp.207-220.

Gosling, D. and Maitland, B., 1976, <u>Design and planning of retail systems</u>, Architectural Press, London.

Gould, J.R. and Preston, L.E., 1965, Resale price maintenance and retail outlets, <u>Economica</u>, n.s., vol.32, pp.302-312; reprinted in Tucker and Yamey, op.cit., Chapter 21.

Green, H.A.J., 1976, <u>Consumer theory</u> (revised edition), Macmillan, London.

Gronhaug, K., 1972, Risk indicators, perceived risk and consumer's choice of information sources, <u>Swedish Journal of Economics</u>, vol.74, pp.246-262.

Gronhaug, K., 1973, Some factors influencing the size of the buyer's evoked set, <u>European Journal of Marketing</u>, vol.7, pp.232-241.

Grubb, E.L. and Grathwohl, H.L., 1967, Consumer self concept, symbolism and market behavior: A theoretical approach, <u>Journal of Marketing</u>, vol.31, no.4, pp.22-27.

Guy, C.M., 1975, Consumer behaviour and its geographical impact, <u>University of Reading, Department of Geography Geographical Paper</u> 34.

Guy, C.M., 1976a, The location of shops in the Reading area, <u>University of Reading, Department of Geography Geographical Paper</u> 46.

Guy, C.M., 1976b, Neighbourhood shops in new towns, <u>Town and Country Planning</u>, vol.44, pp.221-224.

Guy, C.M., 1977a, <u>Local shops in a changing retail environment: Analysis and evaluation for local planning, with special reference to the Reading area</u>, Unpublished Ph D thesis, University of Reading.

Guy, C.M., 1977b, A method of examining and evaluating the impact of major retail developments upon existing shops and their users, <u>Environment and Planning A</u>, vol.9, pp.491-504.

Hall, M., 1971, The small unit in the distributive trades, <u>Committee of Inquiry on small firms, Research Report</u> 8, HMSO, London.

Hall, P., 1974, <u>Urban and regional planning</u>, Penguin, Harmondsworth.

Hall, P. with Gracey, H., Drewett, R. and Thomas, R., 1973, <u>The containment of urban England</u>, Allen and Unwin, London.

Hallsworth, A.G., 1978, A caveat on retail assessment, <u>Area</u>, vol.10, pp.24-25.

Hamilton, F.E.I., 1974, A view of spatial behaviour, industrial organisations and decision making, in Hamilton, F.E.I., (ed), <u>Spatial perspectives on industrial organisation and decision making</u>, John Wiley, London.

Harman, R.G., 1978, Retailing in rural areas: A case study in Norfolk, <u>Geoforum</u>, vol.9, pp.107-126.

Harris, M.R. and Andrew, H.R., 1979, The traffic implications of hypermarket development, <u>Traffic Engineering and Control</u>, vol.20, pp.2-8.

Harrison, E.F., 1975, <u>The managerial decision making process</u>, Houghton Mifflin, Boston.

Hay, A.M. and Johnston, R.J., 1979, Search and the choice of shopping centre: two models of variability in destination selection, <u>Environment and Planning A</u>, vol.11, pp.791-804.

Haynes, P.A., 1974, Towards a concept of monitoring, <u>Town Planning Review</u>, vol.45, pp.5-29.

Heald, G.I., 1972, The application of the automatic interaction detector (AID) programme and multiple regression techniques to the assessment of store performance and site selection, Operational Research Quarterly, vol.23, pp.445-457.

Henderson, R., 1978, Shopping and Mr Shore, The Planner, vol.64, pp.148-149.

Hill, M., 1968, A goals achievement matrix for evaluating alternative plans, Journal of the American Institute of Planners, vol.34, pp.19-29.

Hillman, M., 1973, The social costs of hypermarket developments, Built Environment, vol.2, pp.89-91.

Hillman, M., Henderson, I. and Whalley, A., 1973, Personal mobility and transport policy, PEP Broadsheet 542, London.

Hillman, M., Henderson, I. and Whalley, A., 1976, Transport realities and planning policy: studies of friction and freedom in daily travel, PEP Broadsheet 567, London.

Holton, R.H., 1957, Price discrimination at retail: the supermarket case, Journal of Industrial Economics, vol.6, pp.13-32; reprinted in Tucker and Yamey, op.cit., Chapter 4.

Horton, F.E. and Reynolds, D.R., 1971, Effects of urban spatial structure on individual behaviour, Economic Geography, vol.47, pp.36-48.

Hotelling, H., 1929, Stability in competition, Economic Journal, vol.39, pp.41-57.

Howard, J.A. and Sheth, J.N., 1969, The theory of buyer behavior, John Wiley, New York.

Howe, T.N., 1978, Shopping in Brent Cross: an investigation, Unpublished Diploma dissertation, University of Wales.

Hudson, R., 1974, Consumer spatial behaviour: A conceptual model and empirical investigation in Bristol, Unpublished Ph D thesis, University of Bristol.

Hudson, R., 1976, Linking studies of the individual with models of aggregate behaviour: an empirical example, Transactions of the Institute of British Geographers, n.s., vol.1, pp.159-174.

Huff, D.L., 1966, A programmed solution for approximating an optimum retail location, Land Economics, vol.42, pp.293-303; reprinted in Tucker and Yamey, op.cit., Chapter 18.

IPC Women's Weekly Group, 1970, Shopping in the seventies, London.

Izraeli, D., 1973, The three wheels of retailing: a theoretical note, European Journal of Marketing, vol.7, pp.70-74.

Jameson, C., 1976, Are these the modern follies ? Sunday Times, 25 April.

Jennings, R.G., 1974, Relationship between local authorities and developers, Proceedings of the seminar on Retailing, PTRC Summer Annual Meeting.

Jensen, E.A., 1963, Buying a shop: How to choose, what to pay, Estates Gazette, London.

Jones, P.M., 1978, Trading features of hypermarkets and superstores, Unit for Retail Planning Information, Reading.

Joseph, M.E., 1977, The village shop in rural mid-Wales, St Davids University College, Lampeter.

Kaish, S., 1967, Cognitive dissonance and the classification of consumer goods, Journal of Marketing, vol.31, no.4, pp.28-31.

Kane, B.J. Jr., 1966, A systematic guide to supermarket location analysis, Fairchild, New York.

Kassarjian, H.H. and Robertson, T.S., (eds) 1973, Perspectives in consumer behavior (revised edition), Scott, Foresman, Glenview, Illinois.

Kaufman, G.M. and Thomas, H., (ed), 1977, Modern decision analysis: selected readings, Penguin, Harmondsworth.

Kaye, C., 1975, Planning and management of enclosed shopping centres, Proceedings of the seminar on Retailing, PTRC Summer Annual Meeting.

Keeble, L., 1959, Principles and practice of town and country planning (2nd edition), Estates Gazette, London.

Kelly, G.A., 1955, The psychology of personal constructs, Norton, New York.

Kelly, R.W., 1979, Parking at a hypermarket - six years on, Traffic Engineering and Control, vol.20, pp.257-261.

Kerr, D., 1976, Shop investment, Estates Gazette, vol.237, pp.633-637.

Kirby, D.A., 1974, Shopkeepers go shopping, Geographical Magazine, vol.46, pp.526-528.

Kirby, D.A., 1975, The small shop in Britain, Town and Country Planning, vol.43, pp.496-500.

Kornblau, C.,(ed), 1968, Guide to store location research: with emphasis on supermarkets, Addison-Wesley, Reading, Mass.

Kotler, P., 1965, Behavioral models for analyzing buyers, Journal of Marketing, vol.29, no.4, pp.37-45.

Lakshmanan, T.R. and Hansen, W.G., 1965, A retail market potential model, Journal of the American Institute of Planners, vol.31, pp.134-143.

Langton, R., 1973, White elephant ? Property and Investment Review, May, pp.29-32.

Lee, M., 1976, Retailing: Planning problems, Proceedings of the seminar on Retailing, PTRC Summer Annual Meeting.

Lessig, V.P., 1973, Consumer store images and store loyalties, Journal of Marketing, vol.37, no.4, pp.72-74.

Lewis, W.A., 1945, Competition in retail trade, Economica, n.s., vol.12, pp.202-234; reprinted in Tucker and Yamey, op.cit., Chapter 7.

Lichfield, N., Kettle, P. and Whitbread, M., 1975, Evaluation in the planning process, Pergamon, Oxford.

Likierman, A. and Wilcock, A., 1970, Suburban shopping precincts: an assessment, Journal of the Town Planning Institute, vol.56, pp.138-141.

Lindley, D.V., 1971, Making decisions, Wiley, New York.

Lipsey, R.G., 1975, An introduction to positive economics, (4th edition) Weidenfeld and Nicolson, London.

Lloyd, R.E., 1977, Consumer behaviour after migration: a reassessment process, Economic Geography, vol.53, pp.14-27.

Lock, D., 1976, Small shop survival, Built Environment Quarterly, vol.2, pp.207-210.

Lösch, A., 1954, The economics of location, (trans. W.G. Woglom and W.F. Stopler), Yale University Press, New Haven.

Low, N., 1975, Centrism and the provision of services in residential areas, Urban Studies, vol.12, pp.177-191.

Lowe, J., 1973, Demand, marketing and time, European Journal of Marketing, vol.7, pp.103-111.

Lucas, R.M., 1979, Retailing and planning: An examination of the role of planning in the development of large retail stores in off centre locations, Unpublished Diploma dissertation, University of Wales.

Luce, R.D., 1959, Individual choice behavior, Wiley, New York.

Luce, R.D. and Suppes, P., 1965, Preference, utility and subjective probability, in Luce, R.D., Bush, R.R. and Galanter, E., (eds), Handbook of Mathematical Psychology, Wiley, New York.

Mabey, R. and Craig, L., 1976, Development Plan schemes, The Planner, vol.62, pp.70-72.

McClelland, D.C., 1961, The achieving society, van Nostrand, Princeton.

McDougall, M.J., Slack, J.A. and Trench, S., 1974, The Nottingham Victoria Centre: A policy review, Proceedings of the seminar on Retailing, PTRC Summer Annual Meeting.

Mackay, D.B., Olshavsky, R.W. and Sentell, G., 1975, Cognitive maps and spatial behavior of consumers, Geographical Analysis, vol.7, pp.19-34.

McLoughlin, J.B., 1969, Urban and regional planning: a systems approach, Faber and Faber, London.

McLoughlin, J.B., 1973, Control and urban planning, Faber and Faber, London.

McNair, M.P., 1958, Significant trends and developments in the post war period, in Smith, A.B. (ed), Competitive distribution in a free, high level economy and its implications, University of Pittsburgh Press.

Maltby, D. and Johnston, I., 1979, Traffic implications of hypermarket development, Traffic Engineering and Control, vol.20, pp.261-262.

Mann, H.R., 1977, The Brent Cross shopping centre impact study: the first home interview survey, Greater London Council Research Memorandum 510.

Marcus, M., 1978, Retail blight and planned shopping precincts in England and Wales, Unpublished Ph D thesis, University of Reading.

Maroney, A., 1976, The decline of small shops in Liverpool and the problems involved in providing new facilities, in Jones, P. and Oliphant, R., (eds), Local shops: Problems and prospects, Unit for Retail Planning Information, Reading.

Marriott, O., 1967, The property boom, Hamish Hamilton, London.

Maslow, A.H., 1943, A theory of human motivation, Psychological Review, vol.50, pp.370-396.

Massey, D.B. and Catalano, A., 1978, Capital and land: landownership by capital in Great Britain, Edward Arnold, London.

Massey, D.B. and Meegan, R.A., 1978, Industrial restructuring versus the cities, Urban Studies, vol.15, pp.273-288.

Massy, W.F., Montgomery, D.B. and Morrison, D.G., 1970, Stochastic models of buying behavior, MIT Press, Cambridge, Mass.

Miller, G.A., 1956, The magical number seven plus or minus two: Some limits on our capacity for processing information, Psychological Review, vol.63, pp.81-97.

Ministry of Housing and Local Government, 1966, Planning investment and town centre redevelopment, MHLG Circular 50/66, HMSO, London.

Ministry of Housing and Local Government, 1970, Development plans: A manual on form and content, HMSO, London.

Ministry of Housing and Local Government and Ministry of Transport, 1962, Town centres: approach to renewal, HMSO, London.

Moor, N., 1974, Retailing in London and Paris, Built Environment, vol.3, pp.515-517.

Moor, N., 1975, Structure plans and retailing, Proceedings of the seminar on Retailing, PTRC Summer Annual Meeting.

Moor, N., 1976, Who takes the risk ? Built Environment Quarterly, vol.2, pp.276-278.

Moore, P.G. and Thomas, H., 1976, The anatomy of decisions, Penguin, Harmondsworth.

Moseley, J., 1975, Shopping in Berkshire: survey methods, Unit for Retail Planning Information, Reading.

Mumford, L., 1961, The city in history, Secker and Warburg, London.

Myers, J.H. and Mount, J.F., 1973, More on social class vs. income as correlates of buying behavior, Journal of Marketing, vol.37, no.2, pp.71-73.

Nader, G.A., 1968, Private housing estates: The effect of previous residence on workplace and shopping activities, Town Planning Review, vol.39, pp.65-74.

Narayana, C.L. and Markin, R.J., 1975, Consumer behavior and product performance: An alternative conceptualisation, Journal of Marketing, vol.39, no.4, pp.1-6.

Nelson, P., 1970, Information and consumer behavior, Journal of Political Economy, vol.78, pp.311-329.

Nelson, R.L., 1958, The selection of retail locations, Dodge, New York.

Nicosia, F.M., 1966, Consumer decision processes, Prentice-Hall, Englewood Cliffs, N.J.

Norfolk County Council, 1976, Thresholds for village foodshops, in Jones, P. and Oliphant, R., (eds), Local shops: Problems and prospects, Unit for Retail Planning Information, Reading.

Northen, R.I. and Haskoll, M., 1977, Shopping centres: a developer's guide to planning and design, Centre for Advanced Land Use Studies, Reading.

Nuttall, G., 1976, Is British shoe walking all over you ? Sunday Times, 4 July.

Openshaw, S., 1975, Some theoretical and applied aspects of spatial interaction shopping models, Concepts and techniques in modern geography,4, Geo Abstracts Ltd., University of East Anglia.

Openshaw, S., 1976, An empirical study of some spatial interaction models, Environment and Planning A, vol.8, pp.23-41.

Packard, V., 1957, The hidden persuaders, Longmans, London.

Pickering, J.F., 1972, Economic implications of hypermarkets in Britain, European Journal of Marketing, vol.6, pp.257-269.

Pipkin, J.S., 1977, Some probabilistic revealed-preference models of the choice process in recurrent urban travel, Geografiska Annaler, vol.59B, pp.82-94.

Pipkin, J.S., 1979, Respondent heterogeneity and alternative interpretations of scale values in destination choice models, Professional Geographer, vol.31, pp.16-24.

Pirie, G.H., 1976, Thoughts on revealed preference and spatial behaviour, Environment and Planning A, vol.8, pp.947-955.

Pope, M.P.R., 1975, Store location - a multiple retailer's viewpoint, Proceedings of the seminar on Retailing, PTRC Summer Annual Meeting.

Post Office Users' National Council, 1976, Evidence submitted to the Post Office Review Committee, London.

Potter, R.B., 1977, The nature of consumer usage fields in an urban environment: theoretical and empirical perspectives, Tijdschrift voor Economische en Sociale Geografie, vol.68, pp.168-176.

Potter, R.B., 1979, Designative aspects of consumer perception of urban retailing facilities, Paper given to Annual Conference of the Institute of British Geographers, Manchester.

Prasad, V.K., 1975, Socioeconomic product risk and patronage preferences of retail shoppers, Journal of Marketing, vol.39, no.3, pp.42-47.

Price, F., 1972, Shops and shopping, in Evans, H., (ed) New towns: the British experience, Charles Knight, London.

Raiffa, H. 1968, Decision analysis, Addison-Wesley, Reading, Mass.

Ransome, J.C., 1961, The organisation of location research in a large supermarket chain, Economic Geography, vol.37, pp.42-47.

Reilly, W.J., 1931, The law of retail gravitation, Knickerbocker Press, New York.

Ridgway, J.D., 1976, The future of district shopping centres - a retailer's view, Proceedings of the seminar on retailing, PTRC Summer Annual Meeting.

Riesman, D., Glazer, N. and Denny, R., 1961, The lonely crowd, Yale
University Press, New Haven, Conn.
Rogers, D.S., 1974, Bretton, Peterborough: The impact of a large edge of
town supermarket, Retail Outlets Research Unit, Manchester Business
School, Research Report 9.
Rushton, G., 1969, Analysis of spatial behavior by revealed space
preference, Annals of the Association of American Geographers, vol.59,
pp.391-400.
Sainsbury, J.D., 1973, Food shopping, Journal of the Royal Society of
Arts, vol.121, pp.306-315.
Sainsbury, T.A.D., 1973, Success and survival in retailing, Built
Environment, vol.2, pp.85-88.
Schaffer, F., 1972, The new town story (revised edition), Paladin,
London.
Schewe, C.D., 1973, Selected social psychological models for analyzing
buyers, Journal of Marketing, vol.37, no.3, pp.31-39.
Schiller, R.K., 1971, Location trends of specialist services, Regional
Studies, vol.5, pp.1-10.
Schiller, R.K., 1972, The measurement of the attractiveness of shopping
centres to middle class luxury consumers, Regional Studies, vol.6,
pp.291-297.
Schiller, R.K., 1974, Retailing and planning, The Planner, vol.60,
pp.744-749.
Schneider, C.H.P., 1975, Models of space searching in urban areas,
Geographical Analysis, vol.7, pp.173-185.
Schuler, H.J., 1979, A disaggregate store choice model of spatial decision
making, Professional Geographer, vol.31, pp.146-156.
Scott, P., 1970, Geography and retailing, Hutchinson, London.
Scott, W.G., 1967, Organisation theory, Irwin, Homewood, Illinois;
also reprinted (pp.219-226) in Castles, Murray and Potter, op.cit.,
Chapter 1.
Seeney, L.E.S., 1976, The decline of small shops, in Jones, P. and
Oliphant, R., (eds), Local shops: Problems and prospects, Unit for
Retail Planning Information, Reading.
Senior, M.L., 1979, From gravity modelling to entropy maximising:
a pedagogic guide, Progress in Human Geography, vol.3, pp.179-210.
Sexton, D.E., 1972, Black buyer behavior, Journal of Marketing, vol.36,
no.4, pp.36-39.
Shepherd, P.M. and Thorpe, D., 1977, Urban redevelopment and changes in
retail structure 1961-1971, Retail Outlets Research Unit, Manchester
Business School, Research Report 27.
Sheppard, E.S., 1979, Notes on spatial interaction, Professional
Geographer, vol.31, pp.8-15.
Simon, H.A., 1957a, Models of man, Wiley, New York.
Simon, H.A., 1957b, Administrative behavior (2nd edition), Free Press,
New York.
Simon, H.A., 1959, Theories of decision making in economics and
behavioral science, American Economic Review, vol.49, pp.253-283;
reprinted (in part) in Castles, Murray and Potter, op.cit., Chapter 4.
Smith, A.D., 1971, Small retailers: prospects and policies, Committee of
Inquiry on Small Firms, Research Report 15, HMSO, London.
Smith, D.M., 1971, Industrial location: an economic geographical
analysis, Wiley, New York.
Smith, D.M., 1977, Human geography: a welfare approach, Edward Arnold,
London.

Smith, G.C., 1976, The spatial information fields of urban consumers, Transactions of the Institute of British Geographers, n.s., vol.1, pp.175-189.

Smith, J. and Gray, J.G., 1972, Redevelopment and the small trader: a comparative study between Edinburgh and twenty British towns, Edinburgh.

Sofer, C., 1965, Buying and selling: A study in the sociology of distribution, Sociological Review, n.s., vol.13, pp.183-209.

Solesbury, W., 1975, Ideas about structure plans: past, present and future, Town Planning Review, vol.46, pp.245-254.

Spencer, A.H., 1978, Deriving measures of attractiveness for shopping centres, Regional Studies, vol.12, pp.713-726.

Stewart, M., 1974, Market strategy: a constructive approach, The Planner, vol.60, pp.827-829.

Stocks, N., 1976, Retailing: Planning problems, Proceedings of the seminar on retailing, PTRC Summer Annual Meeting.

Stocks, N. and Gleave, G., 1971, Financial analysis and town centre development, Urban Studies, vol.8, pp.255-284.

Stone, G.P., 1954, City shoppers and urban identification: observations on the social psychology of city life, American Journal of Sociology, vol.60, pp.36-45.

Stopher, P.R. and Meyburg, A.H., (eds), 1975, Behavioral travel demand models, Lexington Books, Lexington, Mass.

Sullivan, L., 1976, Why Marks has lost its sparks, Sunday Times, 21 March.

Sunderland Corporation, 1971, The Sunderland hypermarket survey, Sunderland.

Swedner, H., 1962, Prediction of differences in habits and attitudes towards service establishments in rural and urban settings, Rural Sociology, vol.27, pp.396-417.

Tauber, E.M., 1972, Why do people shop ? Journal of Marketing, vol.36, no.4, pp.46-49.

Taylor, J.W., 1974, The role of risk in consumer behavior, Journal of Marketing, vol.38, no.2, pp.54-60.

Telling, A.E., 1977, Planning law and procedure (5th edition), Butterworth, London.

Tesco Stores Ltd., 1977, Retailing and the inner city, Cheshunt, Herts.

Thomas, C.J., 1976, Sociospatial differentiation and the use of services, in Herbert, D.T. and Johnston, R.J., (eds), Spatial perspectives on problems and policies, Wiley, London.

Thompson, D.L., 1966, Future directions in retail area research, Economic Geography, vol.42, pp.1-18.

Thorncroft, M., 1976, Dynamics of the market place, Built Environment Quarterly, vol.2, pp.203-206.

Thorpe, D., 1966, The geographer and urban studies, University of Durham, Department of Geography, Occasional Paper 8.

Thorpe, D., 1968, The main shopping centres of Great Britain in 1961: their locational and structural characteristics, Urban Studies, vol.5, pp.165-206.

Thorpe, D., (ed), 1974a, Research into retailing and distribution, Saxon House, Farnborough, Hants.

Thorpe, D., 1974b, Locating retail outlets, in Thorpe, D., (ed), Research into retailing and distribution, Saxon House, Farnborough.

Thorpe, D., 1975a, Assessing the need for shops: Or can planners plan ? Proceedings of the seminar on retailing, PTRC Summer Annual Meeting.

Thorpe, D., 1975b, Retail planning: The key policy issues, Paper given at Symposium: Town Planning for Retailing, Retail Outlets Research Unit, Manchester Business School.

Thorpe, D., Kivell, P.T., Pratley, D.R. and Andrews, M., 1972, The Hampshire Centre, Bournemouth: A study of an out of town shopping centre, Retail Outlets Research Unit, Manchester Business School Research Report 6.

Thorpe, D. and McGoldrick, P.J., 1977, Co-op superstore: Failsworth, Manchester, Retail Outlets Research Unit, Manchester Business School Research Report 22.

Thorpe, D. and Rhodes, T.C., 1966, The shopping centers of the Tyneside urban region and large scale grocery retailing, Economic Geography, vol.42, pp.52-73.

Thorpe, D., Shepherd, P.M. and Bates, P., 1976, Food retailers and superstore competition: a study of short term impact in York, Northampton and Cambridge, Retail Outlets Research Unit, Manchester Business School Research Report 25.

Tisdall, P., 1976a, Closed, moved to larger premises, The Times, 19 May.

Tisdall, P., 1976b, Advantages of basing shopping centre rents on turnover, The Times, 22 November.

Townroe, P.M., 1972, Some behavioural considerations in the industrial location decision, Regional Studies, vol.6, pp.261-272.

Tucker, K.A. and Yamey, B.S., (eds), 1973, Economics of retailing, Penguin, Harmondsworth.

Unit for Retail Planning Information, 1976, Hypermarkets and superstores: Report of a House of Commons Seminar, Reading.

Unit for Retail Planning Information, 1977a, District shopping centres: Report of an URPI workshop, Reading.

Unit for Retail Planning Information, 1977b, List of UK hypermarkets and superstores (5th edition), Reading.

WHICH, 1979, Grocery prices, Which, October, pp.547-552.

Williams, J. and Arnott, C., 1977, A new look at retail forecasts, The Planner, vol.63, no.6, pp.170-172.

Wilson, A.G., 1970, Entropy in urban and regional modelling, Pion, London.

Winsten, C.B. and Hall, M., 1961, The measurement of economies of scale, Journal of Industrial Economics, vol.9, pp.255-264; reprinted in Tucker and Yamey, op.cit., Chapter 14.

Wood, D., 1972, Consumer durables: Differentiation strategy and consumer response in relation to real and apparent risk, European Journal of Marketing, vol.6, pp.249-256.

Wrigley, N., 1980, An approach to the modelling of shop-choice patterns: an exploratory analysis of purchasing patterns in a British city, in Herbert, D.T. and Johnston, R.J., (eds), Geography and the urban environment, vol.3, Wiley, London.

Index

Urban sprawl 90,93
Use Classes Order 109-110, 168
Utility functions 8-9, 18, 65,
  87

Value Added Tax 57, 171n
Voluntary groups 160

Walking distance 107, 151-152
Warehouse, retail 53
Wheels of retailing 51
Woolworth, F.W. 50, 115, 130,
  134